Peter Fischer
Grünbauerstr. 23
8 München 71, T.799364

Schmidt 5.2.93

Triumph Herald 1969-71 Autobook

By Kenneth Ball
Graduate, Institution of Mechanical Engineers
Associate Member, Guild of Motoring Writers
and the Autopress Team of Technical Writers.

Triumph Herald 1200 1969-70
Triumph Herald 13/60 1969-71

Autopress Ltd. Golden Lane Brighton BN1 2QJ England

The AUTOBOOK series of Workshop Manuals is the largest in the world and covers the majority of British and Continental motor cars, as well as all major Japanese and Australian models. For a full list see the back of this manual.

CONTENTS

Acknowledgement

Introduction

Chapter 1	The Engine	9
Chapter 2	The Fuel System	25
Chapter 3	The Ignition System	35
Chapter 4	The Cooling System	41
Chapter 5	The Clutch	47
Chapter 6	The Gearbox	53
Chapter 7	Propeller Shaft, Rear Axle and Rear Suspension	65
Chapter 8	The Front Suspension and Hubs	75
Chapter 9	The Steering System	83
Chapter 10	The Braking System	91
Chapter 11	The Electrical System	99
Chapter 12	The Bodywork	111
Appendix		123

ISBN 0 85147 235 4

First Edition   1970
Second Edition, fully revised   1971
Reprinted   1972
Reprinted   1973

© Autopress Ltd 1973

All rights reserved. No part of this publication may be reproduced, stored in a retrieval system, or transmitted in any form or by any means, electronic, mechanical, photocopying, recording or otherwise, without the prior permission of Autopress Ltd.

761

Printed and bound in Brighton England for Autopress Ltd by G Beard & Son Ltd   A

ACKNOWLEDGEMENT

My thanks are due to Standard-Triumph Ltd. for their unstinted co-operation and also for supplying data and illustrations.

I am also grateful to a considerable number of owners who have discussed their cars at length and many of whose suggestions have been included in this manual.

Kenneth Ball
Graduate, Institution of Mechanical Engineers
Associate Member Guild of Motoring Writers
Ditchling Sussex England.

INTRODUCTION

This do-it-yourself Workshop Manual has been specially written for the owner who wishes to maintain his car in first class condition and to carry out his own servicing and repairs. Considerable savings on garage charges can be made, and one can drive in safety and confidence knowing the work has been done properly.

Comprehensive step-by-step instructions and illustrations are given on all dismantling, overhauling and assembling operations. Certain assemblies require the use of expensive special tools, the purchase of which would be unjustified. In these cases information is included but the reader is recommended to hand the unit to the agent for attention.

Throughout the Manual hints and tips are included which will be found invaluable, and there is an easy to follow fault diagnosis at the end of each chapter.

Whilst every care has been taken to ensure correctness of information it is obviously not possible to guarantee complete freedom from errors or to accept liability arising from such errors or omissions.

Instructions may refer to the righthand or lefthand sides of the vehicle or the components. These are the same as the righthand or lefthand of an observer standing behind the car and looking forward.

CHAPTER 1

THE ENGINE

1:1 Description
1:2 Removing the engine and gearbox
1:3 Removing and replacing the cylinder head
1:4 Servicing the cylinder head and valve gear
1:5 Servicing the valve timing gear
1:6 The camshaft and distributor drive
1:7 The clutch and flywheel
1:8 The sump

1:9 The oil pump
1:10 Lubrication, oil filter and relief valve
1:11 Pistons and connecting rods
1:12 Crankshaft and main bearings
1:13 Reassembling a stripped engine
1:14 Adjusting the valve rocker clearances
1:15 Fault diagnosis

1:1 Description

Although the engine and gearbox are bolted together to form a single unit, this Chapter will deal only with the engine, apart from instructions on removing the engine and gearbox from the car.

The engine on all models covered by this manual is basically the same, though variations in compression ratio are produced. The suffix HE after the engine number indicates the standard high-compression ratio of 8.5:1, while the suffix LE indicates that the engine has a lower compression ratio and is for use in countries where high octane fuel is unobtainable. The prefix GE indicates a 13/60 engine and GA before the number indicates a 1200 engine.

FIG 1:1 shows the fixed parts of the engine, and **FIG 1:2** the moving parts. These two figures will be used as a reference throughout this Chapter and should be referred to for all part numbers, unless otherwise stated. From these two figures, it will be seen that the engine is a conventional four cylinder one following the normal Standard-Triumph design. The overhead valves are in one line with the rocker gear mounted on the cylinder head. The camshaft is mounted in the engine block and operates the rocker gear through cam followers and pushrods. Details of bore and stroke, together with further extensive technical information, are given in Technical Data at the end of this Manual.

The crankshaft is mounted in three main bearings. The main bearings and the big-end bearings use renewable steel-backed alloy shells for the crankshaft to turn in. The camshaft drive is taken from the front end of the crankshaft using two sprockets and a timing chain. The pulley fitted to the front of the crankshaft drives the water pump and generator through a belt.

The camshaft is supported in four bearings and is held in place by a keeper plate, which also controls the camshaft end float. Integral with the camshaft is a gear which turns the distributor driving gear. As well as driving the distributor, this gear is connected to the oil pump by driving dogs. An extra circular, but eccentric, cam on the camshaft operates the mechanical fuel pump which is bolted to the side of the crankcase.

The oil is contained and cooled in the sump and is drawn from the sump by the oil pump. The pressure from the oil pump is limited by a non-adjustable relief valve which returns excess oil to the sump. The oil is then passed through a fullflow oil filter before entering the fore and aft oil gallery on the lefthand side of the engine. Internal passages lead the oil to the crankshaft main bearings and camshaft bearings. Drilled oilways in the crankshaft take

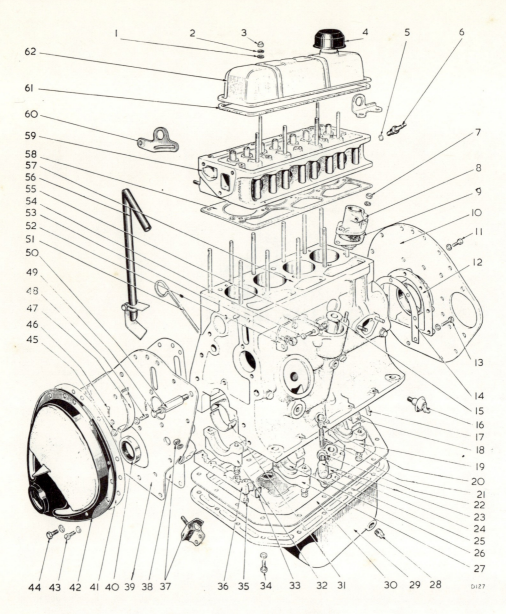

FIG 1:1 Engine details, fixed parts

Key to Fig 1:1 1 Fibre washer 2 Plain washer 3 Nyloc nut 4 Filler cap 5 Copper/asbestos washer
6 Sparking plug 7 Nut 8 Adaptor 9 Gasket 10 Rear engine plate 11 Bolt 12 Rear oil seal 13 Bolt
14 Gasket 15 Oil pump drive shaft bush 16 Oil pressure switch 17 Crankshaft thrust washer 18 Rear bearing shell
19 Rear bearing cap 20 Relief valve 21 Spring 22 Copper washer 23 Cap nut 24 Oil pump body
25 Oil pump end plate 26 Centre bearing shell 27 Centre main bearing cap 28 Sump plug 29 Sump
30 Sump gasket 31 Front bearing shell 32 Front main bearing cap 33 Sealing wedges 34 Sump bolt
35 Slotted screw 36 Front sealing block 37 Front engine mounting 38 Gasket 39 Front engine plate 40 Oil seal
41 Gasket 42 Front timing cover 43 Slotted setscrew 44 Bolt 45 Plain washer 46 Splitpin 47 Chain tensioner
48 Pivot pin 49 Bolt 50 Generator pedestal 51 Dipstick 52 Bracket 53 Nyloc nut 54 Bolt 55 Nyloc nut
56 Breather pipe 57 Cylinder block 58 Cylinder head gasket 59 Cylinder head 60 Generator adjusting link
61 Rocker cover gasket 62 Rocker cover

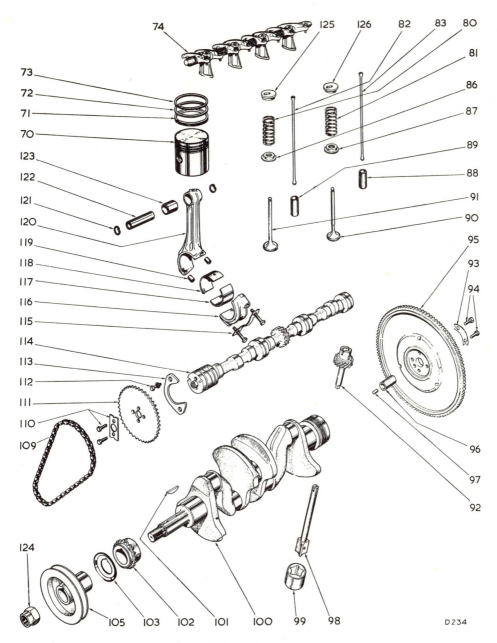

FIG 1:2 Engine details, moving parts

Key to Fig 1:2   70 Piston   71 Oil control ring   72 Taper compression ring   73 Plain compression ring
74 Rocker assembly (See **FIGS 1:4** and **1:5**)   80 Outer spring   81 Outer spring   82 Pushrod   83 Pushrod
86 Lower collar   87 Lower collar   88 Cam follower   89 Cam follower   90 Exhaust valve   91 Inlet valve
92 Distributor and oil pump drive gear   93 Locktab   94 Bolt   95 Flywheel   96 Bush   97 Dowel
98 Inner rotor and spindle   99 Outer rotor   100 Crankshaft   101 Key   102 Sprocket   103 Flinger
105 Crankshaft pulley   109 Timing chain   110 Bolts and locktab   111 Camshaft sprocket   112 Bolt   113 Keeper plate
114 Camshaft   115 Bolt and locktab   116 Conrod cap   117 Lower conrod bearing shell   118 Upper conrod bearing shell
119 Dowels   120 Conrod   121 Circlip   122 Gudgeon pin   123 Gudgeon pin bush   124 Nut   125 Collet
126 Collet

THA/2

FIG 1:3 Cylinder head nut tightening sequence. The sequence used depends on the number of cylinder head studs

the oil from the main bearings to the big-end bearings. A scroll on the front of the camshaft allows oil to seep out and lubricate the camshaft sprocket as well as the timing chain. The rocker gear requires only a small supply of oil and this is metered by a scroll and two flats on the rear end of the camshaft. After lubricating the rockers the oil runs down the pushrod tubes to lubricate the camshaft followers before finally returning to the sump. The pistons, small-ends and cylinder bores are lubricated by oil splash from the crankshaft.

On some engines the crankcase ventilation will be through a simple open pipe vented to the atmosphere. The more usual system will have the aperture for the pipe blocked off and a pipe connecting the rocker cover to the air intake filter.

The only task that cannot be done with the engine in the car is removing and replacing the crankshaft. However, if major work is to be carried out it will probably be easier to have the engine removed from the car and on the bench.

1:2 Removing the engine and gearbox

The gearbox can be removed separately (see **Chapter 6, Section 6:2**), but if the engine is to be removed it is easier to remove them both as a unit and then separate the gearbox from the engine. The combined unit is removed from above but certain operations will have to be carried out under the car. If a pit is not available, securely raise the front of the car on stands. **Any support holding the car must be safe and secure otherwise the car may drop, causing serious injury to anyone working underneath it,** apart from the obvious dangers of mechanical damage.

If the operator is not a skilled automobile mechanic, it is suggested that he will find much useful information in 'Hints on Maintenance and Overhaul' at the end of this Manual, and that he should read it before starting work.

1 Remove the bonnet (see **Chapter 12**). Disconnect the battery. Drain the cooling system, engine and gearbox. Disconnect the fuel supply pipe from the fuel pump. To prevent fuel syphoning out or dirt entering the pipe, block the pipe with a rubber plug.
2 Disconnect the radiator hoses and remove the radiator. Disconnect the control cables from the heater valve, and disconnect the heater hoses.
3 Remove the carburetter and air cleaner (see **Chapter 2**). Disconnect the exhaust from the manifold and free the exhaust pipe from the clip on the clutch housing.
4 Disconnect and label the electrical cables to generator, starter motor, distributor and oil pressure switch. Disconnect the engine earthing strap.
5 Remove the front seats, carpets and gearbox cover. Free the clutch slave cylinder from its mounting and wire it, still attached to its pipe, safely out of the way. Remove the gearbox top cover and blank the aperture with carboard. Disconnect the propeller shaft and speedometer cable from the gearbox. These operations are dealt with in more detail in **Chapter 6, Section 6:2**.
6 Attach a sling to the engine lifting eyes and take the weight of the unit with a hoist. Free the bolts securing the gearbox mounting and the engine front mountings. **Check that all connections from the engine/gearbox to the car are broken.** Lift the unit until the engine sump clears the chassis crossmember. Continue to lift the unit and at the same time move the engine forwards, or the car backwards, until the gearbox is clear of the bulkhead aperture, and then hoist the unit out of the car.

The engine is replaced in the reverse order of removal. Refill the cooling system, engine sump and gearbox. Hand prime the carburetters before starting the engine.

1:3 Removing and replacing the cylinder head

It is essential that whenever the cylinder head nuts are tightened or slackened, they are turned progressively, and part of a turn at a time, in the sequence shown in FIG 1:3. If this precaution is not observed the cylinder head may become distorted and cause early and regular failure of the cylinder head gasket.
1 Drain the cooling system. Disconnect the battery. Disconnect the radiator hoses from the thermostat housing and the water pump inlet (see **Chapter 4**), and remove the complete water pump assembly. Disconnect the heater hoses and heater control cable.
2 Remove the air filter. Either disconnect the carburetter controls or remove the carburetter (see **Chapter 2**). Disconnect the exhaust pipe from the manifold flange and remove the inlet and exhaust manifolds.
3 Label the HT plug leads and disconnect them from the sparking plugs. Remove the Nyloc nuts 3, remove the plain washers 2 and fibre washers 1 and lift off the rocker cover 62 complete with gasket 61. Progressively slacken the four nuts holding on the rocker cover assembly 74 and after removing the nuts lift off the rocker assembly. Remove the eight pushrods 82 and 83, storing them in the correct order for reassembly.
4 Remove the cylinder head nuts in the order shown in **FIG 1:3**. Lift the cylinder head 59 squarely up the studs to remove it. If the head is difficult to free, try

tapping on the sides using a wooden block to hammer on. In particularly obstinate cases rotate the engine by hand (using the flywheel or pushing the car in gear) and use the cylinder compression to free the head.
5 Withdraw the eight cam followers, using a magnet if they are difficult to grasp, and store them in the correct order for reassembly.

Refitting the cylinder head is the reversal of the removal procedure, with special attention to the following points:
1 Examine the cam followers and renew them if they are chipped, cracked or excessively worn. Refit them in their correct positions and ensure that they both rotate and slide freely in their bores.
2 Use a new cylinder head gasket 58, smearing it lightly on both sides with grease to act as an extra seal. Make sure that mating surfaces of the cylinder head and block are scrupulously clean. Tighten the cylinder head nuts, in the order shown in **FIG 1:3**, progressively to a torque of 42 to 46 lb ft (5.807 to 6.36 kg m).
3 Slacken the adjusters on the rocker assembly 74, to prevent them bending the pushrods, and make sure the pushrod ends fit correctly into the cam followers and rocker adjusters. Progressively tighten the four rocker securing nuts to a torque of 24 to 26 lb ft (3.318 to 3.595 kg·m).
4 Set the valve clearances as described in **Section 1:14**. Drive the car for 500 miles and then recheck the torque loading on the cylinder head nuts as well as resetting the valve clearances.

1:4 Servicing the cylinder head and valve gear

Remove the cylinder head as described in the preceding Section. To prevent dirt and carbon chips from falling into the engine, block off the oil and water passages with bits of non-fluffy rags. Make sure the rag pieces are large enough to prevent them falling through into the engine or being forgotten when the cylinder head is replaced. Scrape the carbon from the combustion chambers before removing the valves, so as to avoid damaging the valve seats. Use a blunt tool to remove the carbon. The combustion chambers may be polished using emerycloth, with paraffin as a lubricant, but the cylinder head must be thoroughly cleaned after this to prevent any abrasive particles remaining. A rotary wire brush in an electric drill makes a useful tool for cleaning the inlet and exhaust ports, but take great care not to damage the valve seats or guides.

Use a long straightedge, or surface table and engineers blue, to check the faces of the cylinder head and block for distortion. High-spots may be removed by careful use of a scraper but distortion will require grinding on a surface grinder.

Before cleaning the carbon from the pistons smear a little grease around the tops of the bores. Turn the engine until one pair of pistons are nearly at TDC and use a soft tool (such as a sharpened stick of solder or hardwood) to scrape the carbon from the pistons. Spring an old piston ring into the bore above the piston. This will protect the carbon around the periphery of the piston and the top of the bore. This carbon should be left as it acts as an oil seal as well as protecting the top piston ring from the heat of combustion. **Do not use any abrasives on the pistons** as particles can easily remain to cause expensive damage or scoring. When the first pair of pistons have been cleaned turn the engine to bring the other pair up to TDC. The dirt and carbon chippings will stick to the grease at the top of the bore and are then easily removed.

1 The rocker gear for the Herald 1200 is shown in detail in **FIG 1:4**, and the rocker gear for the 13/60 in **FIG 1:5**. The end caps 2 are held in place by Mills pins 1, which are removed and replaced using a suitable small punch, on the 1200 rocker gear. Splitpins secure the end caps on the 13/60. Remove the end caps and slide the parts off the rocker shaft, taking care to keep the parts in the order in which they were removed. In both cases the rear pedestal is secured to the rocker shaft by a cross-headed screw. Clean all the parts in petrol and renew any that are worn. Examine the working faces of the rockers. Light wear may be cleaned up using a fine carborundum stone, but deeper wear will necessitate renewing the rocker. Reassemble the rocker gear in the reverse order of dismantling. Lubricate the parts with clean engine oil before refitting the assembly to the engine.

2 Lay a block of wood under the cylinder head so that it fits into the combustion chamber holding the valves shut. Press firmly down on the valve collets 125 or 126 to compress the valve springs 80 or 81 and slide the collets sideways so that the valve stem passes into the larger offset hole in the collet. Lift off the collet, valve spring and lower collar 86 or 87. Remove the valve from the combustion chamber. Mark the valves and store them with their associated parts in the correct order for reassembly.

3 Clean the carbon and deposits from the valve head, taking care not to damage the seat. The valve stems must be straight (check using a straightedge) and show no signs of wear or 'picking up'. If satisfactory, but the valve seats are excessively pitted have the seats reground at a garage. Do not attempt to remove deep pitting by using grinding paste, as this will remove metal from the seat in the cylinder head as well. Recut the seats in the cylinder head if they are badly worn or pitted. If the seats are then too wide they may be reduced by using a 15 deg. facing cutter. Seats that are beyond recutting can be restored by fitting inserts, though this operation should be left to a garage.

4 To grind-in valves, put a light spring under the valve head and use medium-grade grinding paste, unless the seats are in very good condition, in which case use

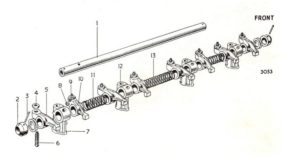

FIG 1:4 Herald 1200 rocker gear details

Key to Fig 1:4 1 Rocker shaft 2 End cap
3 Mills pin 4 Locknut 5 Righthand rocker
6 Adjusting screw 7 Rear pedestal 8 Shakeproof washer
9 Phillips head screw 10 Lefthand rocker 11 Distance spring 12 Pedestal 13 Centre distance spring

FIG 1:5   13/60 rocker gear

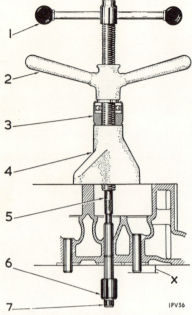

FIG 1:6   Renewing valve guides using Churchill special tool No. S.60A.6

Key to Fig 1:6   1 Handle   2 Threaded handle
3 Thrust race   4 Body   5 Adaptor   6 Distance collar   7 Knurled nut   X = .749 to .751 inch

FIG 1:7   Position of shims on crankshaft

fine-grade paste from the start. Use a suction-cup tool to hold the valve head and grind with a semi-rotary movement, letting the valve rise off its seat occasionally by the pressure of the spring. Use grinding paste sparingly, and when the pitting has been removed, clean away the old paste and transfer to a fine-grade paste. When both seats have a fine matt-grey finish clean away every trace of grinding paste from the valves and bores. If the thickness of the head above the ground seat is less than $\frac{1}{32}$ inch (.8 mm) the valve should be renewed.

5 Insert a new valve into each valve guide in turn. Raise the valve slightly and check that the diametric movement of the valve head does not exceed .020 inch (.508 mm). If this dimension is exceeded then the valve guides are excessively worn and will have to be renewed. **FIG 1:6** shows the method of renewing the valve guides using tool No. S.60A.6. The distance collar 6 ensures that the protrusion X is correct at .75 inch (19.05 mm). If the special tool is not available, use a stepped drift, of which the bottom inch fits snugly inside the valve guide, to drive the old valve guides into the combustion chamber. Drive the new guides, chamfered end leading, down into the head until they protrude .75 inch above the face of the head. The head seats must be recut after fitting new valve guides, to ensure concentricity. Lubricate the guides with engine oil before refitting the valves.

Reassemble the parts in the reverse order of dismantling, after having cleaned away all traces of dirt or grinding paste with petrol or paraffin.

1:5 Servicing the valve timing gear

The components are shown in **FIGS 1:1** and **1:2**. If the engine is still fitted to the car, then drain the cooling system and remove the radiator (see **Chapter 4**). Disconnect the battery. Slacken the generator mounting bolts, pivot the generator towards the block and remove the fan belt.

1 Remove the nut 124 and draw off the crankshaft pulley 105. Remove the timing cover securing bolts and setscrews 44 and 43. Mount them in holes in a sheet of cardboard so that they will be in their correct order for replacement. Carefully withdraw the timing cover 42 and lift off the gasket 41. Take out the oil flinger 103.

2 Lay a straightedge tangentially between the sprockets and along the timing chain. Pull the timing chain firmly away from the straightedge and measure the maximum gap. If this gap exceeds .4 inch (10 mm) the chain and sprockets are excessively worn and must be renewed. **Never renew only the timing chain but renew the timing chain and sprockets as a set.** If the timing chain is noisy but still within the wear limits, renew the timing chain tensioner 47. Part the blades and slip it off the pin on the timing cover. Replace a new tensioner in the same manner.

3 Straighten the ears of the lockplate and remove the two bolts securing the camshaft sprocket 111 to the camshaft 114. Ease off the sprocket and remove the timing chain 109. Withdraw the crankshaft sprocket 102, tap and lever out the key 101 and remove the shims, shown in **FIG 1:7**, from the crankshaft.

4 Refit both sprockets into place, without the shims, key or timing chain. Lay a straightedge across the sides of the teeth. Press the straightedge firmly against the camshaft sprocket 111 and measure, with feeler gauges, the gap between the straightedge and the side of the crankcase sprocket 102. Make up a shim pack equal in thickness to the dimension measured and fit it to the crankshaft after removing the sprocket.

5 Refit the key 101. Turn the crankshaft until Nos. 1 and 4 pistons are at TDC. At this position the key on the crankshaft will be vertically upwards. The markings on the sprockets are shown in **FIG 1:8**. Turn the camshaft until the cut-out (or pop mark) B on the camshaft is approximately at 11 o'clock as shown in **FIG 1:8**. Fit the timing chain around the sprockets so that the scribed lines C align. Refit both sprockets to the crankshaft and camshaft, turning the camshaft so that the threaded holes exactly align with the securing holes in the camshaft sprocket and the pop mark A aligns with the cut-out B. Check that the scribed lines C still align before locking the camshaft sprocket securing bolts in place.

6 If new sprockets are being fitted they will be unmarked and the valve timing will have to be set afresh. Turn the crankshaft so that it is approximately 45 deg. before TDC. This is to prevent the valves from hitting the pistons when the camshaft is turned. Loosely refit the camshaft sprocket and use it to turn the camshaft. Turn the camshaft until No. 1 (front) pushrod reaches its highest point of travel, and adjust No. 8 (rearmost) rocker clearance to .040 inch (1 mm). Turn the camshaft until No. 2 pushrod reaches its highest point of travel and adjust the clearance on No. 7 rocker to .040 inch. Carry on turning the camshaft until the valves on No. 4 cylinder (rearmost cylinder) are at the point of rock. The inlet valve will be at the point of opening and the exhaust (rearmost) valve will be at the point of closing. The position of the cams is shown in **FIG 1:9**. Use feeler gauges and turn the camshaft until the valve clearances on the rear cylinder are exactly equal. **Do not turn the camshaft from this position.** Turn the crankshaft until the key 101 is vertically upwards and Nos. 1 and 4 pistons are exactly at TDC. **Do not turn the crankshaft from this position.** The camshaft sprocket 111 is provided with four holes arranged in equally spaced pairs but so that the pairs are offset from the tooth centre line. Encircle both sprockets with the timing chain and fit them back to the engine so that a pair of holes in the camshaft sprocket exactly align with the threaded holes in the camshaft. Half-tooth adjustment is obtained by rotating the camshaft sprocket 90 deg. from its original position, and quarter-tooth adjustment is made by turning the sprocket back to front. A combination of both these movements produces a three-quarter-tooth adjustment. Simulate the chain tensioner pressure with a finger and check that the valve clearances on the rear cylinder are still equal before locking the camshaft sprocket in place.

7 Lubricate the timing chain with clean engine oil. Replace the oil flinger 103 with its concave side facing forwards. Examine the oil seal 40 in the timing cover. If it has leaked or is worn or damaged carefully drift it out of the cover. Fit a new one so that its lips face into the engine, taking care not to distort the cover. Hold back the blades of the chain tensioner 47 with an Allen key or bent stiff piece of wire and slide the timing cover back into place, after fitting a new gasket 41 to the engine. Remove the Allen key, without damaging the gasket 41, when the blades of the chain tensioner are over the timing chain. Secure the cover lightly in place with the securing bolts and setscrews. Examine the sealing face of the pulley 105. If it is

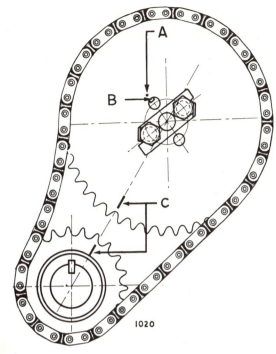

FIG 1:8 Valve timing markings

Key to Fig 1:8   A Centre dot
B Cut-out on camshaft   C Scribed lines

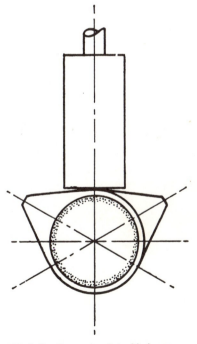

FIG 1:9 Cams at point of balance

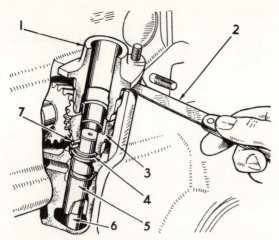

FIG 1:10 Calculating thickness of packing required under distributor adaptor pedestal

Key to Fig 1:10   1 Distributor pedestal   2 Feeler gauge
3 Distributor drive   4 $\frac{1}{2}$ inch (12.7 mm) I/D washer
5 Bush   6 Oil pump drive gear   7 Pin

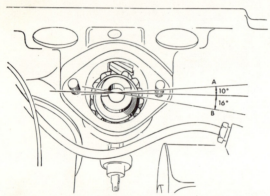

FIG 1:11 Correct position of distributor driving gear when No. 1 piston is at TDC on the compression stroke

FIG 1:12 Correct position of the rotor arm when No. 1 piston is at TDC on the compression stroke

damaged, worn or scored oil will leak between it and the oil seal 40. If satisfactory, oil the face and carefully refit the pulley to the crankshaft. Secure the pulley in place with the nut 124 and tighten evenly all the timing case securing bolts and setscrews.

8 Reset all the valve clearances to .010 inch (.25 mm). After refitting the remainder of the parts and filling the cooling system run the engine and check for leaks.

1:6 The camshaft and distributor drive gear

1 Remove the cylinder head (see **Section 1:3**). Remove the timing cover, chain and sprockets (see previous Section). Undo the two nuts securing the distributor clamp plate to the drive pedestal 8. **Do not slacken the clamp pinch bolt or the ignition timing will be lost.** Withdraw the distributor from the pedestal. Remove the nuts 7 and withdraw the pedestal 8 complete with its shims 7 from the engine. Lift out the distributor drive gear 92. If the bush 15 is worn it can be tapped out from inside the crankcase and a new one driven back, using a stepped drift. Disconnect, and plug, both fuel pipes from the fuel pump and remove the fuel pump.

2 Before removing the camshaft, check the end float with feeler gauges between the keeper plate 113 and the camshaft. The end float should be between .004 and .008 inch (.10 and .20 mm) and if this is exceeded the end float should be reduced by fitting a new keeper plate.

3 Remove the two bolts 112 securing the keeper plate 113, and slide it out of the annular groove in the camshaft. Carefully, so as to avoid damaging the bearings, withdraw the camshaft from the engine. Check the camshaft for damage or chipping.

Refit the camshaft and parts in the reverse order of dismantling. Make sure all the parts are clean and lubricate all bearing surfaces, including the cams, with clean engine oil. Leave the rocker cover off and refit the distributor driving gear 92 as follows.

Remeshing the distributor drive gear:

To ensure the correct positioning of the distributor it is essential that the driving gear 92 is correctly meshed with the camshaft gear. The gear must also be fitted with the correct amount of end float, adjusted by the thickness of the shims 9 under the pedestal, otherwise the rate of wear throughout the valve timing mechanism will be excessive. As the parts are hidden inside the crankcase it is impossible to measure the end float directly and the following method, using a packing washer of known thickness, allows the amount of shimming required to be calculated. Refer to **FIG 1:10**.

1 Measure the thickness of a $\frac{1}{2}$ inch I/D washer with a micrometer. Fit the washer to the drive gear and insert them both into the crankcase, ensuring that the drive gear 3 meshes both with the camshaft gear and the drive dogs on the oil pump shaft 6. Replace the adaptor pedestal and measure the gap between it and the crankcase with feeler gauges 2.

2 Subtract the width of the gap, as measured, from the thickness of the washer 4. A negative answer indicates that there is preload and that sufficient shims will have to be added to bring the preload to zero before adding further shims to give the correct end float. If the answer

is positive, then the difference between the answer and the correct end float of .005 inch (.12 mm) is the total amount of shims required

3 Lift off the adaptor pedestal 1, leaving the gear 3 and washer 4 in place. Make up a shim pack equal in thickness to the dimension calculated and refit the adaptor pedestal with the shim pack between it and the crankcase. Again measure the gap 2 and, provided the shims are correct, the gap should be within .003 to .007 inch (.076 to .178 mm) less than the thickness of the washer 4. Remove the parts and discard the washer 4.

4 Turn the engine until No. 1 piston is at TDC on the compression stroke (both valves closed). Lower the gear 3 back into place, turning it slightly to allow it to mesh both with the camshaft gear and the driving dogs of the oil pump drive shaft 6. When correctly meshed the gear should be aligned as the line A in **FIG 1:11**, note that the larger offset is away from the engine. Secure the pedestal in place and refit the distributor. The rotor arm should then point as shown in **FIG 1:12**. If the pinch bolt on the distributor clamp has been slackened the ignition timing will be lost. Refer to **Chapter 3** for instructions on setting the ignition timing.

1:7 The clutch and flywheel

Full details on servicing the clutch and its associated parts are given in **Chapter 5**. This Section will only deal with removing and replacing the clutch. If the clutch or flywheel are to be examined while the engine is still in the car then the gearbox will have to be removed, refer to **Chapter 6, Section 6:2**.

1 Turn the engine so that Nos. 1 and 4 pistons are at TDC. This will make it easier to replace the flywheel in the correct position. Progressively slacken the ring of bolts securing the clutch cover to the flywheel. Remove the clutch assembly and driven plate.

2 Remove the four bolts 94 securing the flywheel to the crankshaft. Earlier engines had lockplates 93 fitted but later engines use self-locking bolts 94. Pull the flywheel back to clear it from the dowel 97. Take care not to drop the flywheel when it comes free.

3 If the face of the flywheel is scored it may be rectified by skimming off in a lathe. No more than .030 inch (.762 mm) of metal may be removed and if the damage is greater than this the flywheel will have to be renewed.

4 If the spigot bush 96 is worn or shows chatter or fret marks inside it, remove the old bush and press in a new one using zinc oxide grease as a lubricant.

5 The parts are replaced in the reverse order of removal. Before refitting the flywheel, clean off all dirt and particles from the mating faces of the flywheel and crankshaft. Replace the flywheel and progressively tighten the bolts to pull the flywheel back onto the dowel 97. Mount a DTI (Dial Test Indicator) on the engine rear plate and measure the runout on the flywheel. Keep the crankshaft pressed firmly forwards so that crankshaft end float does not falsify the runout figures for the flywheel. The runout should not exceed .002 inch at a radius of 5 inches from the centre of the spigot bush. Use a mandrel to centralize the driven plate while refitting the clutch.

Starter ring gear:

The ring gear will show most wear in the positions where the engine stops, because of the cylinder compressions, and the starter pinion first engages. Worn ring gear teeth will cause the starter to jam or even spin ineffectually. Lay the flywheel, clutch face upwards, on three hardwood blocks. Use a drift to drive the ring gear evenly and in small stages from the flywheel. In difficult cases the ring may be weakened by drilling at the root of a tooth and then split open with a cold chisel, but great care must be taken while using this method to avoid damaging or marking the flywheel.

Use a wire brush to remove all traces of dirt or rust from the flywheel periphery and then lay the flywheel, clutch face downwards, on the hardwood blocks. Heat the ring gear to expand it. It is most important to heat the new ring evenly otherwise it may become distorted. Place the hot ring into position on the flywheel and drive it evenly into place with light taps from a copper drift. Allow it to cool before moving the flywheel.

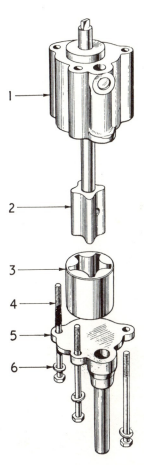

FIG 1:13 Oil pump details

Key to Fig 1:13 1 Body 2 Inner rotor 3 Outer rotor
4 Bolt 5 End plate 6 Spring washer

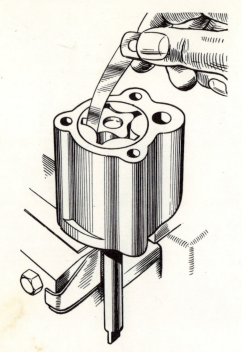

FIG 1:14 Measuring the clearance between the oil pump rotors

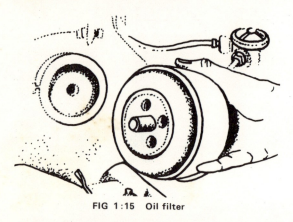

FIG 1:15 Oil filter

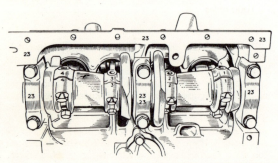

FIG 1:16 Main and connecting rod bearing markings

1:8 The sump

The sump 29 is removable with the engine fitted to the car, though the task will be easier if the bottom two bellhousing bolts are removed first. Removing the plug 28 drains the oil out of the sump. However, the sump will drain faster and better if the oil is hot, so drain after a run long enough to heat it up.

Remove the dipstick and progressively slacken all the securing bolts 34, then lower the sump.

Sludge should be cleaned out with newspapers followed by non-fluffy rags. Examine the flanges of the sump and tap them back to shape if they are damaged. Refit the sump, using a new gasket 30. Hold the gasket in place with either a thin smear of grease or with jointing compound. The two shorter bolts fit into the front sealing block on the engine. Do not overtighten the securing bolts. Replace the two bellhousing bolts. Renew the oil filter if required and fill the sump to the correct level with fresh engine oil.

1:9 The oil pump

This is accessible after the sump has been removed. The details of the pump are shown in **FIG 1:13**, and, as well as holding the parts together, the three bolts 4 also secure the pump to the crankcase.

All the oil for the engine passes through the pump so, because of the continuous lubrication, the pump is unlikely to wear or give trouble in service. Provided that the oil is changed regularly the oil pump should last 200,000 miles before it requires attention, and even then lapping of the end plate should ensure further satisfactory life.

Remove the pump and clean the parts in petrol. Reassemble the pump dry. Use feeler gauges to measure the clearance between the rotors, as shown in **FIG 1:14**. The clearance should not exceed .008 inch (.203 mm). Similarly the clearance between the outer rotor 3 and the body 1 should not exceed .010 inch (.254 mm). Lay a straightedge across the base of the body and measure the end clearance between the rotors and the body. This should not exceed .004 inch (.102 mm). If the end clearance is exceeded or the end plate 5 is badly scored, and a drop in oil pressure is associated with these faults, the parts may be lapped down. Use fine emerycloth laid on plate glass (not window glass as it is not truly flat) and rub the end plate down on this until the scoring is removed. Similarly rub down the end of the body to cure excessive end clearance. Wash the parts thoroughly in petrol to remove all abrasive particles.

Before refitting the pump lubricate it well with clean engine oil. No special precautions are required before starting the engine as, provided there is oil in the sump, the pump is self-priming.

1:10 Lubrication, oil filter and relief valve

The oil circulation through the engine has already been discussed in **Section 1:1**.

The oil filter is shown in **FIG 1:15**. **The unit is a sealed assembly and cannot be cleaned.** A relief valve is incorporated in the filter so that, in the event of the filter element becoming blocked by dirt, oil will still be supplied to the engine. The oil which passes through the oil filter relief valve is unfiltered and, if oil changes have also been neglected, there will be a lot of dirt and particles carried around in the engine. This causes expensive and rapid wear, so renew the filter and change the oil at regular intervals.

Unscrew by hand the old filter assembly from the lefthand side of the engine. **Discard the old filter assembly.** Check that the rubber seal on the new filter is undamaged and smear it with a little clean oil. Screw the new assembly back handtight into the engine. Wipe away any oil spillage, start the engine and check for oil leaks immediately. Switch off the engine and when the oil level has settled, top up the sump to replace any losses from changing the filter.

Check the oil level when the car has not been run for some time and is standing on level ground. Failure to observe this precaution may result in overfilling the sump with consequent oil wastage.

The non-adjustable relief valve parts are shown in **FIG 1:1** as items 20 to 23. Dirt holding the relief valve 20 open may be a cause of a drop in oil pressure. Unscrew the cap 23 and withdraw the parts from the crankcase. Clean the seat in the crankcase with a piece of hardwood. Clean the parts in petrol. Renew the relief valve 20 if it is excessively worn. The free length of the spring 21 should be 1.54 inch (39.11 mm) and if it is shorter than this it has weakened with use and should be renewed. Reassemble the parts using a new copper washer 22. A satisfactory oil pressure is 40 to 60 lb/sq in at an engine speed of 2000 rev/min.

1:11 Pistons and connecting rods

These can be removed with the engine still fitted to the car. To change the big-end bearings only the sump need be removed (see **Section 1:8**), but to remove the pistons and connecting rods the cylinder head also needs to be removed (see **Section 1:3**). For ease of access also remove the oil pump (see **Section 1:9**). **FIG 1:16** shows the positions of the markings on both the big-end caps and connecting rods, as well as the markings on the main bearing caps. Before removing the caps check that these identifications are present, otherwise mark the parts with light punch marks.

1 Remove the securing bolts 115 from each big-end in turn. These bolts are of the self-locking type which do not require locking plates. Pull off the bearing cap 116. Push the connecting rod 120 and piston 70 up the bore of the cylinder to clear the connecting rods from the crankpins on the crankshaft.
2 Lay the big-end bearing caps out in their correct order and slide out the bottom bearing shells 117, keeping them with their respective caps. Similarly slide out the upper bearing shells 118 from the connecting rods and lay them out with their associated caps.
3 Examine and measure the crankpins using a micrometer. If the crankpin is excessively worn, scored, oval or tapered the crankshaft must be removed and reground. **Do not file the caps or the connecting rods in an attempt to take up wear** as the parts will then form an oval hole as well as being unfit for exchange. Check the shell bearings and if any are worn, pitted or scored renew the complete set.
4 If new shell bearings are being fitted they should only be cleaned to remove the protective coating. They are fitted as received and do not require scraping or boring to make them fit. Slide the shells back into their positions in the bearing caps and connecting rods,

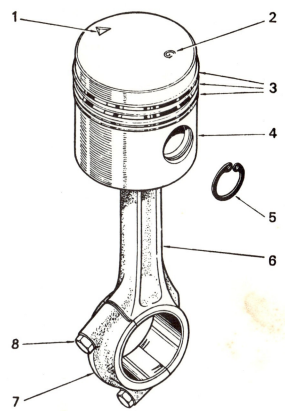

FIG 1:17 Connecting rod and piston assembly, using floating gudgeon pins

Key to Fig 1:17   1 Triangular mark on front of piston
2 Letter indicating grade of piston   3 Piston rings
4 Piston   5 Circlip (used only with floating gudgeon pins)
6 Connecting rod   7 Cap   8 Bolt

making sure that their tags seat in the recesses provided. Lubricate them with clean engine oil.
5 Pull the pistons back down the bores and guide the connecting rods onto the crankpins. Replace the caps in their correct positions and secure them with the bolts 115 tightened to a torque of 38 to 42 lb ft (5.254 to 5.807 kg m).
6 Replace the oil pump and sump, and drive without using full power or 'slogging' the engine for at least 1000 miles.

Cylinder bores:

The pistons and connecting rods are removed by pushing them out of the top of the block when the cylinder head has been removed. Examine the bores. The maximum point of wear will be near the top of the bore and at right angles to the gudgeon pins. The thickness of the unworn ridge at the top of the bore will give a good guide to the amount of wear that has taken place. If the wear is excessive the engine will have to be rebored to take oversize pistons. If the wear is such that oversize pistons are too small then the cylinders will have to be bored oversize and dry liners fitted. These liners can then be bored to

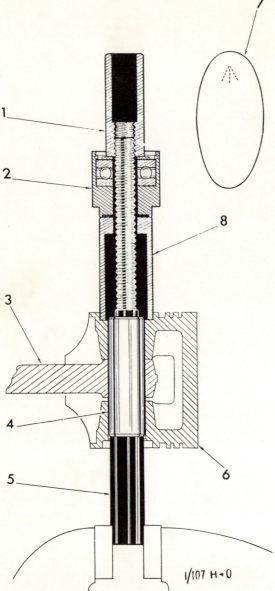

FIG 1:18 Removing interference fit type gudgeon pins, using Churchill special tool No. S334. The gudgeon pins are refitted without using the sleeve 8

Key to Fig 1:18 1 Nut   2 Stop and ball race
3 Connecting rod   4 Gudgeon pin   5 Draw bar
6 Piston   7 View of crown of piston   8 Sleeve

accept standard pistons. This operation should be left to a qualified garage.

If the wear is not sufficient to warrant reboring, but new piston rings are to be fitted, the unworn ridge around the top of the bore should be removed, using garage equipment. A new unworn top ring will hit this ridge, if it is left, and cause early failure of the ring. At the same time the glaze on the cylinder bore should be removed by light honing, or at least scuffed off with careful use of medium-grade carborundum paper. Removing the glaze will allow the new piston rings to bed in better and more quickly.

Pistons:

A connecting rod and piston assembly, using the floating type of gudgeon pin, is shown in **FIG 1:17**. The removal of the interference fit type of gudgeon pin will be dealt with later under 'Connecting rods'. **In all cases the triangular mark 1 on the piston crown indicates the front of the piston.** The letter 2 indicates the grade of the piston, which must be fitted to a matching grade of bore. The dimensions of the three grades of standard piston are given in Technical Data. The dimension B is measured at the bottom of the skirt at right angles to the gudgeon pin axis and the dimension A is measured similarly just below the piston ring grooves. The pistons are separated from the connecting rods by first removing the circlips 5 and then using the fingers to press out the floating gudgeon pin. Tight gudgeon pins will be easier to remove after heating the piston in hot water.

Dry the gudgeon pins and connecting rod bushes. The bushes are satisfactory if the gudgeon pin can be pushed through, using only finger pressure, at room temperature. If the gudgeon pin falls through under its own weight alone then the bush is too slack and should be renewed. After fitting, new bushes have to be jig-reamed to a very close tolerance so this operation is best left to a service station.

Piston rings:

Three rings are fitted to each piston; a plain compression ring at the top, tapered compression ring in the middle and an oil control ring in the bottom groove. The bottom oil control ring fitted to the 13/60 is a three part ring. Lacquering on the sides of the piston indicates that gases are blowing past the piston rings.

A piston ring expanding tool will greatly facilitate removing and replacing the piston rings, but it is not essential. Remove the rings from the top of the piston by sliding a thin piece of metal, such as a discarded feeler gauge, under one end and passing it around the ring, at the same time pressing the raised portion onto the land above. Use three equi-spaced shims to protect the piston when sliding the rings on or off.

Clean carbon from the ring grooves using a piece of broken ring, but taking great care not to remove metal or else the oil consumption will be increased. Carefully clean out the oil drain holes behind the oil control ring.

Before fitting new rings check that the gaps between the ends are correct when the rings are fitted. Fit the ring into the cylinder bore and press it down, using a reversed piston, to about $\frac{1}{4}$ inch from the top of the bore. Use feeler gauges to measure the gap between the ends and, if required, carefully file the ends until the gaps are correct. Ring gaps are given in Technical Data.

The bottom ring is fitted first. On the 13/60 the corrugated spacer of the oil control ring is fitted first then a scraper is slid down the piston and fitted between the bottom edge of the spacer and the bottom side of the ring groove. The other scraper is similarly fitted, but above the spacer. The second ring is fitted with the narrowest diameter of the taper uppermost, and the marking T or Top also uppermost.

The connecting rods:

The big-end bearings and bushes for the floating gudgeon pins are all renewable as already discussed.

The interference fit type of gudgeon pin relies on the interference fit to keep the gudgeon pin in place. They should not be removed without good reason as every time they are moved the interference fit is diminished. A special tool S334 is essential for removing or refitting the gudgeon pins. The method of removal is illustrated in **FIG 1:18**. When the nut 1 is turned the gudgeon pin is drawn out into the sleeve 8. It should be noted that the tool will only fit on the front side of the piston. To replace the gudgeon pin the sleeve 8 is removed and the gudgeon pin is drawn up into the piston until it hits the stop 2. Great care must be taken to ensure that the piston 6 and connecting rod 3 are exactly in line when the gudgeon pin 4 starts entering the connecting rod, otherwise the gudgeon pin will 'pick up' metal. The piston trying to turn with the gudgeon pin will indicate this condition. If the pin is then left in this state rapid wear will take place in the piston bosses. The special tool should be lubricated with ordinary lubricants only (no molybdenum disulphide compounds) and a torque wrench should be used to turn the nut 1. The torque required to turn the nut should be between 5 and 30 lb ft. If the torque is outside these limits the interference fit is unsatisfactory and the connecting rod will have to be renewed (no bushes are fitted with interference fit gudgeon pins). All connecting rods should be checked on a jig by a garage to ensure that they are within the limits of twist and bend.

Refitting the pistons and connecting rods:

When fitted it is essential that the triangular mark on the pistons faces forwards and that the offsets on the connecting rods face the camshaft side of the engine, so the pistons must be refitted to the connecting rods as shown in **FIG 1:17**.

Turn the piston rings so that the gaps are evenly spaced around the piston. Lightly lubricate the rings with clean engine oil and compress them into their grooves with a piston ring clamp of the appropriate size. In an emergency a large Jubilee type clip can be used. Turn the connecting rod so that the offset faces the camshaft side of the engine and lower it down the bore. Enter the skirt of the piston into the bore and gently push the piston into place letting the clamp slide off the piston rings as they enter in turn. Take great care not to force the rings or they will snap. Replace the shell bearings and reconnect the big-ends as already instructed. Reassemble the rest of the engine.

1:12 Crankshaft and main bearings

To remove the crankshaft the engine must be out of the car (see **Section 1:2**). Separate the gearbox from the engine by undoing the ring of bolts around the clutch housing. Draw back the gearbox to clear the input shaft from the clutch. Do not allow the weight of the gearbox to hang on the input shaft.

1 Remove the clutch and flywheel (see **Section 1:7**). Remove the retaining bolts and take off the rear engine plate 10. Remove the valve timing gear (see **Section 1:5**) and the camshaft keeper plate 113. After undoing the securing bolts the front engine plate

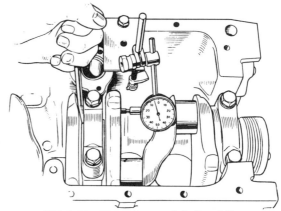

FIG 1:19 Measuring crankshaft end float

39 and gasket 38 can be removed. If full dismantling is required the cylinder head and camshaft should also be taken out. Turn the engine over and remove the sump and oil pump.

2 Remove the two screws 35 holding the front sealing block 36 and pull out the sealing block from the crankcase. Remove the sealing wedges 33 and all traces of jointing compound from the ends of the sealing block 36. Remove the seven screws 13 and take off the rear seal housing 12 and its gasket 14.

3 Check that all the big-ends and main bearing caps are marked as shown in **FIG 1:16**. Disconnect the big-ends, push the connecting rods down the cylinder bores and loosely replace the bearing caps on their respective connecting rods.

4 Mount a DTI as shown in **FIG 1:19** and by levering the crankshaft measure the end float. The end float should be .004 to .008 inch and if this is exceeded new thrust washers, or in bad cases oversize thrust washers, must be fitted on either side of the rear main bearing.

5 Progressively slacken the bolts securing the main bearing caps and remove the caps. Slide the shell bearings out of the caps and lay them all out in the correct order for reassembly. Lift the crankshaft out of the crankcase. Remove the upper row of main bearing shells and lay these in order with their respective bearing caps.

6 Measure with a micrometer, and inspect, the journals of the crankshaft. If they are excessively worn, oval, tapered or scored the crankshaft will have to be reground and undersize bearing shells fitted. Examine the bearing shells. If any of these are pitted, worn or scored the whole set should be renewed. **Never file the bearing caps in an attempt to take up wear.**

7 Clean the crankshaft with paraffin under pressure and then blow through all the oilways with compressed air. This is particularly important if the crankshaft has been reground or a bearing has 'run' as otherwise particles may remain in the oilways and later be forced into the bearings by the oil pressure. Clean out the crankcase, and wash the bearing caps in petrol.

8 Replace the bearing shells in their correct positions, ensuring that the tags on the shells seat in the recesses

FIG 1:20 Aligning front sealing block

14 Fit the front engine plate 39 and a new paper gasket 38 to the front of the engine. If the stud at the top centre of the plate has been removed, it must be replaced with jointing compound on the threads as the tapped hole communicates with the water passages. No paper gasket is fitted under the rear engine plate.

1:13 Reassembling a stripped engine

All dismantling and reassembling operations have been dealt with in detail in the various sections, so that it is simply a matter of tackling the tasks in the correct sequence. **Absolute cleanliness is essential.** All metal parts should be cleaned and degreased. If a trichlorethylene degreasing bath is available use this to degrease the components. Carefully scrape off all remains of old gaskets and jointing compound, and use all new seals and gaskets. Blow through oilways with paraffin followed by dry compressed air. Lubricate all running surfaces with clean engine oil.

Start by fitting the crankshaft, followed by the pistons and connecting rods. Completely refit the valve timing gear, though this is only possible if the original marked sprockets are used. Otherwise the valve timing gear will have to be finalized after the cylinder head has been replaced. Refit the oil pump, sump, flywheel and clutch. The engine can then be turned the right way up for refitting the cylinder head. Leave the accessories till last as they will only get in the way and possibly get damaged if fitted earlier. Refit the engine to the car after mating it up with the gearbox. Torque wrench loads for all important fixings are given in Technical Data or the relevant section.

If will be found simpler to adjust the valve clearances before mating the engine to the gearbox, as the engine can then be turned using the flywheel.

1:14 Adjusting the valve rocker clearance

As no provision is made for a starting handle the engine will have to be turned over by some other method. Remove the sparking plugs and try turning the engine over by

provided. Other than cleaning off protective, no other work should be done on new shells as they are designed to fit as received.

9 Lubricate the bearings with clean engine oil and lay the crankshaft back in place. Refit the upper pair of thrust washers 17 on either side of the rear main bearing so that the whitemetal faces the crankshaft. Refit the bearing caps and lower thrust washers. Progressively tighten all the bolts to a torque of 50 to 55 lb ft (6.913 to 7.604 kg m).

10 Loosely refit the front sealing block 36 to the engine using the two bolts 35. Smear two new wedges 33 with jointing compound and drive them into the slots at the end of the sealing block. Lay a straightedge across the front of the crankcase and align the sealing block to it as shown in **FIG 1:20**. Fully tighten the securing screws 35. Use a sharp knife to trim the sealing wedges flush with the bottom face of the crankcase.

11 Two types of rear crankshaft seal were manufactured and some earlier 1200s may have a scroll type seal on the crankshaft and a plain rear seal housing 12. Later and current engines have a plain end to the crankshaft and an oil seal fitted to the seal housing. Both types are illustrated in **FIG 1:21**. A worn or damaged oil seal may be driven out of the later type of housing by using a small punch through the holes provided. Refit a new seal so that the lips face into the engine.

12 Use special tool No. S335 to refit the later types of oil seal. Coat both sides of a new paper gasket 14 with jointing compound and lay it in place on the crankcase. Fit the special tool to the crankshaft and slide the housing down the tool, using oil as a lubricant. Tighten the securing bolts 13 to a torque of 18 to 20 lb ft and remove the centralizing tool. If no tool is available, secure the housing lightly in place with the bolts and use feeler gauges to even the gap between the housing and the crankshaft, as shown in **FIG 1:22**, then torque load the bolts.

13 The earlier scroll type of seal housing is refitted in the same manner as the later type when no special centralizing tool is available. The gap between the housing and the crankshaft is .002 inch (.0508 mm).

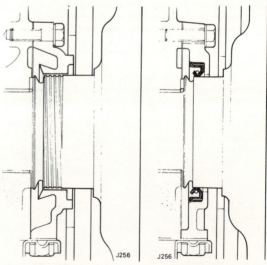

FIG 1:21 Scroll type of rear oil seal is fitted to early engines and the seal type is fitted to later engines

FIG 1:22 Centralizing rear oil seal housing

1:15 Fault diagnosis

(a) Engine will not start

1. Defective coil
2. Faulty distributor capacitor (condenser)
3. Dirty, pitted or incorrectly set distributor points
4. Ignition wires loose or insulation faulty
5. Water on sparking plug leads
6. Battery discharged, or corrosion on terminals
7. Faulty or jammed starter
8. Sparking plug leads wrongly connected
9. Vapour lock in fuel lines (hot weather only)
10. Defective fuel pump
11. Overchoking or underchoking
12. Blocked petrol filter (if fitted) or carburetter jets
13. Leaking valves
14. Sticking valves
15. Valve timing incorrect
16. Ignition timing incorrect

pulling on the fan belt. If the engine is too stiff for this method, engage a gear and turn the engine either by pushing the car or by rotating a jacked up rear road wheel.

1. Remove the rocker cover. **FIG 1:23** shows the valve operating details. All the rocker clearances should be set, with the engine cold, to .010 inch (.25 mm). Check that the working faces of the rockers are not worn. A feeler gauge will bridge any depression and give a false setting for the valves. For extreme accuracy use a DTI to measure the movement on the end of the rocker 2. Feeler gauges are normally sufficient, provided the rocker faces are not pitted.

2. Each valve must be adjusted when its follower is on the base of the cam. This is readily done by turning the engine and working to the following sequence:

    Adjust No. 1 rocker with No. 8 valve fully open
    Adjust No. 3 rocker with No. 6 valve fully open
    Adjust No. 5 rocker with No. 4 valve fully open
    Adjust No. 2 rocker with No. 7 valve fully open
    Adjust No. 8 rocker with No. 1 valve fully open
    Adjust No. 6 rocker with No. 3 valve fully open
    Adjust No. 4 rocker with No. 5 valve fully open
    Adjust No. 7 rocker with No. 2 valve fully open

    Notice that the numbers in each line add up to 9. The table is laid out to turn the engine by the minimum amount between each adjustment, so remembering the number 9, it is easy to go on checking without constant reference to the table.

3. Hold the adjuster 3 with a screwdriver and slacken the locknut 4. Turn the adjuster anticlockwise to open the gap until a .010 inch (.25mm) feeler gauge can easily be passed between the valve stem and the rocker. Turn the adjuster clockwise until resistance is felt on the feeler gauge when it is moved. Hold the adjuster steady with the screwdriver, pressing down hard to take up any slack, and tighten the locknut 4. Recheck the clearance to ensure that the adjuster 3 has not turned when tightening the locknut 4.

4. When all the valves have been adjusted replace the rocker cover, renewing the cork gasket if it is hardened or compressed. Start the engine and after a few minutes check for oil leaks.

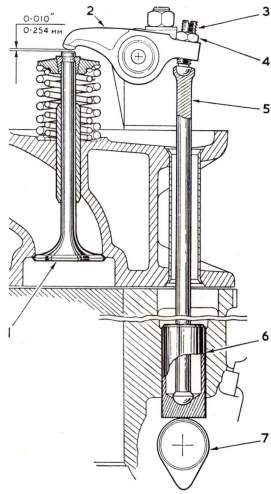

FIG 1:23 Valve operating details

Key to Fig 1:23 1 Valve 2 Rocker 3 Adjusting screw
4 Locknut 5 Pushrod 6 Tappet 7 Cam

(b) Engine stalls
1 Check 1, 2, 3, 4, 5, 10, 11, 12, 13 and 14 in (a)
2 Sparking plugs defective or gaps incorrectly set
3 Retarded ignition
4 Mixture too weak
5 Water in fuel system
6 Petrol tank vent blocked
7 Incorrect valve clearances

(c) Engine idles badly
1 Check 2 and 7 in (b)
2 Air leak at manifold joints
3 Carburetter jet settings wrong
4 Worn piston rings
5 Worn valve stems or guides
6 Weak exhaust valve springs

(d) Engine misfires
1 Check 1, 2, 3, 4, 5, 8, 10, 12, 13, 14, 15 and 16 in (a); also check 2, 3, 4 and 7 in (b)
2 Weak or broken valve springs

(e) Compression low
1 Check 14 and 15 in (a); 4 and 5 in (c) and 2 in (d)
2 Worn piston ring grooves
3 Scored or worn cylinder bores

(f) Engine overheats (see Chapter 4)

(g) Engine lacks power
1 Check 3, 10, 11, 13, 14, 15, 16 and 17 in (a); 1, 2, 3 and 6 in (b); 4 and 5 in (c) and 2 in (d). Also check (e) and (f)
2 Leaking cylinder head gasket
3 Fouled sparking plugs
4 Automatic advance not operating
5 Piston sticking in carburetter

(h) Burnt valves or seats
1 Check 14 and 15 in (a); 6 in (b) and 2 in (d). Also check (f)
2 Excessive carbon around valve head or in cylinder head

(j) Sticking valves
1 Check 2 in (d)
2 Bent valve stem
3 Scored valve stem or guide
4 Incorrect valve clearance
5 Gummy deposits on valve stem

(k) Excessive cylinder wear
1 Check 11 in (a). Also check (f)
2 Lack of oil
3 Dirty oil
4 Piston rings gummed up or broken
5 Badly fitting piston rings
6 Bent connecting rod

(l) Excessive oil consumption
1 Check 4 and 5 in (c) and check (k)
2 Ring gaps too wide
3 Oil return holes in pistons choked with carbon
4 Scored cylinders
5 Oil level too high
6 External oil leaks

(m) Low oil pressure
1 Lack of oil
2 Dirty oil
3 Excessively worn engine
4 Weak relief valve spring
5 Faulty gauge or connections

(n) Crankshaft or connecting rod bearing failure
1 Check 2, 3 and 6 in (k), also check 1, 2, 3 and 4 in (m)
2 Restricted oilways
3 Worn journals or crankpins
4 Loose bearing caps

(o) Internal water leakage (see Chapter 4)

(p) Poor water circulation (see Chapter 4)

(q) Corrosion (see Chapter 4)

(r) High fuel consumption (see Chapter 2)

(s) 'Pinking'
1 Too low a grade of fuel
2 Ignition too far advanced
3 Excessive carbon in the cylinder head

(t) Engine 'knocks'
1 Worn big-end bearings
2 Worn main bearing
3 Piston knock (slap)
4 Worn small-ends
5 Incorrectly adjusted rocker clearances

CHAPTER 2

THE FUEL SYSTEM

2:1 Description
2:2 Routine maintenance
2:3 The fuel pump
2:4 Operation of Solex carburetter
2:5 Adjusting the Solex carburetter
2:6 Dismantling the Solex carburetter

2:7 Operation of Stromberg carburetter
2:8 Servicing the Stromberg carburetter
2:9 Slow-running adjustments on the Stromberg carburetter
2:10 The air cleaner
2:11 Fault diagnosis

2:1 Description

All the models covered by this Manual use an engine driven AC mechanical fuel pump. Fuel is stored in a tank at the rear of the car. On the estate car the larger fuel tank is mounted under the floor extension. Details of the tank are shown in **FIG 2:1**. The other models have a smaller fuel tank mounted inside the luggage compartment. The tank fixings for the smaller tank are shown in **FIG 2:2**. Bi-metal gauge units are fitted to both fuel tanks to measure the quantity of fuel.

Single carburetters are fitted as standard to all models. The Herald 13/60 range has a variable choke sidedraught 150.CD Stromberg and the Herald 1200 range has a Solex B.30 PSEI carburetter fitted.

An air filter is fitted to both types of carburetter to clean the incoming air and to prevent excessive wear by the microscopic particles of dust in the outside air.

The principles of operation of the two types of carburetter and the fuel pump will be dealt with in the relevant sections.

2:2 Routine maintenance

1 Apart from the usual tuning and cleaning operations the Solex carburetter requires no routine maintenance.

2 At periodic intervals remove the hexagon nut from the top of the Stromberg carburetter and fill the oil well with SAE.20 engine oil to within a $\frac{1}{4}$ inch of the end of the rod in which the damper operates.
3 Periodically clean out the sediment bowl and the gauze filter in the fuel pump. Do not use rags or any fluffy material.
4 If water contaminated fuel has been used, or there is an excess of dirt in the fuel pump sediment bowl, remove the fuel tank and clean it out thoroughly. Disconnect the fuel lines and blow through them using an airline.
5 At regular intervals check the carburetter controls for freedom of movement and lightly oil the pivot points.

2:3 The fuel pump

This is an AC mechanical fuel pump driven by a cam on the engine camshaft. The details of the pump are shown in **FIG 2:3**. The operating lever 18 is moved by the engine cam. As the lever moves towards the pump it moves the linkage which draws the diaphragm 12 downwards to create a suction in the pump chamber. The inlet valve opens allowing fuel to be drawn in from the sediment chamber and through the gauze filter 5. When the operating lever 18 moves back under the pressure of the

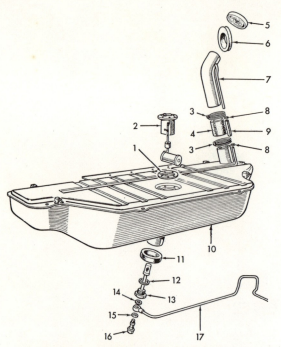

FIG 2:1 Estate car fuel tank details

Key to Fig 2:1   1 Gauge unit washer
2 Bi-metal gauge unit   3 Hose clip   4 Filler pipe connection   5 Filler cap   6 Fuel filler grommet
7 Filler pipe assembly   8 Hose clip   9 Vent pipe connection
10 Fuel tank assembly   11 Sealing ring   12 Sealing washer
13 Pipe assembly   14 Adaptor washer   15 Adaptor washer
16 Adaptor bolt   17 Pipe assembly

FIG 2:2 Standard fuel tank attachments

entering the float chamber. The resultant fuel pressure holds the diaphragm 12 down against the pressure of the spring 13 and the pump linkage 'free-wheels', so that no more fuel is pumped out. As soon as the needle valve in the float chamber opens again, the fuel pressure is lowered, and the diaphragm can once again start to be operated by the linkage. A hand priming lever 22 is fitted so that the pump can be operated, either for tests or priming the carburetter, when the engine is not running.

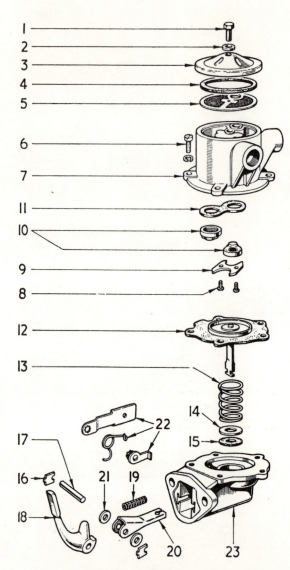

FIG 2:3 Fuel pump details

Key to Fig 2:3   1 Retaining screw   2 Washer
3 Cover   4 Joint   5 Gauze   6 Screw   7 Body
8 Screws   9 Retainer   10 Valves   11 Upper retainer
12 Diaphragm assembly   13 Spring   14 Washer
15 Washer   16 Retainer   17 Spindle   18 Operating lever   19 Return spring   20 Operating fork
21 Distance washer   22 Priming lever assembly
23 Lower body

return spring 19, the diaphragm is forced upwards by the pressure of the spring 13. The inlet valve closes and the outlet valve opens, allowing the fuel to be pumped to the carburetter float chamber. This sequence continues until the carburetter float chamber is full. The needle valve in the float chamber then prevents any more fuel from

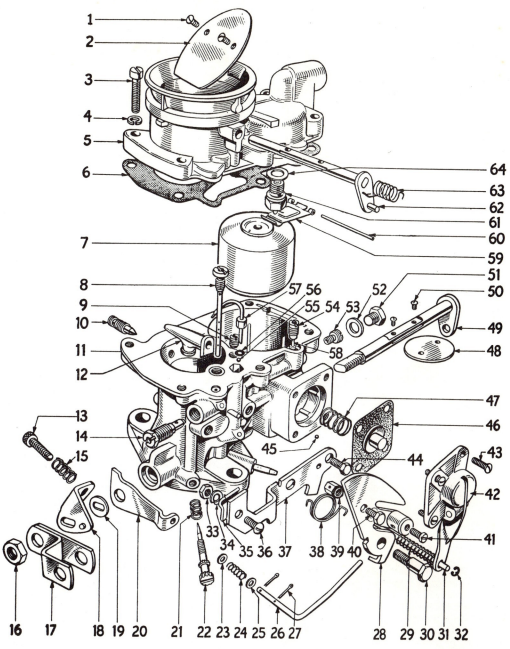

FIG 2:4 Solex carburetter details

Key to Figs 2:4, 2:5, 2:6 and 2:7 1 Screw   2 Strangler   3 Screw   4 Spring washer   5 Top cover
6 Gasket   7 Float   8 Air correction jet   9 Econostat fuel jet   10 Spraying bridge retaining screw   11 Body
12 Spraying bridge   13 Slow-running adjustment screw   14 Slow-running fuel jet   15 Spring   16 Nut   17 Throttle lever
18 Stop lever   19 Slotted washer   20 Strangler, interconnecting lever   21 Spring   22 Volume control screw
23 Washer   24 Spring   25 Washer   26 Strangler, interconnecting pushrod   27 Splitpin   28 Strangler operating cam
29 Spring   30 Pivot bolt   31 Accelerator pump pushrod   32 Circlip   33 Nut   34 Spring washer   35 Cable clip
36 Screw   37 Abutment bracket   38 Spring   39 Solderless nipple   40 Pinch screw   41 Pinch screw
42 Pump cover and lever assembly   43 Screw   44 Setscrew   45 Non-return ball valve   46 Pump diaphragm
47 Diaphragm spring   48 Throttle butterfly   49 Throttle spindle   50 Screw   51 Main jet access plug
52 Fibre washer   53 Main jet   54 Pump chamber non-return valve body   55 Non-return ball valve   56 Fibre washer
57 Accelerator pump jet   58 Pump chamber non-return valve   59 Float lever   60 Float lever pivot   61 Needle valve
62 Strangler cam follower and spindle   63 Return spring   64 Fibre washer   65 Solderless nipple   66 Screw
67 Abutment bracket   68 Choke cable   69 Throttle cable   70 Nuts   71 Rubber sleeve   72 Fuel pipe

Cleaning the sediment chamber:

This operation is carried out while the pump is still fitted to the engine. The fuel level is higher than the pump so, unless precautions are taken, fuel will syphon out through the pump when the cover is removed. Disconnect the fuel supply pipe to the fuel pipe and plug it with a rubber bung. Remove the screw 1 and washer 2 from the top of the pump. Lift off the cover 3 complete with seal 4. Carefully remove the gauze filter 5. Use a thin screwdriver to scrape the sediment loose from the sediment bowl, taking care not to damage the outlet valve. Wash the filter gauze in clean petrol and use an airline to blow away loose dirt from inside the pump and the gauze filter. Check that the sealing ring 4 is undamaged and replace the parts in the reverse order of dismantling. Prime the carburetters by the hand priming lever and start the engine. Check for fuel leaks.

Removing the fuel pump:

The pump is mounted on the lefthand side rear of the engine, and is held in place by two nuts. Disconnect both fuel lines to the pump and plug the supply pipe to prevent fuel syphoning out. Remove the two nuts and withdraw the pump, complete with gasket and any shims, from the crankcase. Replace the pump in the reverse order of removal.

Dismantling the fuel pump:

The pump is dismantled by removing the parts in the numerical order of the key to **FIG 2:3**, but noting the following points:
1 Clean off dirt from the outside of the pump and file a light mark across the flanges of the upper and lower bodies 7 and 23 before starting to dismantle the pump.
2 Invert the upper body 7 before removing the screws 8 which hold the valve assemblies in place.
3 The diaphragm 12 is freed from the link 20 by lightly pressing the diaphragm down and turning it 90 deg. in an anticlockwise direction, then lifting it out of the lower body 23. Examine the diaphragm for fine splits or perishing and renew it if required.
4 Wash all the parts in clean fuel and carefully check the castings for fine hairline cracks or distorted flanges. Renew all worn parts, but if the pump is badly worn consider fitting an exchange unit.

Reassembling the pump is the reversal of the dismantling procedure. It should be noted that the inlet and outlet valves 10 are identical and interchangeable, but they must be reassembled correctly. The inlet valve must be fitted pointing towards the diaphragm and the outlet valve fitted pointing away from the diaphragm, as shown in **FIG 2:3**. Use the file marks made before dismantling to align the upper body to the lower body.

Testing the fuel pump:

The fuel pump should operate at a pressure between 1.5 to 2.5 lb/sq in (.1 to .18 kg). A flow-rig is required to test the fuel pump fully but a functional check can be carried out without using any equipment. Disconnect the fuel pipe from the carburetter float chamber, operate the hand priming lever and catch the fuel in a suitable container. At every stroke of the hand priming lever a good gush of fuel should jet from the pipe. Reconnect the fuel pipe and again use the hand priming lever. Fill the carburetter float chamber. A loss of resistance on the lever indicates that the diaphragm is being held down. Unless there is a fuel leak, the diaphragm should remain in the down position for a reasonable length of time and the hand priming lever should work easily. With pressure in the pump, again check for leaks or hairline cracks in the castings.

2:4 Operation of Solex carburetter

The details of the Solex carburetter are shown in **FIG 2:4**. The main body 11 of the carburetter contains the fixed aperture choke bore and, at the bottom end of the choke bore, pivots the throttle butterfly valve 48 on the spindle 49. The float chamber is integral with the main body 11, and passages and tapped holes for the jets are also integral. The top cover carries the choke (strangler) butterfly valve and the needle valve for the float chamber.

The air for the engine is drawn through the choke bore, and the volume is controlled by the throttle butterfly valve. The choke bore is shaped like a venturi so the airflow is speeded up and there is a pressure drop at the throat. Fuel is sucked through the main jet and is mixed with the air by the action of the spraying bridge 12.

At low speeds the suction is insufficient to draw adequate fuel through the main jet. Instead the pressure drop by the throttle butterfly is used to draw fuel through the slow-running jet 14. Compensators are fitted to provide a smooth transition from slow-running, when the throttle butterfly is nearly shut, through the point where the suction by the butterfly is decreasing and the suction in the throat is not sufficient to make the main jet independent.

To enrich the mixture for acceleration an accelerator pump is fitted to the main body. This operates from the throttle linkage and injects the extra fuel through the jet 57.

The mixture also requires to be enriched for starting the engine from cold. The strangler butterfly 2 is spring-loaded to shut and cut off the air supply but is normally held open by the cam 28. The cam is controlled by the choke knob in the car. Shutting the strangler valve causes extra depression in the choke bore and extra fuel is then drawn through the jets. As the airflow increases the air tries to open the strangler valve against the pressure of the return spring, so the valve assumes a position balanced between these two forces.

2:5 Adjusting the Solex carburetter

Provided the correct jet sizes are used, the only adjustment that the carburetter requires is for idling speed. The carburetter cannot be adjusted satisfactorily if the engine is in poor condition or the ignition is not correctly set. Run the engine until it reaches its normal working temperature. There is no need to remove the air cleaner. **FIG 2:5** shows the carburetter fitted to the car.
1 Turn the slow-running adjustment screw 13 until the engine speed is approximately 500 rev/min.
2 Unscrew the volume screw 22 until the engine begins to hunt. Screw the volume screw back in until the hunting disappears and the engine idles smoothly.
3 The engine speed may increase so adjust it back to 500 rev/min by turning the adjustment screw 13. Slowing down the idling speed may then bring back the hunting so cure this by further slight adjustment of the volume screw 22. **The volume screw 22 should never be tightened fully home.**

2:6 Dismantling the Solex carburetter

The carburetter and jets can be cleaned without removing the carburetter from the car or completely dismantling it.

1 Remove the air cleaner and disconnect the fuel pipe 72 from the float chamber. Remove the screws 3 and washers 4, and lift off the top cover 5 and gasket 6.
2 Remove the needle from the needle valve assembly, and check that the tapered seat is not worn to a step. Unscrew the seat from the top cover and renew the complete assembly if the needle is worn. Blow through the fuel inlet to clear out any dirt.
3 Lift out the float lever and pivot 59 and 60, then withdraw the float 7 from the float chamber. Shake the float to check that no fuel has leaked into it. Renew the float if it is punctured. The carburetter body with the float removed is shown in **FIG 2:6**.
4 Unscrew the plug 51 and use a long screwdriver to unscrew the main jet 53. Unscrew the slow-running jet 14, the Econstat jet 9 and the air correction jet 8. Remove the valve body 54 and the valve 58. Pull out the accelerator pump jet 57, taking care not to lose either the washer 56 or the ball 55 under the jet.
5 Unscrew the volume control screw 22 and remove it with its spring. If the tapered end of the screw is worn to a step renew the screw, otherwise accurate adjustments are impossible. The screw should never be tightened against its seating as this is the main cause of wear.
6 Take out the screws 43 and swing the accelerator pump cover to one side on the pushrod 31. Carefully remove the diaphragm 46 and spring 47, taking extra care not to lose the ball 45 from the pump housing. Renew the diaphragm if it is split, worn or distorted.
7 Clean out the float chamber with petrol and wash the jets in a bowl of clean petrol. Blow carefully through the internal passages in the body using an airline. The jets should also be cleaned with compressed air. **Never use wire or any hard material to clean out the jets.**
8 Reassemble the carburetter in the reverse order of dismantling. Use new seals if possible. Prime the carburetter by hand and check for leaks before starting the engine, then check again for leaks. Use the correct size of screwdriver when removing or refitting the jets. They are made of brass and the wrong screwdriver will quickly tear the slots making the jets difficult to turn.

Removing the carburetter:

1 Remove the air cleaner. Disconnect the fuel pipe 72. Disconnect the vacuum stub by pulling the rubber sleeve 71 off the carburetter stub pipe.
2 Release the inner and outer choke cables 68 from the abutment plate 37. Free the inner cable from the choke cam 28 by slackening the pinch bolt 40. Disconnect the throttle cable 69 from the throttle lever 17.
3 Unscrew the two nuts 70 and lift off the carburetter. Remove the insulating gasket. Check that the gaskets are undamaged and that the carburetter flange is true and flat. Use a scraper to carefully remove any damage. The carburetter is replaced in the reverse order of removal.

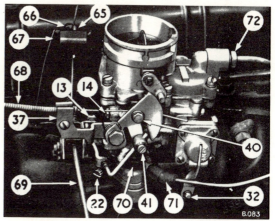

FIG 2:5 Solex carburetter fitted to engine

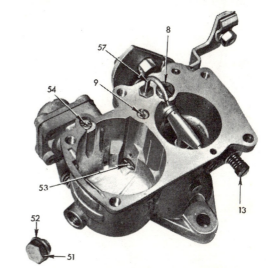

FIG 2:6 Solex carburetter jets

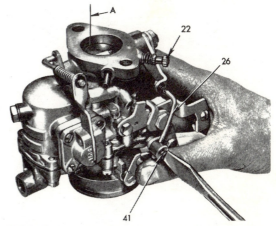

FIG 2:7 Adjusting the throttle and choke interconnection using a .027 inch diameter (.7 mm) piece of wire A

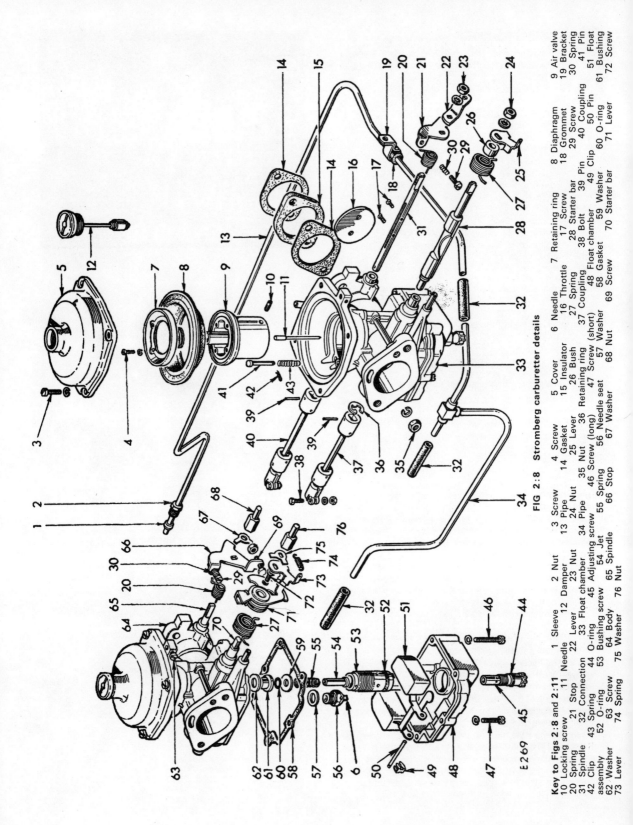

FIG 2:8 Stromberg carburetter details

Key to Figs 2:8 and 2:11
1 Sleeve 2 Nut 3 Screw 4 Screw 5 Cover 6 Needle 7 Retaining ring 8 Diaphragm 9 Air valve
10 Locking screw 11 Stop 12 Damper 13 Pipe 14 Gasket 15 Insulator 16 Throttle 17 Screw 18 Grommet 19 Bracket
20 Spring 21 Spring 22 Lever 23 Nut 24 Nut 25 Lever 26 Bush 27 Spring 28 Starter bar 29 Screw 30 Spring
31 Spindle 32 Connection 33 Float chamber 34 Pipe 35 Nut 36 Lever 37 Coupling 38 Bolt 39 Pin 40 Coupling 41 Pin
42 Clip 43 Spring 44 O-ring 45 Adjusting screw 46 Screw (long) 47 Screw (short) 48 Float chamber 49 Clip 50 Pin 51 Float
assembly 52 O-ring 53 Bushing screw 54 Jet 55 Needle seat 56 Gasket 57 Washer 58 Gasket 59 Washer 60 O-ring 61 Bushing
62 Washer 63 Screw 64 Body 65 Spindle 66 Stop 67 Washer 68 Nut 69 Screw 70 Starter bar 71 Lever 72 Screw
73 Lever 74 Spring 75 Spring 76 Nut

30

Dismantling the carburetter:

1 Remove the carburetter from the car and dismantle it as instructed under the instructions for cleaning the carburetter earlier in this section.

2 The top cover 5 can be completely dismantled by removing the two screws 1 holding the strangler valve 2 to the spindle 62. Slide the valve out of the spindle and withdraw the spindle from the top cover.

3 Free the accelerator pump cover assembly 42 from the pushrod 31 connecting it to the throttle spindle by removing the spring clip 32. Slacken the ferrule screw 41 and ease out the interconnection rod 26 from the cam 40. Remove the cam 40 by taking out the pivot bolt 30, and being careful not to lose the spring 38. The abutment bracket 37 is now held on only by the bolt 44.

4 Unscrew the nut 16. Remove the throttle lever 17, stop lever 18, slotted washer 19 and the interconnection lever 20. Remove the two screws 50 and slide the throttle butterfly 48 out of the throttle spindle 49. The spindle can then be withdrawn from the body. The spraying bridge 12 is secured in place by the screw 10.

5 Thoroughly clean all the parts, using petrol and compressed air, and then examine them for wear. The most likely points of wear are where the spindles join the castings. If renewing the spindles 49 and 62 still leaves an excessive clearance, then it is advisable to fit an exchange carburetter. After a long period of service the jets wear slightly oversize, and this is even more possible if the jets have been incorrectly cleaned. A new set of jets will restore the carburetter.

6 Reassemble the carburetter in the reverse order of dismantling. When reassembled, insert a length of .027 inch diameter (.7 mm) wire A between the throttle butterfly valve 48 and the bore of the body as shown in **FIG 2:7**. Hold the strangler valve 2 fully closed and tighten the screw 41 to set the interconnecting rod 26.

2:7 Operation of Stromberg carburetter

The Stromberg carburetter uses a constant-vacuum variable choke orifice controlled by a vacuum operated air valve. This valve is in the form of a piston attached to a diaphragm which operates in a suction chamber on the top of the carburetter. The suction in the carburetter is fed to the suction chamber by internal passages and this will then raise the piston, opening the throat area of the choke. As the weight of the piston is constant the piston will rise until the vacuum in the carburetter is also a constant.

The amount of fuel is controlled by a tapered needle fixed to the air valve piston and operating in a jet of fixed area. As the piston rises the needle is withdrawn from the jet, increasing the effective area of the jet. As the vacuum is constant more fuel will be drawn through the jet to match the increased volume of air drawn in through the piston. A normal butterfly valve downstream of the air valve controls the volume of air to the engine.

The mixture strength is varied by raising or lowering the fixed area jet so that it operates on a different range of the tapered needle.

An oil filled damper is fitted to the top of the air valve. This serves the dual function of damping out rapid fluctuations of the air valve and also acts as an accelerator pump. On acceleration the damper causes the air valve to lag behind the instantaneous demands of the engine and the choke area is smaller than required. This leads to an

FIG 2:9 Stromberg carburetter, as fitted to the 13/60 engine

FIG 2:10 Checking float chamber fuel level

increased vacuum in the throat and excess fuel for acceleration is then drawn through the jet.

Operating the choke knob rotates a starter bar which lifts the air valve, enriching the mixture for cold starts. The starter bar is connected by a cam to the throttle so the engine idling speed is also increased for cold starts. The design of the carburetter ensures that a single jet is sufficient for all running conditions of the engine.

2:8 Servicing the Stromberg carburetter

The details of the carburetter are shown in **FIG 2:8**. A twin carburetter installation is shown, but the actual single carburetter installation on the Herald 13/60 is shown in **FIG 2:9**.

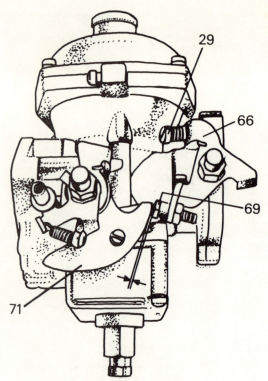

FIG 2:11 Carburetter adjustment

It is advisable to renew all washers and gaskets whenever the carburetter is dismantled. These are available as kits.

Removing the carburetter:

Remove the air filter. Disconnect the choke cable, throttle cable and the fuel supply pipe to the float chamber. Unscrew the two nuts securing the carburetter to the manifold and remove the carburetter. Check the condition of the gaskets between the carburetter and manifold, renewing them if necessary. Examine the face of the carburetter flange, and file or scrape it flat if there is any distortion or damage.

Dismantling the carburetter:

1 Clean the outside of the carburetter, using petrol and an old toothbrush. Lightly file a mark across the flanges of the cover 5 and body 64 to facilitate reassembly. Unscrew and remove the damper assembly 12.
2 Remove the four screws 3 and their washers. Lift off the cover 5 and withdraw the piston 9 and diaphragm 8 assembly. The diaphragm, piston and needle assembly need not be dismantled unless a new needle 11 or diaphragm 8 is to be fitted. **Take great care not to drop these parts or let the weight rest on the needle.** If the needle is bent it must be renewed.
3 Turn the carburetter over and unscrew the two long screws 46 and three short screws 47. Remove the float chamber 48. Spring the clip 49 free and pull out the float pin 50 to free the floats 51. Lift out the needle 6 and unscrew the needle seat 56 and seal 57 from the carburetter.
4 Unscrew and remove the adjusting screw 45 followed by the bushing screw 53. The jet 54, spring 55, washer 59, O-ring 60, bushing 61 and washer 62 can now be removed from the body 64.
5 If either the starter bar 28 or throttle spindle 31 need to be removed first remove the throttle lever and interconnection linkage by undoing the nuts 23 and 24. Make a careful note of the position of the pieces for reassembly. The throttle spindle 31 is freed by undoing the two screws 17 and sliding the throttle butterfly valve out of the slot in the spindle.

Reassembling the carburetter:

1 Clean all the parts in petrol and remove any sediment. Examine the needle 6. If the seat is worn to a step renew both the needle and the seating 56. Examine the jet needle 11. If it is bent or scored slacken the screw 10 and renew the needle, fitting the new needle so that the bottom shoulder of the needle is flush with the face of the piston 9. The diaphragm 8 is secured to the piston by the retaining ring 7 and four screws 4. Examine the spindles 28 and 31, renewing them if they are worn. If new spindles do not cure excessive wear then the carburetter must be exchanged for a new or reconditioned unit.
2 Reassemble the carburetter in the reverse order of dismantling. Use new seals and washers to ensure that the carburetter will not leak when refitted. The diaphragm 8 has a small protruding tag which seats into a recess in the body.
3 Before replacing the float chamber 48 check that the float chamber fuel level is correct.
4 Leave the bushing screw 53 just slack and recentralize the jet before fully tightening the bushing screw.

Float chamber fuel level:

This operation must be carried out with the carburetter removed from the car. Invert the carburetter and remove the float chamber 48. Check that the highest point of the floats 51 is .71 inch (18 mm) above the bottom face of the body 64, as shown in **FIG 2:10** at dimension A. If required, reset by carefully bending the tag on the floats 51 which contacts the needle 6. An additional thin washer under the seating 56 will lower the fuel level.

Centralizing the jet:

This operation must be carried out every time the bushing screw 53 is slackened or a new needle 11 is fitted. Remove the damper 12 and the air cleaner. Raise the piston 9 to the top of its travel and let it fall. It should fall freely and land on the bridge of the body with an audible click. In service, failure of the piston to fall freely can be caused by sticky oil or dirt on the piston rod. Remove the top cover 5 and the piston assembly. Clean out with petrol or methylated spirits and lightly oil the piston rod before reassembling the parts. Also check that the needle 11 is not bent as this can be another cause of the piston sticking. Centralize the jet as follows:

1 Screw the adjusting screw 45 right up until the jet 54 is flush with the bridge in the carburetter. Slacken the

bushing screw 53 half a turn and press the piston 9 down, using a pencil through the threaded hole in the top cover 5.

2 Slowly tighten the screw 53, checking regularly that the needle remains free in the jet orifice. Check by raising the piston $\frac{1}{4}$ inch and allowing it to fall. The piston should stop firmly on the bridge. When satisfied replace the damper, after checking the oil level, and refit the air cleaner.

2:9 Slow-running adjustments to the Stromberg carburetter

Provided that the correct needle and jet are used, setting the carburetter for slow-running is sufficient to set the carburetter for all running conditions. The engine must be in good condition and the ignition correctly set before adjusting the carburetter.

If the carburetter has been dismantled set it to an approximate running position. Unscrew the slow-running adjustment screw 29 until it is just clear of the stop with the throttle valve shut. Slightly open the throttle valve by screwing in the adjusting screw 29 by $1\frac{1}{2}$ turns. Screw the adjusting screw 45 up until the jet is level with the bridge of the carburetter and then unscrew it three turns.

1 Run the engine until it reaches its normal operating temperature. Remove the air cleaner. Adjust the idling speed, using screw 29, until it is approximately 600 to 650 rev/min, making sure that the screw 69 is well clear of the cam 71.

2 Listen to the exhaust beat. If it is smooth and regular then the mixture setting is correct. If there is a heavy rhythmic misfire with black smoke coming from the exhaust then the mixture is too rich. A weak splashy misfire and colourless exhaust indicates a weak mixture. Screw the adjusting screw 44 up to weaken the mixture and down to enrich it.

3 Check the mixture setting by raising the piston $\frac{1}{32}$ inch, either with a long thin screwdriver through the air intake or by using the piston lifting pin 41. If the engine speed rises then the mixture is too rich. Hesitation or stopping indicates a weak mixture. Adjust the mixture until the engine speed remains constant or falls slightly on raising the piston.

4 If required, reset the idling speed back to 600 to 650 rev/min. Refer to **FIG 2:11**. Turn the screw 69 until the clearance between its head and the cam 71 is $\frac{1}{16}$ inch (1.6 mm).

2:10 The air cleaner

The air cleaner is mounted directly on the carburetter intake. A clamp bolt tightens it around the intake of the Solex carburetter but bolts hold it on to the flange of the Stromberg. The majority of cleaners use a renewable paper element. The element should be changed regularly, at intervals depending on the climatic conditions. Halfway through its life it is permissible to remove loose dust and dirt from the element, using gentle air pressure or a soft brush, but once dirty it must be renewed and cannot be cleaned. In very dusty conditions some cars may be fitted with an oil wetted mesh filter. This should be cleaned by washing in petrol or paraffin. The gauze is then soaked in clean engine oil, and the surplus oil allowed to drain away before refitting the air filter.

2:11 Fault diagnosis

(a) Leakage or insufficient fuel delivered
1 Air vent in tank restricted
2 Petrol pipes blocked
3 Air leaks at pipe connections
4 Pump filter blocked
5 Pump gaskets faulty
6 Pump diaphragm defective
7 Pump valves sticking or seating badly
8 Fuel vaporizing in pipelines due to heat

(b) Excessive fuel consumption
1 Carburetter needs adjusting
2 Fuel leakage
3 Sticking controls or choke device
4 Dirty air cleaner
5 Excessive engine temperature
6 Brakes binding
7 Tyres under-inflated
8 Idling speed too high
9 Car overloaded

(c) Idling speed too high
1 Rich fuel mixture
2 Carburetter controls sticking
3 Slow-running screws incorrectly adjusted
4 Worn carburetter butterfly valve

(d) Noisy fuel pump
1 Loose mountings
2 Air leaks on suction side and at diaphragm
3 Obstruction in fuel pipe
4 Clogged pump filter

(e) No fuel delivery
1 Float needle stuck
2 Vent in tank blocked
3 Pipeline obstructed
4 Pump diaphragm stiff or damaged
5 Inlet valve in pump stuck open
6 Bad air leak on suction side of pump

NOTES

CHAPTER 3

THE IGNITION SYSTEM

3:1 Description
3:2 Routine maintenance
3:3 Ignition faults
3:4 Removing and dismantling the distributor

3:5 Timing the ignition
3:6 Sparking plugs
3:7 Fault diagnosis

3:1 Description

The distributor is mounted on the engine and driven by the camshaft at half engine speed (each cylinder only fires once for every two revolutions of the engine). The distributor consists of a shaft, keyed to the engine, which has a cam at the top opening and closing contacts in the body. A rotor arm on top of the cam and a distributor cap mounted on the body feed the HT voltage to the firing cylinder. When the contacts are closed an LT current flows through the ignition coil primary circuit and contact points. There are four lobes on the rotating cam and the distributor position is so set that a lobe is just opening the contacts when the appropriate cylinder is in the exact firing position. As the contacts open the current is sharply cut off, assisted by the action of the capacitor, and the magnetic field in the coil collapses rapidly inducing a high voltage in the secondary turns of the coil. This high voltage is taken by an HT lead to the carbon brush in the centre of the distributor cap and from that directly to the rotor arm. The rotor arm directs the high voltage, through the appropriate contact in the distributor cap and HT lead, to the sparking plug where the spark fires the mixture.

A centrifugal advance mechanism is fitted to the distributor shaft. As the engine speed increases, two weights are flung out by centrifugal force against the restraint of the springs. The movement of the weights turns the cam further in relation to the shaft in the direction of rotation, thus advancing the ignition point as the engine speed rises.

A vacuum unit is connected to the inlet manifold by a small-bore pipe. The vacuum unit is connected to the base plate of the contact breakers, rotating them about the fixed position and so adjusting the ignition timing for the engine load and throttle opening.

The vacuum unit is fitted with a micrometer adjustment so the ignition point can be accurately set for different grades of fuel or adjusted to suit the engine condition.

The various components of the distributor are shown in **FIG 3:1**. **FIG 3:2** shows the distributor shaft, centrifugal weights and cam in greater detail.

3:2 Routine maintenance

Ensure that the outside of the distributor, the HT leads and the top of the ignition coil are always kept clean and dry. Wipe away moisture or oil with a clean, dry cloth, paying particular attention to the crevices between the HT leads on the distributor cap.

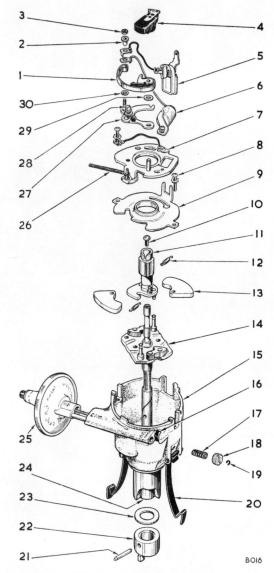

FIG 3:1 Distributor details

Key to Figs 3:1 and 3:2
1 Spring contact
2 Insulating sleeve   3 Nut   4 Rotor arm   5 LT terminal
6 Capacitor   7 Contact plate   8 Screw   9 Base plate
10 Screw   11 Cam   12 Centrifugal spring
13 Centrifugal weights   14 Action plate and shaft assembly
15 Distributor body   16 Ratchet spring   17 Coiled spring
18 Adjusting nut   19 Circlip   20 Cap retainer   21 Pin
22 Driving dog   23 Washer   24 Bearing sleeve
25 Vacuum unit   26 Vacuum connecting spring
27 Fixed contact   28 Screw   29 Insulating washer
30 Insulating washer   31 Collar

Remove the distributor cap and refer to **FIG 3:3**. Lift off the rotor arm and pour a few drops of engine oil over the screw indicated by arrow 1. A clearance is provided around the screw, so it should not be removed. Put a single drop of oil on the contact pivot 2. Work the moving contact to ensure that it is free on the pivot and to allow the oil to spread evenly. If the contact sticks, the points will have to be removed and the pivot lightly polished with a piece of fine emerycloth. Lightly grease the surface of the cam 3. Inject a few drops of oil between the contact breaker base plate and the side of the housing. Wipe away any surplus oil. Wipe the inside of the distributor cap and the rotor arm with soft, dry cloth and replace them on the distributor.

Adjusting the contact breaker points:

Before adjusting the points make sure that they are clean. With the distributor cap and rotor arm removed, slacken the fixed contact securing screw, arrowed in **FIG 3:4**. Insert a screwdriver, as shown, between the slot in the fixed contact and the slotted hole in the base plate. Turn the engine so that a lobe of the cam is under the foot of the moving contact and the contact points gap is widest. Measure the gap with feeler gauges and turn the screwdriver until the gap measures .015 inch (.38 mm). Tighten the securing screw and recheck the points gap before replacing the rotor arm and distributor cap.

Cleaning the contact breaker points:

If the points are dirty they should be cleaned using a small piece of carborundum paper, but if they are pitted it is best to remove them and clean them using a fine carborundum stone or file. Remove the distributor cap and rotor arm. Unscrew the nut 3, shown in **FIG 3:1**, and withdraw the insulating sleeve 2. Lift off the wires for the capacitor 6 and LT terminal 5. The moving contact 1 can now be removed. Lift the two insulated washers 29 and 30 off the fixed contact 27. Remove the securing screw 28 and lift out the fixed contact. **Clean the points, carefully removing metal so that the points are flat and meet squarely when assembled.**

Refit the points in the reverse order of dismantling, fitting the larger insulating washer 29 to the pivot over the fixed contact. If the points are excessively worn a new set should be fitted. Use a spring balance to check that the tension on the moving contact spring is 18 to 24 ozs. Lubricate and then adjust the points as described earlier. **Make sure the rotor arm 4 is replaced before refitting the distributor cap.** It is surprisingly easy to lay the rotor arm in a safe place and then forget to replace it, with consequent frustration when the car will not start.

3:3 Ignition faults

If the engine runs unevenly, and the carburetter is correctly adjusted, set the engine to idle at a fast speed. Taking care not to touch the metal parts, short out or disconnect each plug in turn. Use an insulated handle screwdriver between the sparking plug top and the cylinder head to short the plug. Shorting, or disconnecting, a plug that is not firing will make no difference to the running but doing the same to a plug that is firing properly will make the uneven running more pronounced.

Having located the faulty cylinder, stop the engine and remove any insulator or shroud fitted to that plug lead. Start the engine and using insulated tongs, or taking other precautions to avoid shocks, hold the metal end of the HT lead about $\frac{3}{16}$ inch from an earthed clean bit of metal (not near the carburetter). A strong regular spark shows that the fault may lie with the sparking plug.

Remember that the fault may be in the engine and not in the ignition circuit, as a sticking valve can cause similar symptoms. Stop the engine, remove the sparking plug and either clean it, as described in **Section 3:6**, or else substitute it with a new sparking plug.

If the spark is weak or irregular check that the HT lead is not cracked or perished. If the lead is found to be faulty, renew it and repeat the test. If there is no improvement, remove the distributor cap and wipe the inside with a clean soft cloth. Check that the carbon brush protrudes from the moulding and moves freely against the internal spring. Examine the inside surface of the cap for cracks or 'tracking'. 'Tracking' can be seen as a thin black line between the electrodes or to some metal part in contact with the cap. Scraping away tracking with a sharp knife may effect a temporary cure. Renew the cap if it is cracked or shows signs of 'tracking'. Use a sharp knife to clean away deposits from the distributor cap contacts. Check the rotor arm, though if this is split or faulty all the cylinders will be affected.

Testing the low-tension circuit:

Before carrying out any electrical tests, confirm that the contact points are clean and correctly set.

1 Disconnect the LT cable from the CB terminal of the ignition coil. Connect a low-wattage 12-volt test bulb between the terminal and the cable end. Switch on the ignition and turn the engine slowly over by hand. To turn the engine over by hand first remove the sparking plugs and try turning it by pulling the fan belt. If the engine is too stiff to be turned by this method engage a gear and turn it either by pushing the car or by rotating a jacked up rear wheel. The test lamp should light when the points are closed and go out when the points open. Either staying continuously on, or failing to light at all indicates a fault. The lamp staying on continuously indicates a shortcircuit in the distributor, or a faulty capacitor.

2 If the lamp does not light, remove it and reconnect the cable to the CB terminal on the coil. Disconnect the other cable from the SW terminal on the coil and connect the test bulb between this cable and a good earth. The lamp should now be on continuously with the ignition switched on. If it now lights but did not light previously then the ignition coil is at fault and must be renewed. If the lamp still fails to light, reconnect the cable to the SW terminal and turn the engine until the contact points are open. Using the wiring diagram in Technical Data as a guide, trace through the wiring with either a test lamp or 0–20 voltmeter until the fault is found.

3 Simple tests will help to determine in which part of the circuit the fault lies. Switch on the ignition and operate the direction indicators. If these operate then the ignition is also satisfactory as far as the flasher unit terminal socket. If the direction indicators fail to operate then turn on the windscreen wiper motor. If this now operates then the fault lies between the ignition switch and the flasher unit terminal socket. The wipers also failing to operate show that the fault is in the battery and ignition switch part of the circuit. Check the battery terminals first before testing the remainder of the circuit. Using these simple checks will help to isolate the fault without equipment or tracing all the wires.

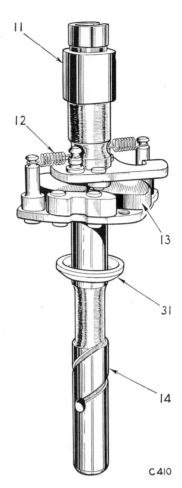

FIG 3:2 Distributor shaft and centrifugal advance mechanism

Capacitor:

The capacitor (condenser) is made up of metal foil insulated with paper. If the insulation breaks down the spark tends to erode away the metal foil in the area, preventing a shortcircuit. However, with the ignition switched on, if a voltmeter connected across the points shows no reading then the capacitor is suspect.

An open circuit capacitor is more difficult to diagnose, but it may be suspected if either the points are badly burnt or 'blued' and starting is difficult.

Specialized equipment is necessary for testing a capacitor so the best method readily available is to substitute it with a known satisfactory one. The capacitor is held to the base plate by a single screw and the wire is held on by nut 3 (see **FIG 3:1**).

3:4 Removing and dismantling the distributor

Before removing the distributor turn the engine until No. 1 piston is at TDC on the compression stroke. The distributor rotor arm should then be pointing as shown in **Chapter 1, FIG 1:12**. If the position is incorrect the

FIG 3:3 Distributor lubrication points

FIG 3:4 Adjusting the distributor contact points gap

FIG 3:5 HT leads correctly connected

distributor driving gear should be remeshed correctly as described in **Chapter 1, Section 1:6**. Do not turn the engine from the TDC position as it will then serve as a check to ensure that the distributor has been correctly reassembled and refitted. Remove the distributor by undoing the two nuts securing the clamping plate to the pedestal. Leave the clamp plate pinch bolt tight and the ignition timing will not be lost. Use **FIG 3:1** as a reference.

1 Remove the distributor cap and rotor arm 4. Disconnect the vacuum control spring 26 from the contact plate 7. Unscrew the two screws 8 and lift out the complete contact breaker assembly. This is dismantled by removing the contacts and capacitor as described earlier.
2 Remove the circlip 19 and unscrew the adjusting nut 18 to free the vacuum control unit 25. Take care not to lose the spring 17 or the ratchet spring 16 which slides into the body.
3 **Before further dismantling, note the relative positions of the rotor arm driving slot in the cam 11 and the offset of the driving dog 22. They must be reassembled in the same relative positions otherwise the ignition timing will be 180 deg. out.**
4 Release both springs 12 from the base of the cam 11. This assembly is shown in greater detail in **FIG 3:2**. **Take care not to twist or distort the springs when removing them** as the timing characteristics depend on their correct tension. Remove the screw 10 and lift off the cam 11. The weights 13 can now be lifted off.
5 Check the end float of the shaft 14 in the body, using feeler gauges. The end float should not exceed $\frac{1}{32}$ inch (.8 mm) and if it is greater than this the nylon spacer 31 and washer 23 will have to be renewed on reassembly.
6 Drive out the pin 21 and remove the driving dog 22 and washer 23. The shaft 14 can now be withdrawn from the distributor body.

Reassembly is the reversal of the dismantling procedure, but note the following points.

1 Use petrol or methylated spirits to clean all the metal parts and remove old grease or oil.
2 Insert a new shaft 14 or a .490 inch diameter (12.45 mm) test bar into the bush 24 to check the wear. Renew the bush if it is excessively worn.
3 Lubricate all the bearing surfaces and pivots with clean engine oil.
4 Ensure that the cam 11, shaft 14 and drive dog 22 are reassembled in their original relative positions.
5 Set the contact breaker gap before refitting the distributor to the car, as it is easier to turn the distributor than the engine.
6 Check that the rotor arm points in the correct direction after refitting the distributor to the engine.

3:5 Timing the ignition

1 Remove the sparking plugs and turn the engine until No. 1 piston is at TDC on the compression stroke. The pointer on the engine timing cover aligns with a small drilled hole in the crankshaft pulley when Nos. 1 and 4 pistons are at TDC. The compression stroke is indicated by both valves being closed and both rockers being at their highest positions. Compression stroke can also be determined without removing the rocker cover. One operator slowly turns the engine over whilst another operator blocks the sparking plug hole on No. 1 piston with a thumb. As the piston rises to TDC on the compression stroke a strong pressure build up will be felt in the cylinder.
2 Set the micrometer adjuster on the distributor to the fully retarded position (turn the adjusting nut in the direction of the arrow marked R on the body). Slacken the pinch bolt on the distributor clamping plate.

3 Ensure that the rotor arm is pointing at the contact in the distributor head connected to No. 1 cylinder spark plug. Turn the distributor until the contact points are just open. This position is more easily checked by disconnecting the cable from the distributor at the CB terminal on the coil and connecting in a low wattage 12-volt bulb. The light will extinguish immediately the points open, when the ignition is switched on. Tighten the clamping plate pinch bolt to prevent the distributor from rotating.

4 Turn the micrometer adjustment nut to advance the ignition (in the direction of the arrow marked A on the distributor body) until the correct ignition timing is set. One division on the micrometer scale equals 4 crankshaft degrees so $2\frac{1}{4}$ divisions equals 9 deg. BTDC which is the correct setting for the low-compression engine of the Herald 1200 and for the standard engine in the Herald 13/60. The correct setting for the standard Herald 1200 engine is 15 deg. BTDC and this equals $3\frac{3}{4}$ divisions on the scale. Replace the sparking plugs.

3:6 Sparking plugs

Inspect, clean and adjust sparking plugs regularly. The inspection of the deposits on the electrodes is particularly useful because the type and colour of the deposit gives a clue to the conditions inside the combustion chamber, and is therefore most useful when tuning the engine.

Remove the sparking plugs by loosening them a couple of turns and blowing away loose dirt from the plug recesses with compressed air or a tyre pump before removing them completely. Store the sparking plugs in the order of removal. Examine the gaskets and renew them if they are less than half their original thickness.

Examine the firing end of the sparking plug to note the type of deposit. Normally the deposit should be powdery and range in colour from brown to greyish tan. There will also be light wear on the electrodes and the general effect is one which comes from mixed periods of high-speed and low-speed driving. Cleaning and resetting the gaps is all that will be required. If the deposits are white or yellowish they indicate long periods of constant-speed or much low-speed city driving. Again the treatment is straightforward.

Black, wet deposits are caused by oil entering the combustion chamber past worn pistons, rings or worn down valve guides or worn valve stems. Hotter running sparking plugs may held to alleviate the problem, but the only cure is an engine overhaul.

Overheated electrodes have a white, blistered look about the centre electrode and the side electrode may be badly eroded. This may be caused by poor cooling, incorrect ignition, running with too weak a mixture, incorrect grade of sparking plugs or sustained high-speeds with heavy loads.

Dry, black, fluffy deposits are usually the result of running with a rich mixture. Incomplete combustion may also be a cause and this might be traced to defective ignition or excessive idling.

Have the sparking plugs cleaned on an abrasive-blasting machine and then tested under pressure after attention to the electrodes. File these until they are clean, bright and parallel. Set the electrode gap to .025 inch (.64 mm). **Do not bend the centre electrode.** Sparking plugs should be renewed every 12,000 miles.

Before replacing the sparking plugs clean the threads with a wire brush and smear the threads with a little graphite grease to prevent them binding in the cylinder head. Never use ordinary grease or oil as it will bake hard and jam the plug. If it is found that the sparking plugs cannot be screwed into place by hand, run a tap down the threads in the cylinder head. Failing a tap, use an old sparking plug with crosscuts down the threads. Grease the tool well so that chips and dirt stick to the grease instead of falling down the cylinder bore. Clean the insulator on the sparking plug with a petrol-moistened cloth to remove all dirt and grease. Screw the sparking plug in hand tight, by hand only, and finally tighten it to a torque of 30 lb ft. If a torque wrench is not available, tighten with a normal box spanner through half a turn.

HT cables:

These are 7 mm neoprene covered and are of the resistive type for suppression of radio and television interference. They should not be replaced by ordinary tinned copper HT cables as the conductor consists of a special nylon or cotton thread impregnated with carbon. Their resistance is approximately 420 ohms per inch so a serviceable cable should give a reading between 3000 and 12,000 ohms. In some cases a short length of tinned copper is inserted in the end of the cable to provide a suitable pick-up point so do not be misled by this into thinking that the conductor is all tinned copper.

The HT cables are held in the distributor cap by spiked screws in the individual contact points. The positions of the HT leads, in the correct firing order of 1—3—4—2 and with the ignition correctly set, are shown in **FIG 3:5**.

3:7 Fault diagnosis

(a) Engine will not fire

1 Battery discharged
2 Distributor points dirty, pitted or out of adjustment
3 Distributor cap dirty, cracked or 'tracking'
4 Carbon brush inside distributor cap not in contact with rotor arm
5 Faulty cable or loose connection in low-tension circuit
6 Distributor rotor arm cracked
7 Faulty ignition coil
8 Broken contact breaker spring
9 Contact points stuck open
10 Faulty capacitor
11 Water on HT leads, distributor cap or ignition coil
12 Faulty HT lead between ignition coil and distributor

(b) Engine misfires

1 Check 2, 3 5 and 7 in (a)
2 Weak contact spring
3 HT leads cracked or perished
4 Sparking plug loose
5 Sparking plug insulation cracked
6 Sparking plug gap incorrect
7 Ignition timing too far advanced

NOTES

CHAPTER 4

THE COOLING SYSTEM

4:1 Description
4:2 Protective maintenance
4:3 The radiator
4:4 Adjusting the fan belt

4:5 The water pump
4:6 The thermostat
4:7 Frost precautions
4:8 Fault diagnosis

4:1 Description

All the models covered by this manual have a pressurized cooling system. The natural thermo-syphon circulation of the water through the system is augmented by a centrifugal impeller-type pump mounted on the front of the cylinder block and driven by a belt from the crankshaft. The belt that drives the water pump also drives the generator. The water is cooled by being passed through the radiator. The radiator core consists of many tubes, through which the water passes, and the external surface area of the tubes is increased by the addition of many thin fins. Air passing over these tubes and fins takes the heat from the water. Cooling fan blades are fitted to the front of the water pump so that there is a continual circulation of air even when the car is stationary or travelling at low speed.

If all the water were to pass through the radiator the engine would take a very long time to warm up and in cold weather would never reach its optimum working temperature. To ensure a quick warm-up and to keep the engine at a reasonably constant temperature a thermostat valve is fitted between the outlet from the cylinder head and the top tank of the radiator. The valve contains a temperature sensitive bellows which opens the valve at a predetermined temperature. When the engine is cold the valve stays shut and the water is bypassed back to the engine. As the water heats up the valve opens, allowing the water to pass through the radiator. The water circulation is shown in **FIG 4:1**.

The heater is fitted into the circuit so that water circulates through it even if the thermostat valve is closed. On the Herald 13/60 models the hot water also passes through the inlet manifold, again even when the thermostat is closed. This ensures that the manifold is heated at the same time as the engine, allowing the choke control to be returned earlier. The circulation through the Herald 13/60 is shown in **FIG 4:2**.

The radiator is fitted with a filler cap, shown sectioned in **FIG 4:3**. As the water heats it expands and pressure builds up in the cooling system. The pressure rises until the pressure valve 4 releases and allows the excess air or water to pass out through the overflow 3. On earlier models the pressure was limited to 7 lb/sq in but on later models this figure was increased to 13 lb/sq in. The pressurization raises the boiling point of the water, allowing a higher temperature to be used for normal running, while still preventing boiling at localized hot spots in the engine.

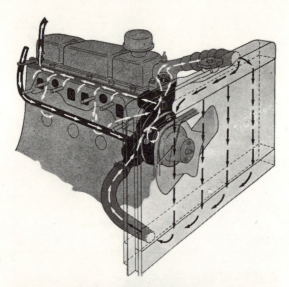

FIG 4:1 Water circulation

FIG 4:2 Herald 13/60 heated inlet manifold

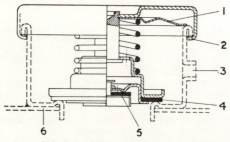

FIG 4:3 Radiator filler cap details

Key to Fig 4:3 1 Spring friction plate 2 Retaining lugs
3 Pressure release pipe 4 Pressure valve 5 Vacuum valve
6 Header tank

When the engine cools the pressure drops and air is drawn in through the vacuum relief valve 5 to prevent a vacuum forming in the cooling system.

The filler cap must not be removed while the engine is hot, and never when the engine is overheated. The pressure will force scalding water out of the filler and the sudden drop in pressure can cause the water to boil and the resultant steam will force even more scalding water out of the filler.

4:2 Protective maintenance

A screwed plug is fitted to the top righthand side of the water pump bearing housing. Every 12,000 miles remove this plug and replace it with a grease nipple. Inject grease through the grease nipple using a hand-operated grease gun and a maximum of five strokes. Remove the grease nipple and replace the sealing plug.

Periodically drain the cooling system and flush it through, either with clean water or with a proprietary flushing compound.

Draining:

Remove the filler cap from the radiator, set the heater to hot, and open the drain taps. The radiator drain tap is shown in **FIG 4:4**, and the cylinder block drain tap is fitted on the righthand rear of the engine. Antifreeze may be left in the system for a period of up to one year, so the coolant should be collected for re-use during that period.

Flushing:

If a proprietary compound is used, follow the instructions given on the tin.

To flush with water, drain the cooling system and unscrew both drain taps to provide an unobstructed flow to the flushing water. Insert a hosepipe into the filler on the radiator and run water through until it comes clean from the drains. Disconnect the heater hoses and flush the heater through in the reverse of the normal direction of flow until the water comes out clean and rust free. If the radiator is blocked, remove it, turn it upside down and flush through in the reverse direction of normal flow. If the radiator still remains blocked it will have to be sent away for specialist attention. A hosepipe fitted to the cylinder block drain will also help to flush out deposits from the cylinder block.

Reconnect the heater hoses and replace the drain taps. **Close the drain taps before refilling.**

Filling:

Leave the heater control on hot and fill the system through the filler on the radiator header tank, using soft clean water, until the system is full. Replace the filler cap and run the engine until it is hot. Stop the engine and allow it to cool. Top up the level in the radiator if required. The header tank should not be filled right up to the filler neck as an air gap is required to allow for expansion of the water. After a short time the level will steady at about half an inch from the top. If constant topping up is required to bring the water to this level, **but no higher,** then the system should be checked for leaks.

If, when the engine is hot, the heater fails to produce hot air after refilling the system, there is probably an air lock in the heater system. Set the engine to run at a fast-idle and slacken each hose clip in turn on the heating system, in the order of the direction of the water flow. Tighten each clip as soon as water leaks out from the connection. Use rags and a bowl to prevent the water drips staining trim or carpets.

4:3 The radiator

The radiators on all models covered by this manual are similar. The details are shown in **FIG 4:4**.

Before removing the radiator drain the cooling system. Disconnect the top hose 4 and the bottom hose 6. The radiator may then be removed by undoing the four sets of nuts, washers and bolts securing it to the car. Examine the fins for damage and the core for leaks or signs of leaks indicated by rust stains. Periodically use a hosepipe to flush water between the fins and pipes in a direction opposite to the normal airflow. This will remove the accumulation of dirt and dead insects that build up.

4:4 Adjusting the fan belt

Refer to **FIG 4:5**. Slacken the adjustment bolt 6 and the two pivot bolts 7 and 8. Pull the generator away from the cylinder block, either by hand or using a wooden lever such as a hammer handle between the generator and block, until the tension on the belt is such that it can only be moved $\frac{3}{4}$ inch (19 mm) by hand pressure at the point 9. Hold the generator in position and tighten all three bolts 6, 7 and 8.

To remove the fan belt, slacken the three bolts as before but push the generator firmly towards the cylinder block. Lift the fan belt and pull as much as possible forwards and off the water pump pulley. The remainder of the fan belt can then be removed from the pulley by turning the fan blades. Once free the belt can be removed from the other two pulleys and then lifted over the fan blades.

4:5 The water pump

The details of this are shown in **FIG 4:6**.

Removing the water pump:

Drain the cooling system and remove the fan belt. Scribe a line across the fan blades, balance weight and water pump pulley to ensure that the parts will be reassembled in the correct relative positions. Undo the bolts and remove the fan blades.

To service the pump body 11 need not be removed from the engine. Undo the nuts and washers securing the bearing housing 6 to the body 11 and withdraw the bearing housing assembly.

To remove the complete water pump, disconnect the water hoses to the top of the radiator, heater and manifold. Disconnect the electrical cable from the water temperature transmitter. Refer to **FIG 4:5** and remove the three bolts 2 and 3, noting their positions as they are all of unequal length. The complete water pump assembly and gasket 10 can then be removed from the engine.

Replacing the pump or bearing housing is the reversal of removal procedure. Clean away all traces of old gasket or jointing compound from the mating surfaces.

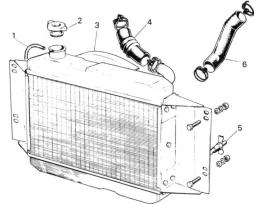

FIG 4:4 Radiator details

Key to Fig 4:4   1 Overflow pipe   2 Filler cap
3 Radiator   4 Top hose   5 Drain tap   6 Bottom hose

FIG 4:5 Fan belt tension and water pump attachments

Key to Fig 4:5   1 Clip   2 Bolts, unequal lengths
3 Bolt   4 Grommet   5 Bracket   6 Generator adjustment bolt
7 Generator pivot bolt (front)   8 Generator pivot bolt (rear)
9 Play in belt, $\frac{3}{4}$ inch (19 mm)

Use new gaskets, smearing both sides lightly with non-setting jointing compound. Note that the fuel pipe is clipped to the bolt 3.

Dismantling the bearing housing assembly:

1 Remove the nut 1 and washer 2. Withdraw the pulley 3 and remove the Woodruff key (not shown) from the spindle 13.
2 Use a suitable extractor to withdraw the impeller 8 from the spindle 13. Remove the seal 7 from the back of the impeller.
3 Remove the circlip 4 and gently tap out the spindle 13 complete with the bearing assembly.
4 Remove the spinner 14, circlip 5 and washer 15 from the spindle. Use a press to remove the two bearings 16 and 18 as well as the distance piece 17 from the spindle.

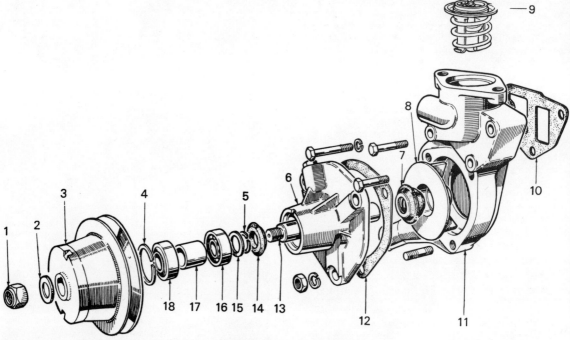

FIG 4:6 Water pump details

Key to Fig 4:6   1 Nut   2 Washer   3 Pulley   4 Circlip   5 Circlip   6 Housing (bearings and spindle)
7 Seal   8 Impeller   9 Thermostat   10 Gasket   11 Body (water pump)   12 Gasket   13 Spindle   14 Spinner
15 Washer   16 Bearing (inner)   17 Spacer (bearings)   18 Bearing (outer)

FIG 4:7 Thermostat removal

Examining the parts:

Scrub the parts in clean water to remove any sediment. If the blades on the impeller are badly eroded or it has lost its tight fit on the spindle the impeller should be renewed. Examine the sealing face in the housing 6. If the surface is worn or scored it may be refaced using a Churchill cutter No. S.126, but it must not be recut so much that the depth from the face of the housing exceeds .265 inch (6.7 mm). Damage deeper than this will require a new housing 6. Wash the bearings in clean fuel and check them for roughness or wear. Renew both bearings if required.

Reassembling the bearing housing assembly:

1 Refit the washer 15, circlip 5 and spinner 14 to the spindle 13. Press the bearing 16 onto the spindle so that the sealed face of the bearing faces the washer 15. Replace the spacer 17 and press on the bearing 18 so that its sealed face is away from the spacer.
2 Pack the bearings with grease and insert the spindle assembly back into the housing 6. Tap the assembly into place and secure it with the circlip 4.
3 Fit the seal 7 into the impeller 8 and use a press to refit the assembly to the spindle. Place a .030 inch (.762 mm) packing piece between the housing and impeller when refitting the impeller. Press the impeller on until it just nips the packing piece, thus ensuring that the clearance between the impeller and housing is correct. Remove the packing piece and solder the impeller to the end of the spindle to prevent leakage.
4 Refit the Woodruff key to the spindle and replace the pulley and fan blades in the reverse order of dismantling. Line up the previously made scribed lines to ensure that the balance of the pulley and fan blade assembly is not lost.

4:6 The thermostat

The thermostat 9 is mounted in the water pump body 11, as shown in **FIG 4:6**. To remove the thermostat, first drain the cooling system so that the level is below the thermostat. The thermostat and top cover are shown in **FIG 4:7**. Undo the two bolts securing the cover and lift it slightly to break the seal. The hose need not be disconnected as the cover can be swung to one side, still connected to the hose. Lift out the thermostat.

Replace the thermostat in the reverse order of removal, noting that the thermostat is fitted into the housing and the gasket is then placed on top of the thermostat. If the gasket is damaged fit a new one in its place. Remove all traces of the old gasket and any old jointing compound. Smear both sides of the new gasket with either jointing compound or grease before fitting it.

The thermostat may be tested by suspending it in water. Heat the water, measuring the temperature with an accurate thermometer, and note the temperature at which the thermostat valve starts to open. If the valve does not start to open at the temperature stamped on the thermostat flange, or the valve sticks in the open position, then the thermostat is defective and must be renewed. The thermostat is a sealed unit and cannot be repaired if defective.

4:7 Frost precautions

It is always advisable to use antifreeze in cold weather. If it is very cold and no antifreeze has been used, the bottom half of the radiator is liable to freeze and become blocked, even when the engine is running. This can cause further damage because with the radiator blocked the engine will boil. In very cold weather therefore if the engine boils, stop the engine and wrap the engine and radiator to allow the heat from the engine to slowly thaw out the ice in the radiator. The use of sufficient antifreeze will prevent this trouble.

Draining the cooling system overnight is not an adequate precaution against frost as some water will remain in the heater.

Most of the branded names of antifreeze are suitable, but ensure that they meet BSI.3152 or BSI.3151 specifications. The total cooling system capacity (including heater) is 8.5 Imperial pints (10.2 US pints, 4.8 litres) and the quantity of antifreeze should be as recommended by the makers for the protection required.

The cooling system should be flushed out before adding antifreeze. It should also be checked for leaks and loose connections before the antifreeze is added, as antifreeze will penetrate through cracks which hold back pure water. **Close the drain taps after flushing.** Pour in the correct quantity of antifreeze first and then add soft clean water to fill the system to the correct normal cold level. Run the engine until it is hot to allow the antifreeze to mix with the water, and again check for leaks. If topping up is required use a mixture of antifreeze and water to prevent dilution of the antifreeze already in the system.

Never use antifreeze in the windscreen washers. A mixture of one part of methylated spirits to two parts of water should be used instead.

4:8 Fault diagnosis

(a) Internal water leakage

1 Cracked cylinder wall
2 Cracked cylinder head
3 Loose cylinder head nuts
4 Faulty head gasket

(b) Poor circulation

1 Radiator core blocked
2 Engine water passages restricted by deposits
3 Low water level
4 Loose fan belt
5 Defective fan belt
6 Perished or collapsed water hoses

(c) Corrosion

1 Impurities in the water
2 Infrequent draining and flushing

(d) Overheating

1 Check (b)
2 Sludge in crankcase
3 Incorrect ignition timing
4 Weak mixture
5 Low oil level in sump
6 Tight engine
7 Choked exhaust system
8 Binding brakes
9 Slipping clutch
10 Incorrect valve timing

NOTES

CHAPTER 5

THE CLUTCH

5:1 Description
5:2 Routine maintenance
5:3 Servicing the master cylinder
5:4 Servicing the slave cylinder

5:5 Bleeding the hydraulic system
5:6 Servicing the clutch
5:7 The clutch release mechanism
5:8 Fault diagnosis

5:1 Description

All the models covered by this manual are fitted with a diaphragm spring-operated clutch. Earlier models of the Herald 1200 were fitted with a clutch operated by coil springs, but these models are outside the scope of this manual. The details of the clutch are shown in **FIG 5:1**. The driven plate 1 may be renewed separately but if the remainder of the clutch is in any way defective it must be renewed as a unit and not dismantled or repaired.

The cover 8 contains the parts and it is bolted to the engine flywheel so that the clutch assembly revolves with the engine. Normally the diaphragm spring 5 presses the pressure plate 2 firmly forwards to grip the driven plate 1 between the pressure plate and the rear face of the flywheel. The driven plate 1 is then forced to revolve with the engine and the drive is transmitted to the gearbox by the splines at the hub of the driven plate.

When the clutch pedal is depressed, hydraulic action presses forward a release bearing which contacts the central fingers of the diaphragm spring 5. Further pressure on the fingers then causes a lever action on the diaphragm spring and the outer edge of the spring releases the pressure on the pressure plate, allowing the driven plate to rotate, or come to a stop, independently of the engine.

The hydraulic system and its operation will be dealt with in more detail in the relevant sections, though it should be noted that the master cylinder and pedal are exactly the same as the master cylinder and pedal assembly in the brake system.

5:2 Routine maintenance

There are no lubrication points in the system, and wear is automatically taken up so there is no adjustment required.

1 At regular intervals check the fluid level in the master cylinder reservoir. Before removing the cap wipe the top clean to prevent any dirt from falling into the reservoir. The correct level is indicated by an arrow on the side of the reservoir. If necessary top up to the correct level using only Castrol-Girling Crimson Clutch and Brake Fluid to specification SAE.70 R3. **The use of an incorrect fluid can be dangerous** as some fluids will attack the material of the seals causing them to swell and then fail.

If the master cylinder needs constant topping up or the level suddenly falls, the system should be inspected for leaks.

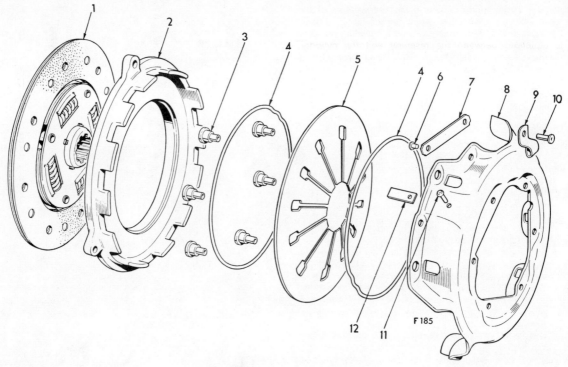

FIG 5:1 Diaphragm spring clutch details

Key to Fig 5:1 1 Driven plate 2 Pressure plate 3 Rivet 4 Fulcrum ring 5 Diaphragm spring 6 Rivet
7 Drive strap 8 Cover pressing 9 Retaining clip 10 Rivet 11 Rivet 12 Balance weight

2 It is strongly recommended that the system be dismantled at three-yearly intervals and old seals and fluid discarded. Before dismantling the system pump the old fluid out through the bleed nipple on the slave cylinder and pump at least a pint of methylated spirits through to remove any dirt or old gummy fluid from the pipes.

5:3 Servicing the master cylinder

The instructions given here apply equally to the brake master cylinder.

Removal:

The master cylinder and pedal assembly is shown in **FIG 5:2**.

1 Syphon out the fluid from the reservoir, and pump the rest out through a small-bore tube attached to a bleed nipple. **Take great care to prevent any fluid falling on paintwork otherwise the paintwork will be quickly damaged.**
2 Undo the union securing the pipe to the outlet on the body and withdraw the pipe without bending it. Use rags to catch any slight spillage of fluid.
3 Pull back the dust cover 11. Extract the splitpin 12 and withdraw the clevis pin 14, collecting the washer 13 to free the master cylinder pushrod from the pedal 8.
4 Unscrew and remove the two bolts 16 with their washers 17 and lift the master cylinder 1 out from the bracket 15.
5 It should be noted that the pedal 8 pivots about a renewable bush 9 and pivot pin 5. If these are excessively worn they should be renewed.

The master cylinder is replaced in the reverse order of removal, using a new splitpin 12 to secure the clevis pin 14. After the master cylinder has been refitted, fill and bleed the hydraulic system as described in **Section 5:5**.

Operation:

A sectioned view of the master cylinder is shown in **FIG 5:3**. The view **A** is with no pressure applied to the pushrod, and the view **B** is with pressure applied.

When the pedal is depressed it exerts pressure on the pushrod 9. This pressure moves the plunger 7 down the bore of the cylinder, causing a rise in pressure in the fluid in front of the plunger. This pressure holds the valve seal 1 firmly closed and is passed out through the outlet in the side of the body to operate the slave cylinder. Fluid leakage past the plunger is prevented by the seals 8 and 13. When the pedal is released the plunger 7 returns back up the bore under the combined action of the hydraulic pressure and the return spring 5. At the end of the plunger return stroke, the head of the valve shank 4 catches in the spring retainer 6 and the pressure of the return spring 5 overcomes the spring washer 2 to open the valve seal 1. With the valve seal 1 open the pressure is equalized between the reservoir and the cylinder, allowing any fluid losses to be replenished. On the initial movement of the plunger the spring washer 2 closes the valve seal allowing the pressure to build up in the cylinder.

Dismantling:

The details of the master cylinder are shown in **FIG 5 : 4**. This figure has the same key as **FIG 5 : 3** and parts may be identified referring to either of these two figures.

1 Remove the dust cover 10 by easing it off the lip on the outside of the cylinder. Lightly press in the pushrod 9 to relieve the pressure on the plunger by the return spring. Use a pair of long-nosed pliers to remove the circlip 11. With the circlip removed the pushrod 9 and its stop 12 can be pulled out.

2 Shake out the internal parts by tapping the open end of the cylinder on the palm of the hand. When the parts are sufficiently far out, withdraw them using only the fingers. If the parts are difficult to remove blow down the outlet to force them out. **Never use pliers or a similar tool to withdraw the internal parts.**

3 Open the coils of the return spring 5 and use a thin screwdriver to lift the leaf on the spring retainer 6 above the level of the shoulder on the plunger 7 (see **B** in **FIG 5 : 3**). Pull the retainer 6 from the plunger 7. The retainer 6 is provided with a large offset hole through which the head of the valve shank 4 will pass. Partially compress the return spring 5 and slide the stem of the valve shank 4 sideways into the larger offset hole in the retainer. Release the spring and allow the head of the valve stem to pass through the larger offset hole to remove the spring retainer.

4 Take off the return spring 5, distance piece 3 and spring washer 2 from the valve shank 4. Use the fingers only to remove the three seals 1, 8 and 13.

Examining the parts:

All three seals should be renewed when reassembling the master cylinder, so unless they are in perfect condition the old seals should be discarded. Clean the remainder of the parts in methylated spirits or clean hydraulic fluid. Other solvents, such as trichlorethylene, can be used on the metal parts but these must be absolutely dry and free from any traces of solvent before reassembly. Solvents other than methylated spirits will attack the material of the seals if it comes in contact with them.

Cleanliness is absolutely essential when working on any part of the hydraulic system so when the parts have been cleaned lay them on a clean sheet of paper to prevent them picking up any dirt.

Examine the bore of the cylinder and the working face of the plunger 7. The bore must be smooth and highly polished, without a trace of pitting, corrosion or wear. Any of these three defects will mean that a new master cylinder assembly must be fitted.

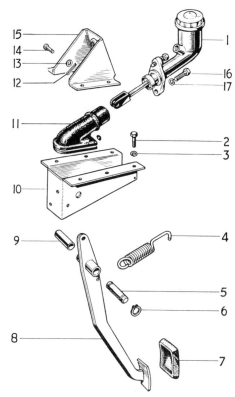

FIG 5:2 Master cylinder, brackets and pedal details

Key to Fig 5:2   1 Master cylinder   2 Bolt
3 Spring washer   4 Return spring   5 Pivot pin   6 Circlip
7 Pedal rubber   8 Pedal   9 Pedal pivot bush
10 Pedal bracket   11 Rubber dust excluder   12 Splitpin
13 Plain washer   14 Clevis pin   15 Master cylinder bracket
16 Bolt   17 Spring washer

Reassembling:

1 Dip the parts in clean hydraulic fluid as they are being reassembled, and fit them wet. This applies to all stages of reassembly.

2 Use only the fingers, no other tool, to refit the three seals 1, 8 and 13. When each seal is in place work it round, again using the fingers, to make sure that it is fully and squarely seated in its recess.

3 Replace the spring washer 2 so that its convex side is facing the flange on the valve shank 4. Replace the distance piece 3 so that its legs will face into the cylinder bore, and then the return spring 5 on top of this. Fit the head of the valve shank 4 through the larger offset hole in the spring retainer 6 and slide the retainer into position in the spring. Make sure that the stem of the valve shank is central in the spring retainer to prevent the spring retainer from coming off again.

4 Press the spring retainer 6 back onto the plunger 7 so that the leaf on the retainer seats squarely behind the shoulder on the plunger. Use a thin screwdriver between the coils of the spring to press the leaf gently into place if it will not seat on its own.

Maximum stroke available—
1·38″ (35·05 mm.)

Stroke position at maximum cut off—
0·099″ (2·5 mm.)

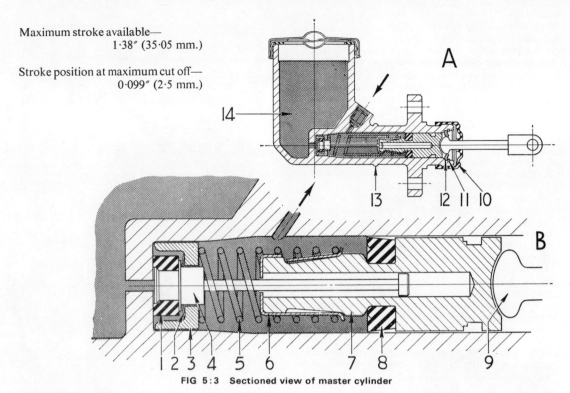

FIG 5:3 Sectioned view of master cylinder

Key to Figs 5:3 and 5:4 1 Valve seal   2 Spring (valve seal)   3 Distance piece   4 Valve shank   5 Plunger return spring
6 Spring retainer   7 Plunger   8 Plunger seal   9 Pushrod   10 Dust cover   11 Circlip   12 Pushrod stop
13 Identification ring(s)   14 Fluid reservoir

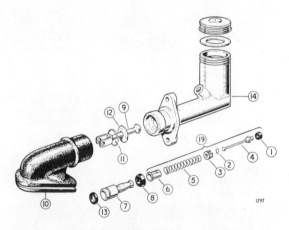

FIG 5:4 Master cylinder details

5 Though the individual parts should have been wetted as they were replaced, dip the complete internal assembly into clean hydraulic fluid and insert it wet into the bore of the cylinder. When the seal 8 starts to enter the bore take great care not to bend back or damage its lips, which should be facing into the bore. Use the fingers to press the edges into the bore and, when satisfied that all the edges of the lips are properly in the bore, press the plunger in further.

Take similar care of the seal 13 which is liable to roll back.
6 Refit the pushrod 9 and its stop 12, using the pushrod to press the plunger down the bore while refitting the circlip 11. Press the plunger fully down the bore and make sure that it returns under the action of the return spring before refitting the dust cover 10. Check that the breathing hole in the filler cap is clear.

5:4 Servicing the slave cylinder

The details of the slave cylinder are shown in **FIG 5:5**. The cylinder is held by the mounting to the clutch housing. Pressure from the master cylinder is led into the slave cylinder by the metal pipe and union 3. The pressure then acts on the seal 6 and piston cup 7 to press the pushrod attached to the clutch operating mechanism and to release the clutch. The spring 5 keeps the piston cup in contact with the pushrod and allows the wear in the clutch to be taken up without excessive pedal movement.

Removal and replacement:

1 Drain the hydraulic system as described in operation 1 of Removal in **Section 5:3**. The whole operation will be found easier if the trim and gearbox cover is removed as access from underneath the car is limited.
2 Unscrew the union 3 and carefully withdraw the metal pipe from the slave cylinder, so as not to bend the pipe.

Undo the locknut 13 and withdraw the securing bolt 11. The cylinder assembly may now be withdrawn from the mounting and removed from the car. Replacement is the reversal of the removal procedure. When replacing, make sure that the pushrod on the operating lever fits properly into the piston cup. Once refitted, fill and bleed the hydraulic system as described in **Section 5:5**.

Dismantling the slave cylinder:

The cylinder is easily dismantled by removing the dust cover 9 and circlip 8, and shaking out the internal parts. The parts should be washed in methylated spirits and the bore of the cylinder examined for scores, wear or pitting. If the bore is defective the slave cylinder assembly must be renewed. **Cleanliness is essential.** Lubricate the parts with clean hydraulic fluid as they are refitted. Use only the fingers to refit the seal to the piston, making sure that it is properly seated in its recess between the piston face and flange on the stem. The lips of the seal are fitted facing away from the piston. Fit the spring 5, narrow diameter leading, onto the stem of the piston and then insert the parts back into the bore. Take great care when entering the seal 6 into the bore to prevent it being damaged. Hold the parts in place with the circlip and then refit the dust cover.

5:5 Bleeding the hydraulic system

This is only necessary when air has entered the system. Air can enter either by dismantling or by allowing the fluid level in the reservoir to fall so low that air is drawn into the master cylinder.

Before starting bleeding operations, fill up the master cylinder reservoir as full as possible without fluid spilling out. During the bleeding operation keep it constantly topped up as fluid will be drawn through the system and, if the level is allowed to fall too low, air will again be drawn into the master cylinder. Always use fresh clean fluid and discard the dirty fluid which comes out of the bleed nipple. Only when the fluid comes out clean may it be used again, and even then it must not be returned direct to the reservoir. Fluid that has been bled should be allowed to stand in a sealed clean container for at least 24 hours to allow it to de-aerate.

FIG 5:6 Centralizing the clutch driven plate

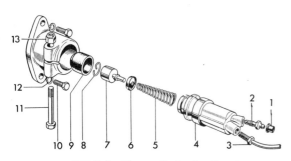

FIG 5:5 Slave cylinder details

Key to Fig 5:5 1 Bleed nipple cover   2 Bleed nipple
3 Pipe union   4 Cylinder body   5 Spring   6 Seal
7 Piston cup   8 Circlip   9 Dust cover   10 Mounting securing bolt   11 Cylinder securing bolt   12 Spring washer
13 Locknut

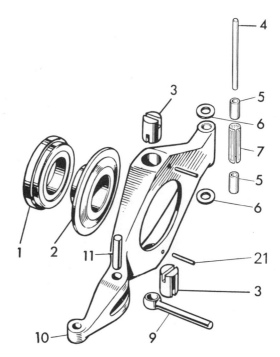

FIG 5:7 Clutch release mechanism details

Key to Fig 5:7 1 Release bearing   2 Release bearing sleeve
3 Plugs   4 Pivot pin   5 Bush   6 Washer
7 Spring clip   8 Plug retaining pin   9 Pushrod
10 Operating lever   11 Operating lever pivot pin

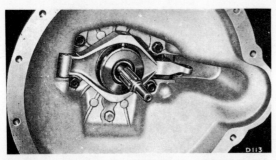

FIG 5:8 Release mechanism fitted to clutch housing

1 Attach a length of small-bore plastic or rubber hose to the bleed nipple 2 on the slave cylinder, after removing the cover 1 and wiping the nipple clean. Dip the free end of the tube in a little clean hydraulic fluid contained in a clean glass jar.
2 Open the bleed nipple one-quarter of a turn and have a second operator pump the clutch pedal with full fast strokes, giving a short pause between each stroke.
3 When air ceases to be ejected from the bleed tube, have the clutch pedal pumped with faster strokes, using only the bottom half of the range of movement so as to expel any remaining air. Tighten the bleed nipple either on a downstroke of the pedal or when it is held in the fully down position.
4 Top up the reservoir to the correct level. Remove the bleed tube and container, wiping away any spillage from around the slave or master cylinders. Have the second operator apply heavy pressure to the clutch pedal and examine the system for leaks.

5:6 Servicing the clutch

The removal of the clutch from the engine has been dealt with in **Chapter 1, Section 1:7**. The clutch is replaced in the reverse order of removal. When progressively tightening the ring of bolts securing the clutch, centralize the driven plate with a mandrel, as shown in **FIG 5:6**. If the driven plate is not centralized it will be practically impossible to refit the gearbox.

The condition and rectification of the flywheel face has already been dealt with in **Chapter 1, Section 1:7**. If the clutch is defective or the presssure plate is scored or burnt, then the clutch assembly must be renewed as the unit cannot be dismantled.

Examine the driven plate, which if it is in poor condition may be renewed. The friction linings should stand well proud of the securing rivets. If the linings are worn flush with the rivet heads then the driven plate must be renewed. Check that all the rivets are tight and secure and make sure that the cushioning springs are also tight in their mountings. Renew the plate if it is defective.

For maximum efficiency the friction linings should have a light-coloured polished glaze through which the grain of the material is clearly visible. A small amount of oil leaking into the clutch will produce darker smears on the linings, while a larger amount of oil will produce an even, dark coloured glaze which hides the grain of the material. Large amounts of oil leaking into the clutch will be obvious from the free oil in the housing and the oil-soaked appearance of the linings. The source of an oil leak must be found and rectified before replacing the clutch. If the grain of the friction material is still visible the driven plate may be used again. If the grain is hidden a new driven plate should be fitted, as the old one will always be a source of drag or slip.

5:7 The clutch release mechanism

The components are shown in **FIG 5:7** and the assembly fitted to the clutch housing is shown in **FIG 5:8**. If the release bearing 1 is noisy or worn it must be renewed, as it is a sealed unit and can neither be lubricated or repaired.

1 If the engine is still fitted to the car, remove the gearbox as instructed in **Chapter 6, Section 6:2**.
2 With a suitable punch drive out the pivot pin 4 to free the assembly from the clutch housing, collecting the two washers 6.
3 Drive out the securing pins 8 and extract the two plugs 16 that secure the bearing sleeve 2 to the operating lever 10.
4 Lever off the old bearing 1 from the sleeve 2 and press the new bearing firmly back into position. Replace the parts in the reverse order of removal, making sure that the pushrod 9 seats correctly through the dust cover and in the piston of the slave cylinder. Refit the gearbox to the car.

5:8 Fault diagnosis

(a) Drag or spin

1 Oil or grease on the driven plate linings
2 Leaking master cylinder, slave cylinder or connecting pipes
3 Driven plate hub binding on splines of gearbox input shaft
4 Distorted driven plate
5 Warped or damaged pressure plate
6 Broken drive plate linings
7 Air in the clutch hydraulic system

(b) Fierceness or snatch

1 Check 1, 2, 4 and 5 in (a)
2 Worn clutch linings

(c) Slip

1 Check 1 in (a) and 2 in (b)
2 Seized piston in slave cylinder

(d) Judder

1 Check 1 and 4 in (a)
2 Contact area of driven plate linings not evenly distributed
3 Faulty engine mountings

(e) Tick or knock

1 Badly worn driven plate hub splines
2 Worn release bearing

CHAPTER 6

THE GEARBOX

6:1 Description
6:2 Removing the gearbox
6:3 Dismantling the gearbox

6:4 Reassembling the gearbox
6:5 The top cover and gearchange extension
6:6 Fault diagnosis

6:1 Description

The gearbox is fitted with four forward and one reverse speeds. Only the top three speeds are fitted with synchromesh engagement, first and reverse gears selected by sliding spur gears into mesh. A sectioned view of the gearbox fitted to the Vitesse models is shown in **FIG 6:1**. The differences are only minor in that a different type of clutch release mechanism is fitted and the clutch on the models covered by this manual uses a diaphragm spring. From this figure it can be seen that the gearlever is mounted on a separate gearchange extension so as to bring it within easy reach of the driver's hand. The gear selector forks are mounted in the top cover of the gearbox so that both the selector mechanism and gearlever parts can be removed from the gearbox without dismantling or taking the unit out of the car. It can also be seen that the gears for the top three speeds are always in mesh and selection is achieved by sliding the synchromesh sleeve (or first gear) so that the gears are connected into drive, the synchromesh allowing the parts to be brought to the same speed before the final toothed engagement of the sleeve. Not clearly shown is that reverse is engaged by sliding into mesh an idler gear, which alters the direction of rotation of the mainshaft.

The mainshaft at the centre and rear runs in ball-bearings and the input shaft is similarly supported at the front end. A spigot on the front end of the mainshaft revolves in a Torrington needle roller bearing in the rear end of the input shaft. The countershaft gear cluster revolves about the countershaft on two renewable bushes. Thrust washers are fitted to take the end thrust of the gears and to control the end float.

A drain plug is fitted underneath the gearbox casing and a combined level and filler plug is fitted to the front of the righthand side. The gearbox is filled with the correct grade of hypoid oil so that the level is just at the bottom of the filler hole. The internal parts are lubricated either by immersion or by splash thrown up from the revolving gears.

A clutch housing connects the gearbox casing to the rear of the engine and rubber mountings on the rear extension support the back end of the gearbox. The gearbox can be taken out of the car without removing the engine.

6:2 Removing the gearbox

Before removing the gearbox raise the car on stands or a ramp so as to have sufficient room to work underneath

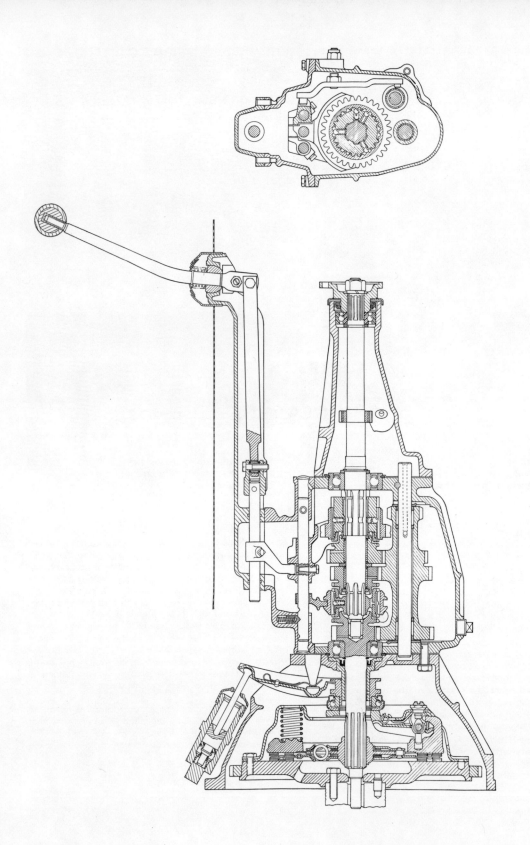

FIG 6:1 Sectioned view of the gearbox. The coil spring operated clutch and clutch release mechanism are not of the type fitted to the models covered by this manual

the car. **Do not rely on odd stacks of bricks and make sure that the car is adequately and safely supported.**

1. Disconnect the battery. Drain the oil out of the gearbox. Next remove the front seats and carpet. Unscrew the gearlever knob, after slackening its locknut, and remove the rubber gaiter from around the bottom of the gearlever. Take out the gearbox cover 7 after undoing the fasteners 5 and 6 shown in **FIG 6:2**.

2. The gearbox will now appear as shown in **FIG 6:3**. If the outside is very dirty clean it off using a stiff brush and suitable solvent. Petrol, paraffin or a proprietary dirt and grease remover are all suitable. Trichlorethylene should not be used as it attacks both rubber and paint.

3. Undo the locknut and remove the clamping bolt 8. Pull the clutch slave cylinder 9, still attached to the hydraulic pipe 10, out of its mounting bracket on the clutch housing and use a length of wire to hold it safely out of the way. **Take great care not to bend or kink the metal pipe 10.**

4. Remove the Nyloc nuts and tap out the bolts 11. Repeat the operation on the similar nuts and bolts securing the rear end of the propeller shaft to the driving flange on the differential. The nuts must be stiff enough to require a spanner for the whole length of the thread on the bolt. **If the nuts are slack enough to be turned by finger pressure only, then they are worn and must be renewed on reassembly.** Partially withdraw the propeller shaft rearwards. It may be necessary to lever the engine and gearbox forwards so as to clear the propeller shaft flange from the driving flange on the gearbox.

5. Disconnect the speedometer drive cable from the side of the rear extension. Undo the nuts 13 and lift off the gearchange extension 14. Blank the aperture with a sheet of cardboard to stop dirt from falling into the gearbox.

6. Remove the starter motor. Release the front exhaust pipe from the manifold and clutch housing.

7. Remove the nuts 15 from the rear mounting rubbers. Place a jack as far rearwards as possible under the engine sump and, using a block of wood to protect the sump, jack-up the engine until the rear extension is clear of the mounting bracket. Remove the two mounting rubbers 16.

8. Undo the ring of nuts 17 securing the clutch housing to the engine. Support the gearbox, check that all connections are free, and draw the gearbox back until the input shaft is clear of the clutch. The gearbox may be difficult to draw back at first but, whatever happens, **always support the weight of the gearbox and do not allow it to hang on the input shaft,** otherwise damage will be caused. Once the gearbox is free lift it out of the car.

To refit the gearbox reverse the removal operations, **taking great care to prevent the weight of the gearbox hanging on the input shaft.** Fill the gearbox with oil to the correct level before replacing the gearbox cover. Make sure that the pushrod on the clutch release mechanism seats properly into the piston cup of the slave cylinder when refitting the slave cylinder.

FIG 6:2 Gearbox cover and its attachments

FIG 6:3 Gearbox attachments

6:3 Dismantling the gearbox

The task will be extremely difficult without the proper special tools and if the owner has any doubts as to his ability to carry out satisfactory work he is strongly advised to take the gearbox to a suitably equipped garage.

The details of the gearbox are shown in **FIG 6:4**. Servicing the selector mechanism and top cover will be dealt with separately in **Section 6:5**.

1. Take off the top cover 29 assembly and its gasket 19 after taking out the seven short bolts 17 and two longer bolts 47 complete with their washers. Note that the cover is located by two dowels and that it will have to be eased off these before it comes free.

2. Drive out the clutch release mechanism pivoting pin 55 using a suitable pin-punch. Remove the assembly 56 and collect the two washers that fit between it and the casing. Remove the clutch slave cylinder bracket 74. Unscrew the four bolts 59 and the Wedgelock bolt 57. Discard the old copper-plated washer 58, as a new one should be fitted to prevent leaks after reassembly. Slide off the clutch housing 54, discarding the old gasket 60 unless it is in excellent condition.

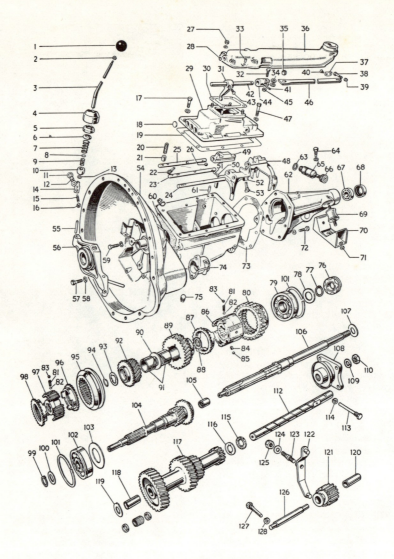

FIG 6:4 Gearbox details

Key to Fig 6:4
1 Knob   2 Locknut   3 Gearchange lever   4 Cover   5 Shield   6 Plate   7 Spring
8 Circlip   9 Spring   10 Nylon sphere   11 Stepped nylon washer   12 Bush   13 Washer   14 Lever end
15 Reverse stop pin   16 Locknut   17 Bolt   18 Welch plug   19 Gasket   20 Spring   21 Plunger
22 Taper locking pin   23 First/Second selector shaft   24 Third/Top selector shaft   25 Reverse selector shaft
26 Interlock ball   27 Nut   28 Rubber O-ring   29 Top cover   30 Gasket   31 Selector ball end   32 Bolt
33 Dowel   34 Washer   35 Bonded rubber bush   36 Gearchange extension   37 Reverse stop   38 Bolt
39 Nyloc nut   40 Screw   41 Mills pin   42 Remote control shaft (front)   43 Taper locking pin   44 Fork
45 Nut   46 Remote control shaft (rear)   47 Bolt   48 First/Second selector fork   49 Reverse selector
50 Interlock ball   51 Interlock plunger   52 Top/Third selector fork   53 Taper locking pin   54 Clutch housing
55 Pin   56 Clutch release mechanism   57 Wedgelock bolt   58 Plain washer (copper-plated)   59 Bolt
60 Gasket   61 Dowel   62 Rear extension   63 Rubber O-ring   64 Peg bolt   65 Speedo drive gear housing
66 Speedo drive gear   67 Extension ballrace   68 Oil seal   69 Gearbox mounting rubber   70 Mounting bracket
71 Nut   72 Bolt   73 Gasket   74 Clutch slave cylinder bracket   75 Sump plug   76 Speedo driving gear
77 Circlip   78 Distance washer   79 Ballrace   First-speed gear   81 Spring   82 Shim   83 Synchromesh ball
84 Plunger   85 Ball   86 Second-speed synchro hub   87 Second-speed synchro cup   88 Thrust washer
89 Second-speed mainshaft gear   90 Thrust washer   91 Bushes   92 Third-speed mainshaft gear   93 Thrust washer
94 Circlip   95 Third/Top synchro sleeve   96 Third/Top synchro cup   97 Third/Top inner synchro hub   98 Top synchro hub
99 Circlip   100 Distance washer   101 Circlip   102 Ballrace   103 Oil deflector   104 Input shaft
105 Torrington needle roller bearing   106 Mainshaft   107 Distance washer   108 Driving flange   109 Spring washer
110 Nut   112 Countershaft   113 Peg bolt   114 Spring washer   115 Rear fixed thrust washer   116 Rear rotating thrust washer
117 Countershaft gear cluster   118 Countershaft bush   119 Front fixed thrust washer   (needle rollers and retaining rings not fitted)
120 Reverse gear bush   121 Reverse gear   122 Reverse gear actuator   123 Actuator pivot   124 Plain washer
125 Nyloc nut   126 Reverse gear shaft   127 Reverse shaft retaining bolt   128 Spring washer

3 Remove the peg bolt 64 and withdraw the speedometer drive parts as shown in **FIG 6:5**. Prevent the drive flange 108 from rotating by holding it with the special peg spanner No. 20.SM.90 and remove the nut 110 and washer 109. Alternative methods of holding the drive flange are to select two gears at once or to use a large adjustable spanner with lead or wood as protection. Draw off the drive flange. Take off the rear extension by tapping with a hide-faced hammer as shown in **FIG 6:6**. Drift out the rear bearing 67 and oil seal 68 using a long drift through the extension.

4 Remove the peg bolt 113 and withdraw the countershaft 112, as shown in **FIG 6:7**, allowing the countershaft gear cluster to fall to the bottom of the casing free from the mainshaft gears.

5 Attach an adaptor S.4235A-2 securely to the front end of the input shaft and assemble the remainder of the Special Tool No. 4235A as shown in **FIG 6:8**. Repeatedly slide the moving weight smartly along the shaft so that it impacts on the handle. This action will draw the input shaft assembly out of the gearbox. Remove the circlip 99 and the distance washer 100. Take off the locating circlip 101 from its groove in the bearing 102 and press the bearing off the mainshaft 104. Lift off the oil thrower 103. **Do not attempt to remove the needle roller bearing 105.**

6 Use a soft-nosed drift and drive the mainshaft assembly rearwards until the bearing 79 is clear of the gearbox casing. Tilt the mainshaft assembly front end upwards and slide off the top speed synchromesh cup 98 by the top/third synchromesh unit as shown in **FIG 6:9**. Re-locate the mainshaft assembly by driving the rear bearing 79 partly back into position. Remove the mainshaft circlip 94 using Special Tool No. S.144 as shown in **FIG 6:10**. The circlip will probably be damaged as it is removed but keep the parts and do not discard them yet.

7 Again drive the mainshaft assembly rearwards until the rear bearing is free. Completely withdraw the mainshaft at the same time sliding the parts off, as shown in **FIG 6:11**. Use a Churchill handpress and adaptors to draw off the speedometer drive gear 76. Remove the circlip 77 and distance washer 78. Take off the circlip 101 and press the rear bearing 79 off the mainshaft 106.

8 Lift out the countershaft gear cluster 117 and collect the three thrust washers 115, 116 and 119. Push the rear gear 121 rearwards and remove it through the aperture in the rear face of the casing. Take out the dowel bolt 127 with its washer 128 and remove the reverse gear shaft 126. Remove the nut 125 and washer 124 to free the reverse gear actuator 122 and its pivot 123.

9 The synchromesh units are dismantled by sliding off their outer sleeves. However, before dismantling them wrap each one completely in a piece of cloth and dismantle them inside this so as to catch and keep the balls, plungers and springs. If this precaution is not taken then the small parts can easily be lost.

FIG 6:5 Removing speedometer drive parts

FIG 6:6 Driving off the rear extension

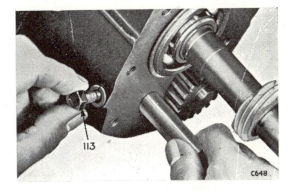

FIG 6:7 Withdrawing the countershaft

FIG 6:8 Removing the input shaft assembly using Churchill tool No. 4235A and adaptor No. S.4235A.2

FIG 6:9 Removing the top/third synchromesh unit

FIG 6:10 Removing the mainshaft circlip using Churchill tool No. S.144

FIG 6:11 Removing the mainshaft parts

6:4 Reassembling the gearbox
Examining the parts:

Before starting reassembly the parts should be thoroughly cleaned and examined. The best way of cleaning is to use a trichlorethylene vapour bath as this removes not only dirt but every trace of grease or oil. If this is not available use a solvent in a bath and wash the parts twice, using perfectly clean solvent for the second wash. If a degreasing agent such as trichlorethylene is used the parts should be wiped over with a clean, oily cloth so as to provide a thin oil film to prevent the parts from rusting.

Examine all the gears for chipped, worn or missing teeth and renew any where necessary. If one gear is damaged, minutely examine the mating gear to ensure that this has not also become damaged. Examine the shafts and bearing surfaces for chatter or fret marks and at the same time check splines for wear. Check all bushes for accurate fit. The bushes 118 in the countershaft gear cluster 117 are renewable. Examine all the bearings for wear or roughness. If the needle roller bearing 105 is damaged it cannot be removed from the input shaft 104 and both parts must be renewed. A new bearing 105 is pressed into the input shaft using a special drift shown in **FIG 6:12**. Note especially the stop pin on the drift which ensures that the bearing is pressed in to the correct depth.

Smear bearing surfaces with a little clean oil to facilitate reassembly. Use new gaskets and seals throughout to prevent oil leaks after reassembly. Jointing compound should not be necessary on paper gaskets but a thin smear of grease will help to keep them oiltight. Make sure that the mating faces of the castings are not damaged or distorted. Clean off any burrs or high-spots using a smooth file.

Torque loads are given in Technical Data.

Synchromesh units:

Refit the shims 82, springs 81 and balls 83 to the synchromesh hubs 86 and 97, holding them in place with thick grease. The second speed synchromesh hub 86 is also fitted with the interlock plunger 84 and interlock ball 85. Compress the balls into the hub using a large hose clip around the hub. Tap the inner hub assembly into the outer sleeve, allowing the hose clip to slide off as the balls enter. Press the hub in until the balls click into place in the detent grooves in the outer sleeve. The correct relationship of the parts on the second-speed synchromesh unit are shown in **FIG 6:13**.

When the synchromesh units have been reassembled they should be tested for axial release load in a type of jig shown in **FIG 6:14**. The flange on the jig prevents the inner hub from moving too far and allowing the balls and springs to fly out. Apply gradually increasing pull to the hook of the jig, through a spring balance, and note the pull required to move the inner hubs out of the detent position. The correct load should be 19 to 21 lbs (8.618 to 9.525 kg). If the load is outside these limits, evenly adjust the quantity of shims 82 under the springs and balls until the correct release load is obtained.

1 Refit the front thrust washer 119 to the casing so that its tag seats in the recess provided and the bronze face is towards the gears, using thick grease to hold it in place. Similarly refit the rear thrust washer 115. Lower the gear cluster 117 into position (small spur gear towards the rear) and, with the cluster pressed firmly forwards, insert the thrust washer 116 so that the bronze faces of the thrust washers 115 and 116 are together and the tags on the thrust washer 116 seat correctly in the gear cluster. Align the thrust washers and gear cluster and slide the countershaft 112 into place. A bullet-nosed dummy shaft of .655 inch (16.64 mm) diameter will help in aligning the parts so that the countershaft can be fitted. Measure the gap between the thrust washers 115 and 116, using feeler gauges as shown in **FIG 6:15**. The correct limits for the end float are .0015 to .0125 inch (.04 to .31 mm) but experience shows that the best amount of end float is .006 inch (.15 mm). The correct end float is obtained by selective fitting of the thrust washers. Minimum end float may be increased by lapping down the steel faces of the thrust washers on fine emerycloth spread over a truly flat surface, such as a surface plate or plate glass. **Under no circumstances may the bronze faces be lapped down or in any way reduced.** Withdraw the countershaft 113 and allow the gear cluster to slide to the bottom of the casing.

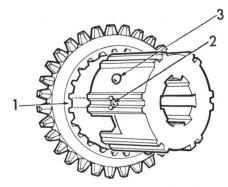

FIG 6:13 Assembly of second-speed synchromesh unit

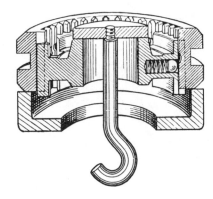

FIG 6:14 Jig for testing the axial release loads on synchromesh units

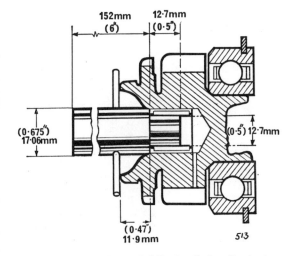

FIG 6:12 Dimensions of drift for fitting Torrington needle roller bearing to the input shaft

FIG 6:15 Measuring the countershaft gear end float

FIG 6:16 Refitting the reverse gear idler

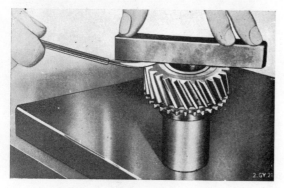

FIG 6:17 Measuring gear end float

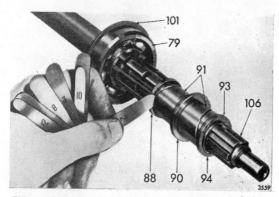

FIG 6:18 Measuring the total end float on the mainshaft assembly

2 Refit the reverse gear idler shaft 126, securing it in place with the bolt 127 and washer 128. Screw the pivot 123 back into the reverse gear actuator 122 so that one thread protrudes through the actuator. Secure the parts back to the casing using the washer 124 and nut 125. Check that the actuator pivots freely. Insert the reverse gear through the aperture in the rear of the casing, making sure that the pip on the actuator fits into the groove in the gear, as shown in **FIG 6:16**.

3 Fit the third-speed mainshaft gear 92 to its bush 91. Stand them on a surface table and measure the end float of the gear on the bush as shown in **FIG 6:17**. Similarly measure the end float of the second-speed mainshaft gear 89 on its bush 91. The correct end float is .002 to .006 inch (.05 to .1524 mm). To increase end float a new bush must be fitted, but the end float may be decreased by lapping down the end of the bush. The total end float of the gears on the mainshaft is partially controlled by the lengths of the bushes, so take care not to reduce the length of either bush excessively or the total end float may be increased beyond the correct limits.

4 Assemble the bushes and thrust washers only to the mainshaft 106, securing them in place with part of the old circlip 94 as shown in **FIG 6:18**. Measure the end float with feeler gauges and if required adjust it to .004 to .010 inch (.1016 to .254 mm) by selective fitting of the thrust washers. Remove and discard the old circlip 94 and slide the bushes and thrust washers off the mainshaft.

5 Press the rear bearing 79 back onto the mainshaft, making sure that it is fully in place and that the annular groove for the circlip 101 is at the rear end of the bearing. Refit the circlip 101 and secure the bearing in place with the distance washer 78 and circlip 77. Press the nylon speedometer drive gear 76 back into position on the mainshaft.

6 Insert the front end of the mainshaft back into the casing, tilt it up and slide the parts back onto the mainshaft in the following order: second-speed synchromesh assembly with its gear portion facing forwards, the second-speed synchromesh cup 87 so that its lugs locate in the synchromesh hub, the rear thrust washer 88 with its scrolled face forwards, second-speed gear 89 and bush 91, centre thrust washer 90, third-speed gear 92 with bush 91 and finally the front thrust washer 93 with its scrolled face rearwards.

7 Drive the mainshaft assembly forwards so that the rear bearing slides partially into the casing and locates the assembly. Use Special Tool No. S.145 to fit the new circlip 94 onto the mainshaft, as shown in **FIG 6:19**. Again drive the mainshaft back, tilt it and slide on the top/third synchromesh assembly with the longer boss facing forwards and baulk rings attached.

FIG 6:19 Refitting the mainshaft circlip using Churchill tool No. S.145

Finally drive the mainshaft assembly forwards until the circlip 101 on the rear bearing is in firm contact with the face of the casing.

8. Place the oil thrower 103 into position, holding it there with a little thick grease. Without moving the oil thrower from its position press on the front bearing 102 with the annular groove for the circlip to the front. Secure the bearing in place with the distance washer 100 and the circlip 99. Refit the circlip 101 to the bearing. Place the top speed synchromesh cone 93 onto the cone on the input shaft and drive the input shaft assembly back into the front of the casing, making sure that the baulk ring lugs fit into their respective slots as shown in **FIG 6:20** as well as guiding the spigot on the mainshaft into the needle roller bearing in the input shaft. Drive the input shaft in until the circlip 101 is in firm contact with the front face of the casing.

9. Use the dummy countershaft described earlier to lift up the countershaft gear cluster and align the thrust washers. Turn the countershaft 112 so that it is at the correct angle to accept the locating bolt and press the countershaft into position, using it to eject the dummy countershaft. Secure the countershaft in place using the peg bolt 113 and its washer 114.

10. Drive the ballbearing 67 back into the rear extension 62 and then drive in the oil seal 68 with its lips facing forwards. Place the paper gasket 73 into position, holding it there with a thin smear of grease and drive the rear extension back into place. Secure the extension using the bolts and washers 72. Lubricate the shaft of the drive gear 66 and feed it back into the housing 65. Make sure that the O-ring 63 is in place and refit the parts of the speedometer drive back into the rear extension, securing them with the peg bolt 64 (see **FIG 6:5**). Refit the drive flange 108 securing it in place with the washer 109 and nut 110.

11. Refit the clutch housing, using a new gasket 60, in the reverse order of removal. Fit a new copper-plated steel washer 58 under the Wedgelock bolt 57 to ensure against oil leaks. Refit the clutch release mechanism and clutch slave cylinder mounting bracket.

FIG 6:21   Fitting the top cover assembly to the gearbox

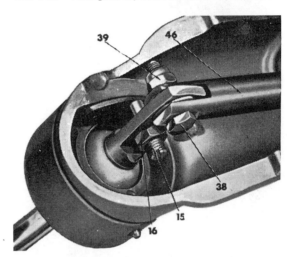

FIG 6:22   Gearlever attachments

FIG 6:20   Refitting the input shaft assembly

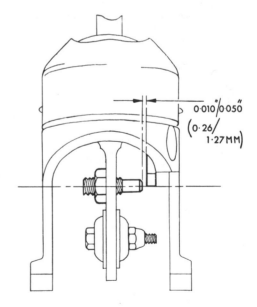

FIG 6:23   Adjustment of reverse stop plate and pin

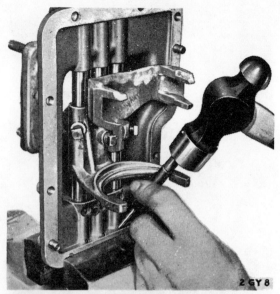

FIG 6:24 Removing the selector shaft Welch plugs

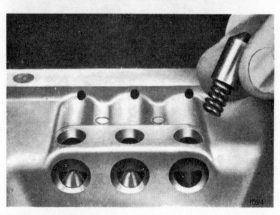

FIG 6:25 Refitting the selector plungers and springs to the top cover

12 Set the gears into the neutral position and similarly set the three gear selectors in the top cover to the neutral position. Refit the top cover, with a new gasket 19, ensuring that the selectors fit correctly into position. The two longer bolts 47 fit at the rear end of the top cover. The top cover being fitted is shown in **FIG 6:21**.

6:5 The top cover and gearchange extension

The details of these parts are shown in **FIG 6:4**. Both can be removed from the gearbox while the unit is still fitted to the car. Removal of the gearchange extension has already been dealt with in **Section 6:2**. The complete assembly can be removed in a similar manner but take out the bolts which secure the top cover to the gearbox casing instead of the nuts securing the extension to the cover.

Gearchange extension:

1 The gearlever knob should already have been removed when taking the extension out of the car. Undo the locknut 39 and withdraw the bolt 38, also shown in **FIG 6:22**, to free the bottom end of the gearlever 14 from the rear extension shaft 46. Slacken the locknut 16 and unscrew the reverse stop pin 15. Press the cap 4 slightly downwards and rotate it in an anticlockwise direction to free its bayonet-type fastening.

2 Lift the gearlever assembly out of the extension and remove the cups 5 and 6 together with the outer spring 7 from the extension. Remove the circlip 8 and slide the inner spring 9, nylon sphere 10 and washer 13 up off the gearlever. Remove the stepped nylon washers 11 and bush 12 from the end 14 of the gearlever.

3 Remove the tapered locking pin 43 and slide the shaft assemblies out of the extension, collecting the ball end 31 as it comes free. Remove the nut 45 and bolt 32 to separate the front extension shaft 42 from the rear shaft 46. Collect the washers 34 and bonded rubber bush 35 when the bolt 32 is withdrawn. The coupling fork 44 can be detached from the front shaft by driving out the hollow steel pin 41 with a suitable pin punch. If required the reverse stop 37 can be removed from the extension 36 by taking out the two countersunk screws 40. Remove the O-ring 28 from its recess using a small blunt screwdriver.

The gearchange mechanism is reassembled in the reverse order of dismantling. Renew any parts that are worn and fit new O-rings 28. After reassembly adjust the gap between the reverse stop 37 and the reverse stop pin 15 to .010 to .050 inch (.26 to 1.27 mm) when the gearlever is in the neutral position of the first/second gate, as shown in **FIG 6:23**.

FIG 6:26 Replacing the interlock balls. The top cover has been cut away for the purposes of illustration

Top cover assembly:

Tap out the six Welch plugs 18 using a ⅛ inch (3.17 mm) pin punch as shown in **FIG 6:24. Take care that the selector shafts are moved clear while removing the Welch plugs.** Remove the three tapered locking pins 22 and 53 to free the selector forks. First press the selector shaft 25 out of the cover, removing the reverse selector 49 as it comes free. Similarly remove the other two selector shafts 23 and 24 and their selectors. Collect the two interlock balls 26 and 50 and slide the interlock plunger 51 out of the selector shaft 23. Shake out the three sets of plungers 21 and springs 20 from the cover.

After cleaning the parts and renewing any that are worn or damaged, refit the three springs 20 into the plungers 21 and refit the three assemblies back into their positions in the top cover as shown in **FIG 6:25.** Slide the top/third selector shaft 24 into position from the front of the cover. Depress the appropriate plunger until the shaft has passed over it and pick up the selector 52 onto the shaft as the latter is pushed in. Press in the shaft until the detent plunger seats in the middle neutral position detent on the shaft. Similarly refit the reverse selector shaft 25 and selector 49. There are only two detents on this shaft but still set it into the neutral position. Refit the interlock plunger into the first/second selector shaft 23 and partially slide in the selector shaft. This shaft also passes through the top/third selector fork 52. Hold the cover up as shown in **FIG 6:26** and with the first/second selector shaft in the position shown drop the two interlock balls 26 and 50 into position. Press the shaft fully home so that the balls are held in place between the shafts. Secure the selector forks in place using the tapered pins 22 and 53. Make sure that the recesses for the Welch plugs are perfectly clean and free from burrs and press the new plugs into position with a little jointing compound around the edges as a seal. Slightly flatten the Welch plugs with a soft drift so as to lock them into position.

6:6 Fault diagnosis

(a) Jumping out of gear

1 Broken spring behind locating plunger for selector shaft
2 Excessively worn detent in selector shaft
3 Worn coupling dogs
4 Fork to selector shaft securing screw loose

(b) Noisy gearbox

1 Insufficient oil
2 Worn or damaged bearings
3 Worn or damaged gear teeth
4 Excessive end float in countershaft gear

(c) Oil leaks

1 Damaged gaskets or oil seals
2 Faces damaged on castings

NOTES

CHAPTER 7

PROPELLER SHAFT, REAR AXLE AND REAR SUSPENSION

7:1 Description
7:2 Routine maintenance
7:3 Servicing universal joints
7:4 The propeller shaft

7:5 The hub and outer axle shaft assembly
7:6 The differential
7:7 The rear suspension
7:8 Fault diagnosis

7:1 Description

FIG 7:1 shows the details of the rear suspension and rear axle assembly. The differential unit is held by rubber mountings to the chassis. The transverse road spring 2 is bolted to the top of the differential casing and secured by the clamp plate 3. Drive is taken from the differential unit by an inner axle shaft mounted one on either side of the casing. The inner shafts are connected by universal joints to the outer axle shafts so as to allow for movement of the suspension. The outer axle shaft rotates in the trunnion housing 26 in one needle roller bearing and one ballbearing 24, oil seals being fitted to prevent the escape of grease, and drives the wheel hub 19 which is keyed to it. The trunnion housing is pivoted to a vertical link whose upper end is attached to the road spring. A telescopic damper 9 is fitted between the chassis and the vertical link so as to control the movements of the road spring. The vertical link 10 is prevented from moving in a fore and aft direction by the radius arm 32.,

The propeller shaft takes the drive from the gearbox to the differential unit. This shaft is fitted with universal joints at either end to allow for any misalignment or movement between the gearbox and differential unit.

7:2 Routine maintenance

1 At periodic intervals grease the universal joints fitted to the propeller shaft. At the same time check the security of the nuts and bolts holding the universals to the flanges. This includes the universal joints fitted to the outer axle shafts.

2 At 6000 mile intervals remove the combined filler and level plug 2 from the rear axle, shown in **FIG 7:2**, and top up with the correct grade of oil, using an oil gun. Allow surplus oil to drain out before refitting the plug, and **never leave the unit in an overfilled condition.** At longer intervals remove the drain plug 1 and drain out the old oil, preferably when it is hot after a long run. Do not flush out the unit with any solvents. Replace the drain plug and refill to the correct level with fresh oil.

3 At 12,000 mile intervals remove the sealing plug, arrowed in **FIG 7:3**, and replace it with a grease nipple. Inject grease until it exudes from the bearing. Remove the grease nipple and replace the sealing plug. Wipe away surplus grease.

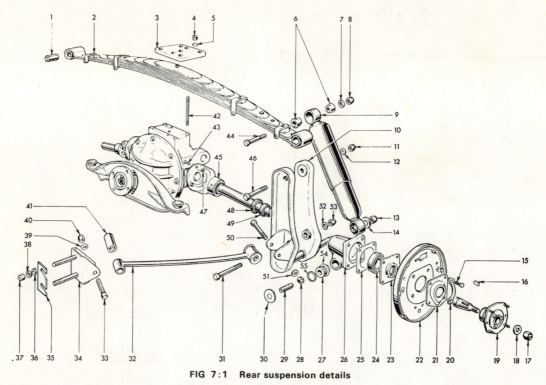

FIG 7:1 Rear suspension details

Key to Fig 7:1   1 Spring eye bush   2 Road spring   3 Spring clamp plate   4 Nut   5 Washer   6 Rubber bush
7 Washer   8 Nut   9 Damper   10 Vertical link   11 Nut   12 Washer   13 Nut   14 Washer   15 Bolt
16 Key   17 Nut   18 Washer   19 Hub   20 Locktab   21 Grease retainer   22 Brake backplate   23 Seal housing
24 Bearing   25 Gasket   26 Trunnion housing   27 Nyloc bush   28 Nut   29 Steel bush   30 Dust seal   31 Bolt
32 Radius arm   33 Bolt   34 Radius arm bracket   35 Shim   36 Washer   37 Nut   38 Washer   39 Washer
40 Nut   41 Rubber bush   42 Stud   43 Bolt   44 Bolt   45 Axle shaft coupling   46 Bolt   47 Nut
48 Flinger   49 Seal   50 Bolt   51 Washer   52 Washer   53 Nut   54 Dust seal   55 Rubber ring

7:3 Servicing universal joints

A typical universal joint fitted to the propeller shaft is shown in detail in **FIG 7:4**. The universal joints fitted to the outer axle shafts are of very similar construction except that no grease nipple is fitted and the seal fits onto the bearing cup and is replaced and refitted with the cup.

Do not attempt to renew individual parts but instead renew all the parts supplied in the service kit. The kit includes a new spider 6 complete with all the bearing parts. Service only one universal joint at a time to avoid mixing the parts between different joints.

1 Clean rust, dirt and enamel from the bore and use a pair of circlip pliers to remove all four circlips 2. If, despite cleaning the bore, the circlips are still stiff to free then lightly tap in each bearing cup 3 so as to ease the pressure on the circlips.

2 Holding the yoke as shown in **FIG 7:5,** lightly tap on the shaft, preferably using a soft-faced hammer, in order to make the bearing cup emerge. Carry on tapping until sufficient of the cup 3 has emerged to allow it to be removed, with either the fingers or a pair of grips. Turn the shaft over and tap out the opposite bearing in a similar manner.

3 Press the shaft firmly up against the trunnion and ease the opposite arm of the other trunnion. Swivel the spider and free the shaft from the trunnion that is holding it. Lay the exposed trunnions on two blocks of wood or lead and, by tapping on the arm as shown in **FIG.7:6,** remove the remaining pair of bearing cups.

4 Thoroughly clean all the parts and check that the bearing cups 3 are a light drive fit through their bores. After a long period of service and inadequate lubrication the bores can wear oval. The flanges 7 can be renewed but, if the bores for the actual shaft have worn, then the only cure is to fit a new shaft assembly.

5 Replace the needle rollers in the bearing cup, holding them in place with a little grease. The correct number of rollers will exactly fill the bearing cup. Replace the seals. If they fit onto the spider use a hollow drift to drive them squarely and accurately into position. Refit the spider into the flange 7, making sure that if a nipple is fitted it will face towards the shaft.

6 Shell Dentax 250, Retinax A or the equivalent should be used for the bearings. On universal joints not fitted with grease nipples the bearings must be well lubricated before reassembly, but if a grease nipple is fitted the lubricant can be injected after reassembly.

7 Press the bearing cups into position, using a mandrel of diameter just smaller than the actual cup, by the method shown in **FIG 7:7. Take great care not to**

FIG 7:2 Rear axle drain and level plugs

FIG 7:3 Rear hub grease plug

allow any needles to become displaced during this operation otherwise excess pressure will snap the displaced needle. If the cup sticks it should be removed and checked, not forced into place.
8 Refit the shaft to the spider and press the remaining pair of bearings back into place. If after reassembly the joint is stiff to swivel, lightly tap on the arms to ease the pressure on the bearings.

7:4 The propeller shaft

Three different propeller shafts are fitted to the models covered by this manual. If there is radial play or end float in the shaft then the universal joints should be serviced as described in **Section 7:3**. Ideally the shaft should be renewed to preserve the balance of the unit, but the cost usually means that the universals have to be serviced instead.

Removal:

This covers all three types of propeller shaft.
1 Raise the car onto chassis stands. Remove the front seats, front carpet and gearbox cover.
2 Remove the four Nyloc nuts securing the propeller shaft to the gearbox driving flange and tap out the bolts. On solid-type shafts the gearbox and engine will have to be levered forwards to free the propeller shaft from the gearbox driving flange.
3 Remove the Nyloc nuts and bolts securing the rear of the propeller shaft to the driving flange on the differential unit. Lower the rear end of the shaft and remove the shaft by drawing it out under the rear of the car.

The propeller shaft is replaced in the reverse order of removal. **The Nyloc nuts must be tight enough to require a spanner for the full threaded length of the bolt.** If they are so slack that they can be turned by finger pressure alone then they are worn and will not provide adequate locking. New nuts must then be fitted. Sliding or strap joints are always fitted to the rear of the car.

Solid shaft:

This, as the name implies, is a continuous shaft with no means of adjusting the length, so that the distance between universal joints is always a constant.

Frictionless shaft:

This is fitted with a sliding joint. The sliding joint uses four rows of rollers, ten rollers in each row, to ensure that it is virtually frictionless in the sliding plane. Under no circumstances may this sliding joint be dismantled and any fault in it requires renewal of the complete propeller shaft.

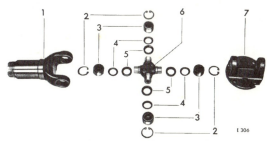

FIG 7:4 Universal joint details

Key to Fig 7:4   1 Sliding yoke   2 Circlips
3 Bearing cups   4 Seals   5 Retainers   6 Spider
7 Flange

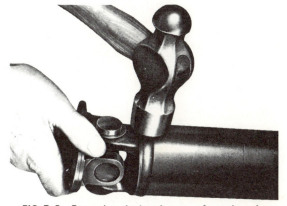

FIG 7:5 Removing the bearing cups from the yoke

FIG 7:6 Removing the bearing cups

FIG 7:7 Refitting the bearing cups

7:5 The hub and outer axle shaft assembly
Removal:

Refer to **FIG 7:1**, which has the same key as the figures following.

1 Remove the hub caps and slacken the wheel nuts on the rear wheels. Jack-up the rear of the car, placing it securely on stands and then remove the rear road wheels.
2 Refer to **FIG 7:10** which shows the details of the rear suspension. Hold the hexagon on the flexible pipe 57 with a spanner and undo the union 56 on the metal pipe. Still holding the hexagon, remove the locknut 58 and free the flexible pipe from the bracket on the chassis.
3 Refer to **FIG 7:11**. Remove the clevis pin 61 and free the spring 63 to disconnect the handbrake cable from the brake unit. Place a jack under the vertical link 10 and raise it to take the load off the damper. Unscrew the nut 28 and withdraw the bolt 50 to free the radius arm 32 from the vertical link.
4 Remove the nut 13 and washer 14. Pull the bottom of the damper rearwards to free it from the mounting pin on the vertical link. Remove the nuts 47 and tap out the bolts 43 to free the axle shaft coupling 45 from the flange on the inner axle shaft attached to the differential casing.
5 Remove the jack from underneath the vertical link and support the brake assembly by hand. Remove the nut 11 and withdraw the bolt 46 to free the upper end of the vertical link from the spring. Withdraw the hub and axle shaft assembly from the car.

The parts are replaced in the reverse order of removal. Leave the nuts 11 and 13 finger tight until the suspension has been loaded to its normal working position and then tighten them to the correct load. Bleed the brakes before refitting the road wheels.

Strap-drive shaft:

A sectioned view of the shaft is shown in **FIG 7:8** and the details of the parts in **FIG 7:9**. The sliding yoke 7 can be removed after the nuts 5, washers 4 and bolts 3 are taken out. On reassembly pack the bore at **Y** with Duckhams Q.5648 grease and lubricate at **X** with either Shell Dentax 250 or Retinax A. Renew the O-ring 2 if it is damaged or worn.

Dismantling:

The details of the rear axle assembly are shown in **FIG 7:12** and the hub and outer axle assembly is further amplified in **FIG 7:13**.

1 Remove the two countersunk screws and take off the brake drum. Unscrew the hub nut 31 and remove the plain washer. Use extractor No. S.109C to withdraw the hub 30 from the shaft 43. Drift the key 42 out of its slot.

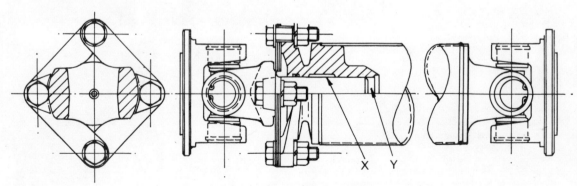

FIG 7:8 Strap drive propeller shaft

2 Remove the nut 74 and its plain washer then withdraw the bolt 73. Slide off the vertical link 75. Take out from the trunnion housing 37, the shims 25, seals 26, nylon inserts 27, shims 28 and the distance piece 38.

3 Free the tabs on the lockplates 71 and take out the bolts 70. The grease trap 32, brake backplate 72, seal 34 in its housing 33 and the joint washer 36 will all now come free.

4 Remove the flinger 44 and the trunnion housing assembly from the axle shaft using the handpress No. S.4221A and adaptors S.4221A/14. Extract the oil seal 41, needle roller bearing 40 and bearing 35 from the trunnion housing 37.

Reassembly:

1 Throughly clean all the parts by washing them with clean fuel. Trichlorethylene or similar solvents may be used provided that they do not come into contact with any rubber parts. Renew any parts that are worn, damaged or seem doubtful.

2 Press the needle roller bearing 40 back into the trunnion housing, preferably using the handpress and tool No. S.300A, so that the lettered end faces out and the bearing is .5 inch (12.7 mm) from the trunnion face. Drift the oil seal 41 into place, lips trailing. Drive the flinger 44 back into place on the shaft using a tool of the dimensions shown in **FIG 7:14**.

3 Pack the needle rollers with grease and slide the shaft 43 through the trunnion housing, taking great care not to damage the oil seal. Mount the shaft in the padded jaws of a vice. Pack the bearing 35 with grease and drive it back into the trunnion housing, preferably using tool No. S.304.

4 If required fit a new oil seal 34 into the housing 33, again with its lips trailing. Smear the joint washer 36 lightly with grease and lay it in position on the trunnion housing. Refit the seal and its housing, brake backplate (wheel cylinder uppermost), and grease trap (duct downwards) and secure them in place with the bolts 70. Lock the bolts with the lockplates 71.

5 Make sure that the tapers are clean and then tap the key 42 back into its slot in the shaft. Refit the hub 30 securing it in place with the plain washer and a new nut 31. Make sure that the brake drum is clean and grease free. Refit the drum.

6 Refit the vertical link 75 and its associated part in the reverse order of dismantling.

7:6 The differential

The details of the differential are shown in **FIG 7:12**. However, it is extremely unwise for the average owner to attempt to fully dismantle or service the unit. The meshing of the pinion and crownwheel is set by the accurate measurement and shimming of the parts, for which specialized equipment is essential. On many rear axles the differential gears may be removed from the casing but on the Triumph range a special tool is required to spread the casing by exactly the right amount to allow the parts to be removed.

If the unit causes any trouble, other than oil leaks, the unit (or car) should be taken to a suitably equipped garage. The fitting of an exchange unit should also be considered.

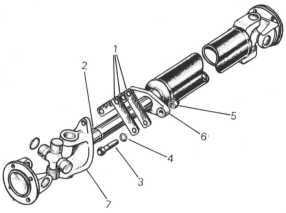

FIG 7:9 Strap drive propeller shaft details
Key to Fig 7:9   1 Straps   2 O-ring   3 Bolt
4 Washer   5 Nut   6 Driving yoke   7 Sliding yoke

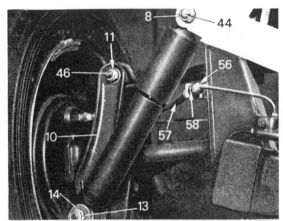

FIG 7:10   Rear suspension attachments

FIG 7:11   Handbrake connections

Inner axle shaft assemblies (including oil seals):

1 Drain the oil from the rear axle. Remove the hub and outer axle assemblies (see **Section 7:5**).

2 The parts are shown in more detail in **FIG 7:15**. Use a $\frac{3}{16}$ inch (6.763 mm) Allen key to remove the socket-headed screws 16. Withdraw the complete assembly from the differential casing.

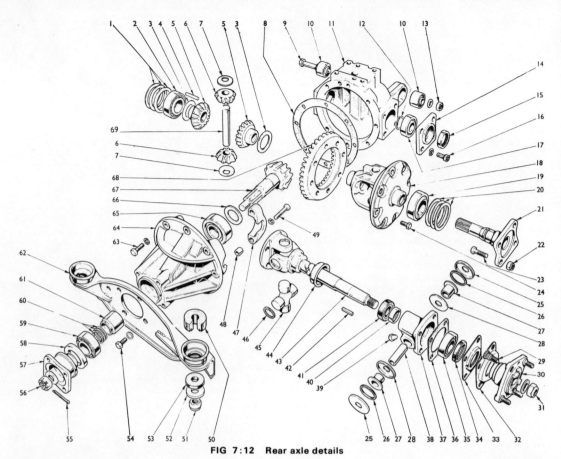

FIG 7:12 Rear axle details

Key to Figs 7:12 and 7:13 1 Shims   2 Differential side bearing   3 Thrust washer   4 Cross-shaft locking pin
5 Sun gear   6 Planet gear   7 Thrust washer   8 Joint washer   9 Rear mounting bolt   10 Metalastik bush
11 Hypoid rear casing   12 Circlip   13 Nyloc nut   14 Seal housing plate   15 Oil seal   16 Hexagon socket screw
17 Ballrace   18 Differential carrier   19 Differential side bearing   20 Shims   21 Inner axle shaft   22 Nyloc nut
23 Bolt   24 Bolt   25 Shim   26 Rubber sealing ring   27 Nylon bush   28 Shim   29 Stud   30 Hub
31 Nyloc nut   32 Grease trap   33 Outer seal housing   34 Seal   35 Ballrace   36 Joint washer   37 Trunnion housing
38 Distance tube   39 Grease plug   40 Needle roller bearing   41 Inner oil seal   42 Key   43 Outer axle shaft
44 Grease flinger   45 Universal joint assembly   46 Circlip   47 Bearing cap   48 Tubular dowel   49 Bolt
50 Mounting rubber   51 Nyloc nut   52 Plain washer   53 Rubber pad   54 Bolt   55 Splitpin   56 Slotted nut
57 Coupling flange   58 Oil seal   59 Pinion tail bearing   60 Shims   61 Spacer   62 Mounting plate   63 Bolt
64 Hypoid nose piece casing   65 Pinion head bearing   66 Spacer   67 Pinion   68 Crownwheel   69 Cross-shaft
70 Bolt   71 Lockplate   72 Brake backplate   73 Bolt   74 Nyloc nut   75 Vertical link

3 Remove the circlip 12. Use the handpress and adaptor set No. S.4221A–7B to withdraw the bearing 17 from the shaft 21. Take off the seal housing plate 14 complete with the seal 15 and remove the seal from the plate.

4 Wash the parts in clean fuel. Drive a new oil seal 15 into the plate 14 so that when reassembled the seals lips will face the differential. Wrap the splines on the shaft with a cylinder of thin shim steel and slide the housing and seal back onto the shaft. Remove the protective cylinder.

5 Press the bearing 17 back onto the shaft, securing it with the circlip 12. Refit the assembly to the differential. Fill the differential to the correct level with oil and replace the hub and outer axle shaft assemblies. Bleed the brakes (see **Chapter 10**) before refitting the road wheels.

Pinion oil seal:

1 Drain the oil from the rear axle. Remove the exhaust tail pipe. Disconnect the propeller shaft from the driving flange 57. When non-extending propeller shafts are fitted it may become necessary to remove the propeller shaft so as to have sufficient room to work in (see **Section 7:4**).

2 Remove the splitpin 55. Prevent the driving flange 57 from rotating, preferably holding it with the special peg spanner No. 20.SM.90, and remove the nut 56 and plain washer. Withdraw the driving flange from the nose piece casing 64 and prise out the old oil seal 58.

3 Squarely drive in a new oil seal and refit the driving flange. Reconnect the propeller shaft and fill the differential to the correct level with oil.

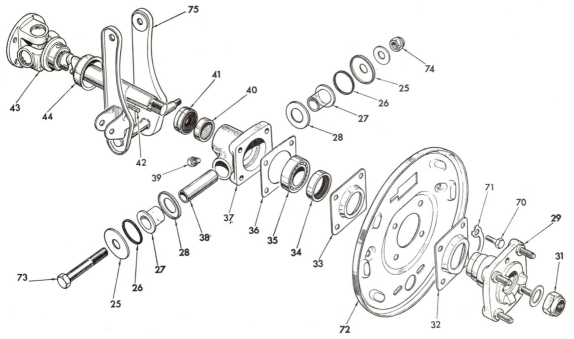

FIG 7:13 Outer axle shaft and hub assembly details

Removing the differential unit:

1 Jack-up the rear of the car and place it securely on chassis stands. Remove the rear road wheels. Remove the exhaust silencer and tail pipe.
2 Support each suspension assembly using a jack under the vertical link. Free the dampers from the vertical links after removing the locknuts and washers.
3 Disconnect the propeller shaft from the driving flange on the differential unit. Disconnect the outer axle shaft couplings.
4 Take out the rear seat assembly and remove the coverplate from the road spring mounting plate. Remove the six Nyloc nuts 4 and the three rear studs 42 from the spring attachment, as shown in **FIG 7:16**. Lift out the washers 5 and plate 3.
5 The differential attachments are shown in **FIG 7:17**. Undo the Nyloc nuts 13 and withdraw the bolts 9, collecting the plain washers. Have an assistant support the weight of the unit and remove the nuts 51, plain washers 52 and the rubber pads 53. Manoeuvre the unit downwards and forwards to clear it from the car.

The unit is replaced in reverse order of removal. Make sure that the Metalastik bushes 10, mounting rubbers 50 and rubber pads 53 are all in good condition before refitting the unit. Leave the Nyloc nuts 13 slack until after the differential assembly is fully in place and the Metalastik bushes are in their normal positions.

7:7 The rear suspension

The details of the rear suspension are shown in **FIG 7:1**. The parts of the trunnion housing and vertical link have already been dealt with in **Section 7:5**.

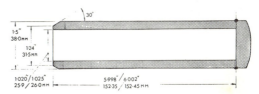

FIG 7:14 Dimensions of tool for refitting grease flinger

FIG 7:15 Inner axle shaft details

FIG 7:16 Spring clamp plate attachments

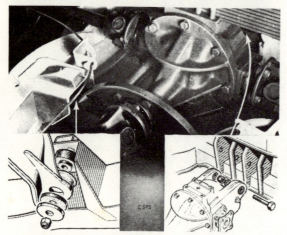

FIG 7:17 Differential unit attachments

The radius arms:

The radius arm attachments are also shown in **FIG 7:18**. To remove a radius arm, jack-up the car, remove the road wheel and support the suspension with a screw-jack. Remove the nuts 28 and 40 together with their washers 51 and 39. Raise or lower the jack under the suspension until the bolts 50 and 33 can easily be withdrawn and the radius arm removed.

Renew the bushes in the ends of the radius arm if they are worn or damaged and refit the radius arm in the reverse order of removal.

The quantity of shims 35 under the radius arm bracket 34 controls the amount of toe-in on the rear wheels. The addition of shims under the bracket will decrease the amount of toe-in. If the bracket is removed, make sure that the original shims are replaced under it when it is refitted.

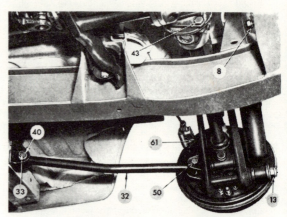

FIG 7:18 Radius arm attachment

The dampers:

Refer also to **FIG 7:10**. To remove the dampers jack-up the rear of the car, remove the road wheels and support the suspension with a jack under the vertical link 10. Undo the nuts 13 and 8. Take off the washer 14 and withdraw the bolt 44. Pull the damper clear from its attachment points and remove it from the car. Replace the damper in the reverse order of removal, tightening the nuts 8 and 13 fully when the suspension is in its normal operating position. Renew the rubber bushes in the damper if they are worn or perished.

Before fitting a new damper, or replacing a damper which has been off the car for some time, the air must be bled out of the operating parts and into the space above the fluid. Mount the damper vertically in the padded jaws of a vice. Pump it up and down, using only short strokes, until there is no lost motion. Test the damper by extending and compressing it fully through several strokes. There should be equal and constant resistance to motion in both directions. If the resistance is weak in either direction, excessively stiff or there are pockets of no resistance then the unit is defective and a new unit must be fitted in its place.

Always renew a damper which shows physical damage.

FIG 7:19 Rear road spring removal

The road spring:

1 Jack-up the rear of the car and place it securely onto chassis stands. Disconnect the brake flexible hoses from their brackets on the chassis (see **Section 7:5,** operation 2 of Removal). Disconnect the handbrake cables and springs from the brakes.

2 Remove the dampers as described earlier. Still supporting the vertical link with a jack, remove the nut 11 and washer 12 and then withdraw the bolt 46 to free one side vertical link from the road spring. Repeat the operation on the other side.

3 Remove the rear seat assembly and take off the access plate to the spring mounting. Remove the six Nyloc nuts 4, washers 5, plate 3 and three rear studs 42 from the attachment (see **FIG 7:16**). Remove the spring from the car as shown in **FIG 7:19**.

The road spring, marked FRONT for correct replacement, is refitted in the reverse order of removal. Check that the spring has no broken leaves and that the clips holding the spring together are tight and secure. Press out the old spring eye bushes 1 if they are damaged or worn, and press new bushes into place. Do not fully tighten the suspension nuts until the suspension had been loaded to its normal working position. Use sealant around the edges of the access panel for the spring attachment so as to prevent the ingress of water or dirt into the car.

7:8 Fault diagnosis

(a) Noisy axle
1 Insufficient or incorrect lubricant
2 Worn bearings
3 Worn gears

(b) Excessive backlash
1 Worn gears, bearings or bearing housings
2 Worn universal joints

(c) Oil leakage
1 Defective oil seals
2 Blocked breather on differential case
3 Too high an oil level in differential

(d) Vibration
1 Propeller shaft out of balance
2 Worn universal joints
3 Tyre defects

(e) Rattles
1 Worn rubber bushes on damper
2 Worn bushes in suspension
3 Worn rubber pads and bushes on differential attachments
4 Loose clips on road spring

(f) 'Settling'
1 Broken leaf or leaves in road spring

NOTES

CHAPTER 8

THE FRONT SUSPENSION AND HUBS

8:1 Description
8:2 Routine maintenance
8:3 Front hubs
8:4 Separating tapers on ball joints
8:5 The suspension sub-assembly
8:6 Road spring and damper assembly

8:7 The upper wishbone and ball joint
8:8 The vertical link and lower wishbone assembly
8:9 Suspension geometry
8:10 Fault diagnosis

8:1 Description

Each front wheel is mounted on an independent suspension sub-assembly as shown in **FIG 8:1**. The wheel is fitted to a hub which revolves around a stub axle on two opposed tapered bearings. This stub axle is in turn fitted to a vertical link which pivots between the outer ends of the wishbones to provide the steering movement. The inner ends of the wishbones are attached to the sub-frame and chassis so that they are free to pivot vertically and allow the suspension to move. All the pivots on the wishbones are fitted either with rubber and steel bushes (inner ends) or nylon bushes (on the outer end of the lower wishbone assembly). The vertical link pivots about a ball joint at its top end and a special screwed trunnion bearing at its lower end. The suspension can either be removed from the car as a sub-assembly or the parts can be serviced in situ.

An anti-roll bar interconnects the lower wishbone assemblies of both suspension units. On fast cornering the weight of the car acts as though it were transferred outwards, putting a greater load on the outside wheels. The outside suspension is forced up relative to the car by the increased load, whilst the inside suspension tends to move down so that the body assumes a roll angle.

The anti-roll bar transfers some of the load from the outside suspension to the inside one, evening up the loads and cutting down body roll. Not only does this improve comfort but it also improves roadholding as the suspension units do not reach exaggerated inefficient angles and weight is always kept on the inside wheel. The details of the anti-roll bar are shown in **FIG 8:2** and its attachments in **FIG 8:3**.

The load on the suspension is taken by a coil spring acting between the lower wishbone assembly and the sub-frame (which is attached to the chassis). The spring movement is controlled by a telescopic sealed damper mounted concentrically with the spring.

The details of the Herald 1200 suspension are shown in **FIG 8:4**. Disc brakes are fitted to the Herald 13/60 instead of the drum brakes on the 1200 models. The suspension for the 13/60 is basically the same but the mountings for the disc brakes are shown in **FIG 8:5**.

8:2 Routine maintenance

1 Jack-up the car under the chassis. Remove the plug 27 from each lower trunnion 42, shown arrowed in **FIG 8:6**, and replace it with a grease nipple. Apply a grease gun filled with Hypoid oil, **not engine oil**,

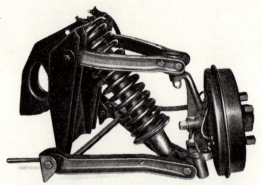

FIG 8:1 Complete suspension sub-assembly

and inject oil until it exudes from the steering swivel. Repeat on the other side suspension. Remove the grease nipples and replace the sealing plugs. This operation should be carried out every 6000 miles.

2 The front hubs should be checked and adjusted every 12,000 miles. Grease may be packed around the outer bearing, not in the dust cap, but it is a better policy to remove the hub from the car and remove old grease before packing both bearings with grease and replacing the hub.

8:3 Front hubs

The hubs and vertical link swivels should all be tested for wear with the road wheel fitted. Check that the wheel nuts are tight and then jack-up the front of the car. Grasp the tyre at the six and twelve o'clock positions and try to rock the top of the tyre in and out. There should be very little play, and if it is excessive it is caused by either worn, maladjusted bearings or wear in the vertical link swivels. Repeat the test, this time grasping the wheel at the nine and three o'clock positions. Play, not to be confused with movement of the steering, indicates that the hub bearings are the source. If the play has gone then the most likely cause is wear in the vertical link swivels. Spin the wheel and check that the bearings rotate smoothly and freely. Noises from the brake should not be confused with the noise from a defective bearing. If the bearings are suspect then the hub should be removed and the bearings checked visually.

A sectional view of the hub assembly fitted to the Herald 1200 is shown in **FIG 8:7** and a similar view of the hub assembly fitted to the Herald 13/60 appears in **FIG 8:8**.

Dismantling:

1 Apply the handbrake and securely jack-up the front of the car. Remove the front road wheels.
2 **1200 only.** Slacken the brake adjusters. Remove the two countersunk screws securing the brake drum and draw off the brake drum. If the drum is difficult to remove it may be left in place and removed with the hub and the parts, then separated later.

13/60 only. Referring to **FIG 8:5**, take out the two bolts 72 and their washers 71 which secure the brake caliper 70 to its bracket 68. Slide back the caliper

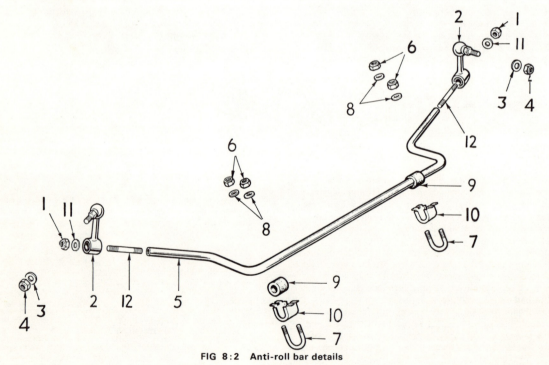

FIG 8:2 Anti-roll bar details

Key to Figs 8:2 and 8:3   1 Nyloc nut   2 Link   3 Plain washer   4 Nyloc nut   5 Anti-roll bar   6 Nyloc nut
7 U-bolt   8 Plain washer   9 Rubber bush   10 Clamp   11 Plain washer   12 Stud

FIG 8:3 Anti-roll bar attachments

from the brake disc 65, noting the position of any shims fitted between the caliper and bracket. Wire the caliper safely out of the way so that the flexible hose is not strained.

3 Remove the dust cap 66, extract the splitpin 62, undo the nut 61 and remove it as well as the D-washer 60. Draw off the hub assembly 57, taking care not to drop the inner race of the bearing 59 as it comes free.

4 Use a soft-metal drift to drive out the oil seal assembly 53 and 54 from the rear of the hub. If the felt 53 is damaged strip it off from the retainer 54 and glue a new felt back into position, using a little jointing compound. This should be done during the dismantling stage so as to allow the jointing compound to dry before the parts are reassembled.

5 Remove the inner race of the bearing 55 and, if required, drift out the outer races of both bearings from the hub 57. Also if required, the brake disc 65 can be separated from the hub 57 on the 13/60 models by removing the bolts 69.

The parts are replaced in the reverse order of removal. Before reassembly wipe away surplus grease using newspapers and rags, then wash the parts in fuel to remove the remainder of the grease. Wash the bearings separately

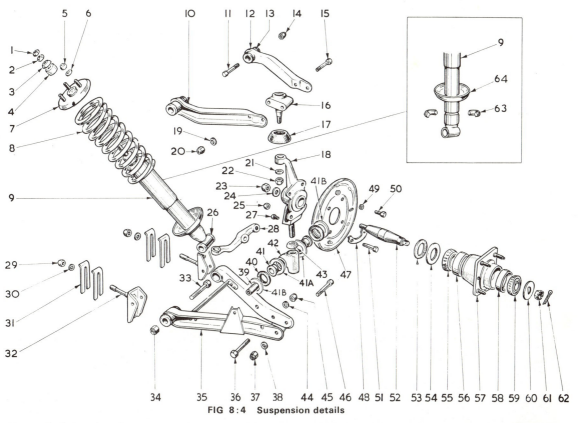

FIG 8:4 Suspension details

Key to Fig 8:4 1 Locknut   2 Nut   3 Washer   4 Rubber bush   5 Nyloc nut   6 Plain washer
7 Upper spring pan   8 Road spring   9 Damper   10 Front upper wishbone arm   11 Bolt   12 Rear upper wishbone arm
13 Rubber bush   14 Nyloc nut   15 Bolt   16 Ball joint   17 Rubber gaiter   18 Vertical link   19 Plain washer
20 Nyloc nut   21 Plain washer   22 Nyloc nut   23 Nyloc nut   24 Plain washer   25 Nyloc nut   26 Rubber bush
27 Plug   28 Steering arm   29 Nyloc nut   30 Plain washer   31 Shim   32 Inner fulcrum bracket   33 Fulcrum bolt
34 Nyloc nut   35 Lower wishbone assembly   36 Suspension unit fulcrum bolt   37 Nyloc nut   38 Plain washer
39 Steel bush   40 Rubber seal   41 Nylon bush   41A Washer   41B Washer   42 Lower trunnion   43 Rubber seal
44 Plain washer   45 Nyloc nut   46 Fulcrum bolt   47 Brake backplate   48 Locking plate   49 Spring washer
50 Setscrew   51 Bolt   52 Stub axle   53 Felt seal   54 Seal retainer   55 Taper roller bearing (inner)
56 Roller bearing outer ring   57 Hub   58 Roller bearing outer ring   59 Taper roller bearing (outer)   60 D-washer
61 Slotted nut   62 Splitpin   63 Spring retaining collet   64 Spring cup

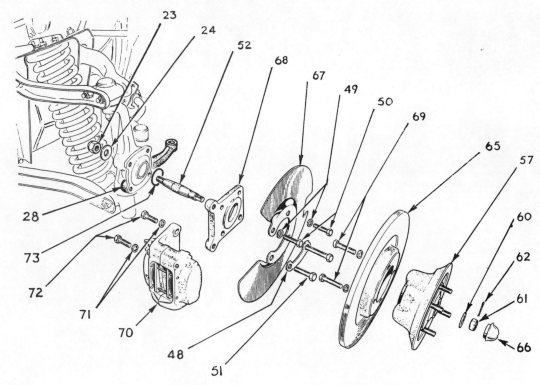

FIG 8:5 Disc brake mounting details

in clean fuel to ensure that no dirt is washed into them. Check the bearings for wear or pitting. Press the two halves of the bearings firmly together between the palms and rotate them to check if the bearing runs roughly. Reject bearings with defects, ideally fitting both new bearings if either of the old ones are defective. On reassembly pack both bearings with grease and also liberally spread grease inside the hub. After the inner bearing 55 has been completely replaced, soak the oil seal in engine oil and drive it back into the hub, felt outwards, after the surplus oil has been squeezed out of the felt 53.

On 1200 models the brakes will have to be adjusted (see **Chapter 10**).

FIG 8:6 Trunnion lubrication point

Adjusting the hubs:

Tighten the nut 61 to a torque of 5 lbft (.7 kgm), while spinning the hub to ensure that the bearings are settled into their running positions. The torque is only just above finger tight so a spanner gently applied will produce very nearly the right torque. Unscrew the nut one flat and secure it with a new splitpin 62. The correct end float is .002 to .008 inch (.05 to .2 mm), and between these figures the hub should spin quite freely without any drag from the bearings.

8:4 Separating tapers on ball joints

Ball joints are fitted where two parts are required to swivel about each other while motion or pressure is also being transmitted from one to the other. On one member a socket can rotate freely about the ball head end of a tapered pin. The tapered end of the pin fits into a very accurately machined mating taper on the other member and the two tapers are pulled into tight contact by the action of a nut. The nut has a locking system to ensure that it does not come free and allow the parts to separate.

With use the two tapers bed together and can be extremely difficult to separate after the nut and washer have been removed. Extractors are obtainable but they may not be readily available. Do not fall into the trap of hammering on the end of the tapered pin, as even with a slave nut fitted there is danger of damaging the threads or even the ball and socket. Instead use a wedge, such as a screwdriver, or some other method to pull the two members firmly apart. To prevent distortion, lay a block

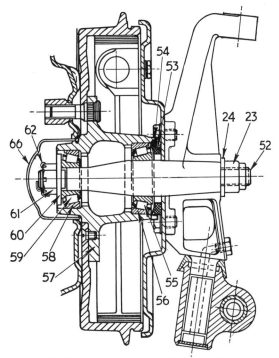

FIG 8:7 Sectioned view Herald 1200 hub

5 Disconnect the anti-roll bar link 2 from the lower wishbone assembly (see **FIGS 8:2** and **8:3**). Remove the Nyloc nut and washer from the tie rod end and disconnect the tie rod from the steering arm as described in **Section 8:4**.

6 Remove the Nyloc nuts 29 and plain washers 30 securing the lower inner fulcrum brackets 32 to the chassis, carefully noting the position and number of shims 31 under each bracket.

7 Refer to **FIG 8:9**. Remove the four bolts 1 from the outer face of the sub-frame and take out the spring washers, plain washers and tapping plates. Support the assembly and remove the single bolt 2, spring and plain washers securing the inner end of the sub-frame to the car. Remove the suspension assembly from the car.

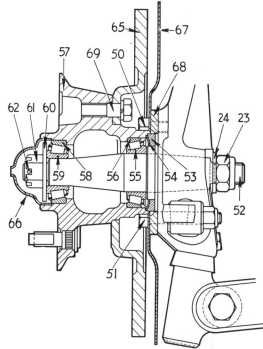

FIG 8:8 Sectioned view of Herald 13/60 hub

of metal against one side of the tapered eye (so that it is parallel to the tapered pin) and give the opposite side of the tapered eye a few smart blows with a copper-faced hammer. By this action the tapers will be quickly and safely freed. If hand pressure is used to pull the parts apart it is a wise precaution to leave the securing nut on the last few threads of the pin. This is to prevent the parts from flying apart suddenly and the hands hitting sharp projections.

8:5 The suspension sub-assembly

All the pivots and swivels can be renewed without removing the sub-assembly from the car. The road spring and damper assembly can also be removed and replaced with the sub-assembly fitted. Because of accident damage, or for other reasons, it may be necessary to remove the unit complete from the car, in which case proceed as follows:

1 Jack-up the front of the car and place it securely onto chassis stands. Remove the front road wheels (slacken the wheel nuts before jacking up the car).

2 If the driver's side sub-assembly is being removed, then slacken the impact clamp on the steering column and disconnect the lower steering coupling from the steering rack pinion (see **Chapter 9**).

3 On Herald 1200 models remove the nut and bolt securing the valance to the sub-frame.

4 Pump out the brake fluid from the brake hydraulic system and disconnect the brake flexible hose from its mounting on the car. Hold the hose with a spanner and remove the metal pipe union followed by the locknut so as to avoid twisting the hose (see **Chapter 10**).

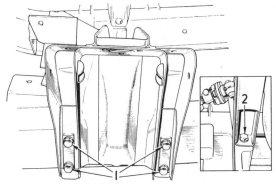

FIG 8:9 Sub-frame attachments

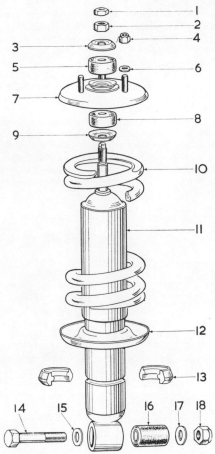

FIG 8:10 Road spring and damper details

Key to Fig 8:10 1 Locknut 2 Nut 3 Washer
4 Nyloc nut 5 Rubber bush 6 Washer
7 Upper spring pan 8 Rubber bush 9 Washer
10 Road spring 11 Damper 12 Lower spring pan
13 Collets 14 Bolt 15 Washer 16 Metalastik bush
17 Washer 18 Nyloc nut

Refit the assembly to the car in the reverse order of removal. Before refitting the road wheels the brakes must be filled and bled as described in **Chapter 10**. When the assembly has been refitted check both the steering and suspension geometry and adjust them if required. This part of the operation is best left to a suitably equipped garage, as specialized and accurate equipment is necessary for the correct checking of the geometry.

8:6 Road spring and damper assembly

The details of the assembly are shown in **FIG 8:10**. Before the assembly is removed, the front of the car must be placed securely on chassis stands and the road wheels removed. Then proceed as follows:

1 Disconnect the anti-roll bar from the lower wishbone assembly (see **FIGS 8:2** and **8:3**).
2 Remove the three sets of nuts 4 and plain washers 6 which secure the upper spring pan 7 to the sub-frame.
3 Remove the nut 18 and washer 17. Support the assembly and withdraw the bottom attachment bolt 14, after which the assembly can be lowered down and removed from the car.

Replace the assembly in the reverse order of removal. On lefthand drive cars a packing piece is fitted between the upper spring pan 7 and the sub-frame on the lefthand suspension unit, so do not forget to replace this if applicable.

Dismantling:

Once the assembly has been removed from the car it may then be dismantled so as to change a damper or spring.

1 Compress as many coils of the spring 10 as possible sufficiently to relieve the pressure on the upper spring pan 7. Use handpress No. S.4221A in conjunction with adaptor S.4221A–5 as shown in **FIG 8:11**.
2 Remove the locknut 1 and carefully unscrew the nut 2. Once the nut is safely off remove the washer 3 and rubber bush 5. Carefully release the pressure on the spring and when all the pressure is gone withdraw the assembly from the press.
3 Remove the upper spring pan 7, rubber bush 8 and washer 9. Lift off the spring 10. On Woodhead-Monroe dampers tap up the lower spring pan 12 and remove the collets 13.

Reassemble the parts in the reverse order of dismantling, after having checked the spring and damper. Renew the rubber bushes 5 and 8 if they are distorted or worn. If the Metalastik bush 16 is damaged or worn press out the old bush. Press a new bush into place using a pilot tool and a little soft soap as lubricant.

Road spring:

The spring should be examined for cracks or other damage. Measure the free length of the spring and compare it with the dimension given in Technical Data. If the spring is short it should be renewed, as it has weakened with service.

Damper:

A defective damper cannot be repaired and must be replaced with a new unit. Before fitting a new damper, or one that has been in storage, mount it vertically in

FIG 8:11 Compressing the road spring using handpress No. S.4221A and adaptor No. S.4221A-5

the padded jaws of a vice and pump it several times using short strokes. This will expel any air from the internal mechanism and allow it to pass to the sealed air space in the top of the unit.

Test a damper by pumping it through several full strokes. The resistance must be constant and appreciable in both directions. If the resistance varies, lacks resistance at the end of the stroke, or is so excessive that the unit can hardly be moved by hand, then the unit is defective and must be rejected. Similarly reject a damper that has physical damage, such as a bent ram or dented body.

8:7 The upper wishbone and ball joint

Check wear using the method described in the first paragraph of **Section 8:3**, as it is difficult to detect excessive wear when the parts have been dismantled.

1 Place the front of the car on chassis stands and remove the road wheel. Support the suspension, using a jack and block of wood underneath the vertical link.
2 The ball joint 16 alone can easily be removed by separating it from the vertical link (see **Section 8:4**) and removing the nuts 20, washers 19 and bolts 15. Refit a ball joint in the reverse order of removal. When the ball joint is freed from the vertical link, tie up the vertical link assembly with a piece of string or wire to prevent the flexible hose from becoming strained.
3 After the ball joint 16 has been freed, the wishbones 10 and 12 can be removed by taking off the nuts 14 and withdrawing the bolts 11. Label the wishbones to ensure that they are correctly replaced. If play is caused by wear in the bushes 13, remove the old bushes and press new ones in so that they protrude evenly on either side of the wishbone. Use a pilot tool and soft soap as lubricant when fitting new bushes. Refit the wishbones in the reverse order of removal, only fully tightening the nuts 14 when the suspension is at its normal working position.

8:8 The vertical link and lower wishbone assembly

Test for wear in the trunnion bearing and wishbone bushes as described in the first paragraph of **Section 8:3**.

1 Remove the road spring assembly (see **Section 8:6**). Remove the hub assembly (see **Section 8:3**). On 1200 models, disconnect the brake flexible hydraulic pipe from its mounting on the car (see **Chapter 10**). This is not necessary on 13/60 models as the brake caliper can safely be wired out of the way.
2 Disconnect the ball joint 16 from the vertical link 18. Either remove the nuts 29 and washers 30, carefully noting the position and number of the shims 31, or else take off the nuts 34 and withdraw the bolts 33 in order to free the parts from the car.
3 Remove the nut 37 and washer 38 and then withdraw the bolt 46 to free the wishbone assembly 35 from the trunnion 42. The bushes in the inner ends of the lower wishbones are renewable if worn.
4 Free the lockwashers 48 and remove the bolts 50 and 51 to free the brake parts and steering arm 28 from the vertical link 18. Unscrew the trunnion 42 and remove the seals, bushes and washers from the trunnion.

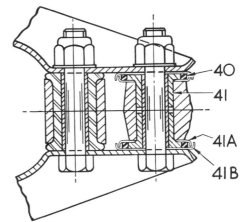

FIG 8:12 Sectioned view of lower wishbone outer attachments

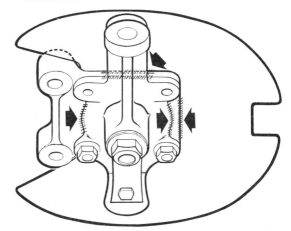

FIG 8:13 Sealing around dust shield for disc brake

5 If the trunnion 42 is worn or defective then both it and the vertical link must be renewed as a set. Remove the nut 23 and washer 24 and press out the stub axle 52 from the old vertical link. Renew the stub axle if it has any hairline cracks or is worn. Press the stub axle back into the new vertical link and secure it with the nut and washer.

The trunnion 42 and vertical link 18 are supplied in handed sets. The righthand trunnion can readily be identified as it has a reduced diameter machined at its base. The righthand assembly uses a righthand thread while the lefthand assembly uses a lefthand thread.

Reassembly:

1 Refit the seal 43 to the vertical link. Plentifully lubricate the thread in the trunnion with hypoid oil and screw in the vertical link till the threads just bottom. Unscrew the vertical link just sufficiently to prevent the threads from bottoming when the vertical link moves through its normal arc of operation.
2 A sectioned view of the lower wishbone outer attachments is shown in **FIG 8:12**. Fit the washers 41A into place on the nylon bushes 41 and then slip

FIG 8:14 Lower inner fulcrum brackets

Key to Fig 8:14   1 Front bracket   2 Rear bracket

the nylon bushes into position in the trunnion. Insert the steel bush 39 into position through the fitted nylon bushes. Place the rubber dust excluders 40 over the flanges of the nylon bushes and fit the washers 41B. Refit the wishbone assembly 35 and secure it loosely in place with the bolt 46, washer 38 and nut 37.

3 Refit the steering arm 28 and brake backplate 47 on Herald 1200 models. On the 13/60 refit the steering arm, caliper bracket 68 with the seal 73 between it and the vertical link, and then the dust shield 67, using Expandite Seal-a-Strip 105S between the parts as shown in **FIG 8:13**. In all cases secure the parts with the bolts 50 and 51, locking them with the washers 49 and lockplate 48.

4 Reassemble the parts to the car in the reverse order of removal. If the brackets 32 have been removed they must be refitted as shown in **FIG 8:14**. Tighten all the nuts to their correct torques (given in Technical Data) only after the suspension is in its normal working position. On 1200 models fill, bleed and adjust the brakes before refitting the road wheels (see **Chapter 10**).

8:9 Suspension geometry

The suspension geometry requires specialized and accurate equipment to check it satisfactorily and for this reason it is beyond the scope of the average owner. The geometry should be checked at a garage after major work has been carried out on the suspension, or if it is suspected that the suspension has been accidentally damaged. **Indiscriminate or inaccurate adjustments can be dangerous.**

Camber:

This is the amount in degrees by which the wheels are inclined from the vertical, when viewed from in front of the car. Camber angle is counted as positive when the tops of the wheels lean outwards. The camber angle is decreased by adding equal amounts of shims under each of the inner fulcrum brackets and increased by the equal removal of shims.

Castor:

This is the angle in side elevation between the vertical and a line drawn through the two steering swivel points. Positive castor is when the steering axis is inclined backwards. To decrease castor either add shims under the front inner fulcrum bracket or remove shims from under the rear bracket.

Steering axis inclination (KPI):

This is the angle between the vertical and a line drawn through the steering swivel points, when viewed from in front of the car.

8:10 Fault diagnosis

(a) Wheel wobble (see also Chapter 9)

1 Worn hub bearings
2 Weak front springs
3 Uneven tyre wear
4 Worn suspension bushes
5 Loose wheel nuts
6 Unbalanced wheels

(b) Bottoming of suspension

1 Check 2 in (a)
2 Dampers not working

(c) Rattles

1 Check 2 and 4 in (a)
2 Worn damper mountings
3 Worn anti-roll bar bushes

(d) Excessive rolling

1 Check 2 in (a) and 2 in (b)
2 Broken anti-roll bar.

CHAPTER 9

THE STEERING SYSTEM

9:1 Description
9:2 Routine maintenance
9:3 Removing and replacing the steering unit
9:4 Servicing the steering unit
9:5 Front wheel alignment (Track)
9:6 The steering column removal and replacement
9:7 Servicing the steering column
9:8 Fault diagnosis

9:1 Description

The steering system is similar on all the models covered by this manual. Rack and pinion steering is fitted as standard and, as the connections are direct with no idler or drag links required, the control is more precise and accurate than on other types of steering unit. The pinion is attached to a coupling on the steering column so that it rotates with the steering wheel. The rotation of the pinion is converted into a sideways linear motion of the rack, and the ends of the rack are connected to the steering arms on the vertical links by the tie rods. The tie rods operate through ball joints so that the motion of the suspension is not impeded. No steering stops are fitted to the suspension units, and the maximum lock of the wheels is controlled by the locknuts on the outer ends of the rack contacting the rack tube. For this reason it is essential that the steering unit is reassembled to the correct dimensions. The tie rod outer ends are fitted to the tie rods on screw threads so that the effective length of the tie rod may be altered to adjust the front wheel alignment. Specialized equipment should preferably be used to check both the front wheel alignment and the maximum steering lock. If the steering unit is dimensionally correct but the steering geometry is found to be considerably out, then the suspension and steering should be checked for accident damage.

The steering column is fitted with an impact clamp so that it telescopes in the event of a head-on collision, instead of impaling the driver. This impact clamp allows a limited adjustment for the distance that the steering wheel protrudes from the facia. The horn push, direction indicator switch and overdrive switch (if fitted) are all mounted in the head of the steering column and the cables are led out through holes in the outer column. By this design no stator tube is required down the centre of the column.

9:2 Routine maintenance

The bellows should be checked regularly for damage or splits as otherwise dirt may enter the assemblies and cause premature wear or failure of the parts. At the same time check the steering unit mountings for security and the ball joints for wear. The lubrication of the lower steering swivels with hypoid oil has already been dealt with in **Chapter 8, Section 8:2**.

FIG 9:1 Steering unit grease plug

At 12,000 mile intervals remove the grease plug, arrowed in **FIG 9:1**, from the top of the steering unit. Replace the plug with a grease nipple and use a hand grease gun to pump in a maximum of five strokes of grease. **Do not over-lubricate** and avoid filling the bellows with grease as otherwise they will split. Remove the grease nipple and replace the engine earthing strap and grease plug.

9:3 Removing and replacing the steering unit

The details of the steering unit are shown in **FIG 9:2**, and its mountings are shown in **FIG 9:3**. The correct dimensions to which the unit must be assembled are shown in **FIG 9:4**.

1 Remove the nut 8 and bolt 9 from the lower steering coupling 7. Disconnect the engine earth strap from the unit by removing the grease plug 28.
2 Remove the nuts 19 and washers 18, then disconnect the tie rod outer ends 44 from the steering arms, either using an extractor No. S.160 or by the method described in **Chapter 8, Section 8:4**.
3 From under the car remove the four sets of nuts and washers 24. As the appropriate nuts and washers come free take off the steering column earth cable 45 and the engine earth cable 46. Take off the plates 23 and remove the shrouded U-bolts 20. Take off the rubber bushes 21 from the rack tube. These bushes are split for easy removal and replacement.
4 Pull the steering unit forwards so that the coupling 7 is freed from the pinion shaft on the unit and manoeuvre the unit out of the car through the hole in the valance on the driver's side. Loosely replace the plug 28 to prevent the entry of dirt.

Replacement:

Before replacing the steering unit make sure that it conforms to the dimensions given in **FIG 9:4**. Free the inner clip 42 and lockwire 40 and slide the bellows 41 outwards to gain access to the inner ball joints. The distance between the locknuts 33 must be 24.40 inches (61.976 cm).

1 Set the steering wheel in the straight-ahead position, with its spokes level. Rotate the steering unit pinion from lock to lock, counting the exact number of turns required. Turn the pinion back exactly half the number of turns counted so that this also is in the straight-ahead direction and refit it in this position.

2 Manoeuvre the unit back into position through the aperture in the driver's side valance. Fit the splines on the pinion shaft back into the lower coupling 7 on the steering column.
3 Refit the rubber bushes 21 to the steering rack tube and place the U-bolts into position over the bushes. Fit back the plates 23 and earthing cables 45 and 46, securing the parts loosely with the nuts and washers 24.
4 At this point an assistant is essential. Press both U-bolts firmly outwards against the rubber bushes until the gap at **A** in **FIG 9:3** between the U-bolt retainers and the flange plates on the rack tube is $\frac{1}{8}$ inch (3.175 mm). Hold the U-bolts in this position while the assistant slides the plates 23 inwards until their inner edges fully abut along the chassis frame flange and then fully tightens the nuts 24. The two flanges which must abut are shown at **B** in **FIG 9:3**.
5 Secure the lower coupling 7 to the pinion shaft using the bolt 9 and nut 8. Reconnect the engine earthing strap to the steering unit under the plug 28. Reconnect the tie rod outer ends to the steering arms on the suspension.
6 Before road testing the car, jack-up the front end and check that the steering moves freely from lock to lock without binding or catching. It is also advisable to check the front wheel alignment (see **Section 9:5**).

9:4 Servicing the steering unit

Remove the unit from the car as described in the previous section.

1 Slacken all three clips 42 and the locking wire 40 which secure the bellows 41 in place. Push both bellows outwards to expose the inner ball joints. Slacken the locknuts 33 and unscrew both tie rod assemblies. Remove the springs 36 from the ends of the rack 32 and also unscrew both locknuts 33 from the rack.
2 Unscrew the cap 27 and remove the shims 29, spring 30 and plunger 31 from the housing 25. Remove the circlip 10 and withdraw the pinion assembly from the housing, taking care not to lose the securing dowel 5. Slide the retaining ring 11, shims 12, bush 13 and thrust washer 14 off the pinion shaft. Extract the O-ring from its annular groove inside the retaining ring 11.
3 Withdraw the rack 32 from the tube 25 and shake out the thrust washer 16 and bush 17 from the pinion housing.
4 Free the ears on the locktab 35 and unscrew the sleeve nut 34 from the cup nut 39. Remove the shims 26 and cup 37 from inside the cup nut. Slacken the locknuts 43 and unscrew the tie rod ends 44 from the tie rods 38. Remove the locknuts 43 and slide off the bellows 41 and cup nut 39 from the tie rod.
5 Wash all the metal parts in clean fuel or some suitable solvent to remove all the grease and dirt. Examine the parts and renew any that are worn or defective. Clean the bellows using newspaper and rag but do not use any solvent that may attack the rubber. Renew the bellows if they are split, torn or wearing through.

The parts are reassembled in the reverse order of dismantling but the correct clearances and dimensions must be adhered to as the parts are fitted.

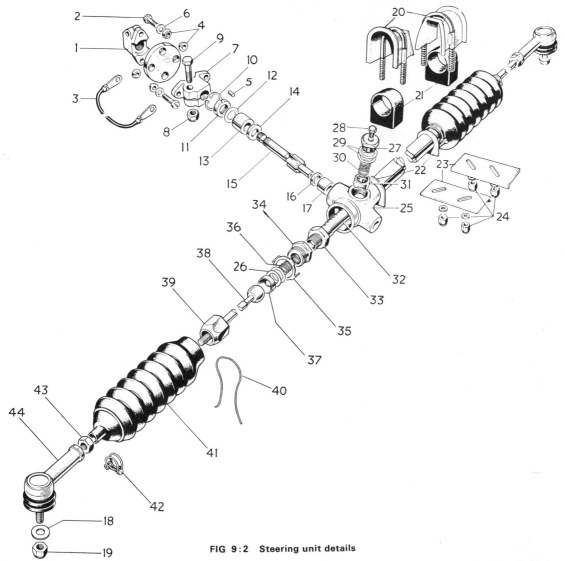

FIG 9:2 Steering unit details

Key to Fig 9:2 1 Steering coupling (upper) 2 Bolt 3 Earth cable 4 Rubber bushes 5 Dowel 6 Washer
7 Steering coupling (lower) 8 Nyloc nut 9 Pinch bolt 10 Circlip 11 Retaining ring 12 Shims 13 Bush
14 Thrust washer 15 Pinion shaft 16 Thrust washer 17 Bush 18 Washer 19 Nyloc nut 20 U-bolts
21 Rubber bushes 22 Abutment plates 23 Locating plates 24 Nyloc nuts 25 Rack assembly 26 Shims
27 Cap 28 Grease plug 29 Shims 30 Spring 31 Plunger 32 Rack 33 Locknut 34 Sleeve nut
35 Lock tab 36 Spring 37 Cup 38 Tie rod 39 Cup nut 40 Locking wire 41 Rubber gaiter 42 Clip
43 Locknut 44 Tie rod end

Pinion end float:

1 Fit the bush 17 and thrust washer 16 back into the housing as shown in the sectioned view of the pinion assembly in **FIG 9:5**. Insert the rack 32 back into the tube.

2 Fit the thrust washer 14, bush 13 and retaining ring 11 back to the pinion 15 and insert the assembly back into its housing, securing the assembly with the circlip 10.

3 Mount a DTI (Dial Test Indicator) on the rack tube so that its stylus rests vertically on the pinion shaft as shown in **FIG 9:6**. Press the pinion firmly down into the housing and zero the DTI. Pull the pinion out of the housing so that it is tightly against the circlip 10 and note the reading on the DTI.

4 Remove the circlip 10 and take out the retaining ring 11. Fit a new O-ring back into the retaining ring. Make up a shim pack 12 which is just thinner than the dimension measured with the DTI. Fit the shim pack into position and replace the retaining ring 11, dowel 5 and circlip 10. Check that the pinion rotates freely with the minimum end float.

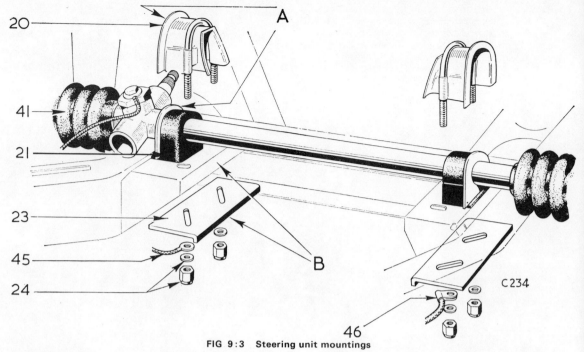

FIG 9:3 Steering unit mountings

Key to Fig 9:3 20 U-bolts   21 Rubber bushes   23 Locating plates   24 Nyloc nuts   41 Rubber gaiter   45 Steering column earth cable   46 Engine earth cable

5 If a DTI is not available the thickness of the shim pack can be judged by a process of trial and error, again ensuring that the pinion rotates freely with the minimum end float.

Pinion pressure pad:

1 Fit the plunger 31 and cap nut 27 to the housing, omitting the shims and spring. Tighten the nut until all end float is removed.
2 Measure the gap between the cap 27 and housing 25 using feeler gauges as shown in **FIG 9:7**. Remove the cap nut and plunger.
3 Make up a shim pack 29 so that its thickness is .004 inch (.1 mm) greater than the gap measured in operation 2. The extra thickness is to provide the correct end float.
4 Pack the unit with grease and refit the plunger 31, spring 30 and shim pack 29, securing them in place with the cap nut 27. Make up a bar of wood or metal as shown in **FIG 9:8** and check that the pinion rotates under a load of 2 lb (.9 kg) applied at the correct radius. Adjust so that it moves at the correct load by either removing or fitting shims under the cap nut 27.

Tie rod inner ball joints:

1 Slide the cup nut 39 into position down the tie rod 38 and insert the cup 37 over the ball and into the cup nut. Fit the tabwasher 35 to the nut 34 and screw the sleeve nut fully back into the cup nut.
2 Hold the cup nut in a vice and roughly estimate the total amount of end float by pulling and pushing on the tie rod. Make up a shim pack 26 which is thicker than the estimated end float. Unscrew the sleeve nut, fit the shim pack into position and refit the sleeve nut.
3 Use feeler gauges to measure the gap between the cup nut, tabwasher and sleeve nut. This dimension plus .002 inch (.05 mm) for end float is the thickness of shims 26 that must be removed for correct assembly.
4 Dismantle the ball joint and pack it with grease. Remove the required amount of shims and completely reassemble the ball joint. Loosely attach the outer tie

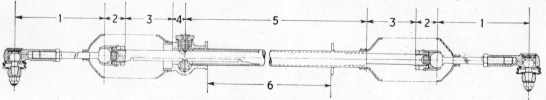

FIG 9:4 Steering unit dimensions

Key to Fig 9:4   1 8.715 inch (221.36 mm)   2 1.42 inch (36.07 mm)   3 3.325 inch (84.45 mm)   4 .875 inch (22.23 mm)   5 16.875 inch (428.63 mm)   6 12.78 inch (324.62 mm)

rod end and screw the assembly slackly back onto the rack. Use a spring balance on the tie rod end and check that the tie rod assembly articulates freely at a load of 1½ lb (.681 kg). If necessary adjust the shim pack until the tie rod articulates satisfactorily.

5 When the adjustment is correct lock the sleeve nut and cup nut together by tapping one ear of the tabwasher over each nut.

Refitting the tie rods:

1 Remove the temporarily fitted tie rod ends. Slide the bellows 41 together with their clips into place on the tie rods.
2 Screw the locknuts 43 onto the tie rods and then refit the tie rod ends so that the distance between the ball centres is dimension 1 in **FIG 9:4**. Lock the tie rod ends in place with the locknuts.
3 Screw the locknuts 33 back onto the rack so that the distance between the inner faces corresponds to the dimensions 3+4+5+3 shown in **FIG 9:4** and the total distance is 24.40 inches (619.76 mm). Screw the tie rod assemblies into position until the sleeve nuts just touch the locknuts and then lock them together after replacing the springs 36.
4 **Recheck all the dimensions shown in FIG 9:4.** It is important that the dimensions are correct as otherwise the front wheel alignment and the maximum steering lock will both be affected.
5 Pack each bellows 41 with ½ oz of Retinax A grease and secure them back into place with the clips 42 and a piece of locking wire 40.

9:5 Front wheel alignment (Track)

This should be checked whenever the steering or suspension has been dismantled or if a front wheel has hit the kerb heavily. An indication of the front wheels being out of alignment is the tyres wearing unevenly and the edge of the tread having a feathered appearance.

On all the models covered by this manual the correct front wheel alignment is 0 to $\frac{1}{16}$ inch (0 to 1.6 mm) toe-in. The wheel alignment is adjusted by slackening the locknuts 43 on the tie rods as well as the outer clips 42 securing the bellows 41. Rotate the tie rod so that it screws in or out of the tie rod end 44 and varies the effective length of the tie rod. When the alignment is correct then tighten the clips and locknuts. To prevent the steering wheel spokes not being level when the front wheels are in the straight-ahead position it is advisable to adjust both tie rods equally, unless the adjustment required is only very small.

It is best to carry out the measurement using special equipment designed for the task, but if care is taken then the operation can be performed satisfactorily without the use of such equipment.

Put the car onto a level piece of ground with the front wheels in the straight-ahead position. Push the car forwards a few yards to settle the suspensions and wheel bearings. Measure, as accurately as possible, the distance between the inner wheel rims at the front of the wheel and at wheel centre height. Push the car forwards so that the wheels rotate exactly half a revolution. Mark the tyre with chalk to assist in getting the right distance to push the car. **If the distance is overshot do not push**

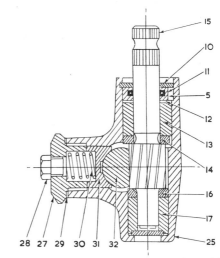

FIG 9:5 Cross-section of steering unit at pinion

Key to Fig 9:5   5 Dowel   10 Circlip   11 Retaining ring
12 Shims   13 Bush   14 Thrust washer   15 Pinion shaft
16 Thrust washer   17 Bush   25 Rack assembly   27 Cap
28 Grease plug   29 Shims   30 Spring   31 Plunger   32 Rack

FIG 9:6   Measuring pinion end float

FIG 9:7   Measuring the gap between the body and the cap nut

THA/2

87

FIG 9:8 Measuring the load required to rotate the pinion

the car back but carry on pushing it forwards until the correct position is again reached. Again measure the distance between the inner wheel rims at wheel centre height, but at the rear of the wheels. By pushing the car forwards for half a revolution the distance is again measured between the same two points on the rim, thus allowing for any minor defect in the rims. The difference between the two dimensions measured gives the wheel alignment. When the rear dimension is larger than that of the front then the wheels have toe-in.

9:6 The steering column removal and replacement

The steering column details are shown in **FIG 9:9**, and the attachments on the 1200 models in **FIG 9:10**.

1 Remove the nut and bolt securing the lower steering column clamp to the steering unit pinion shaft. Disconnect the electrical cables for the switches and horn at the snap connectors under the facia. Label the cables if the colours are faded or difficult to tell apart.
2 Undo the nuts 47 and remove the washers 45 and 46, lower outer clamp 48 and felt 49. Support the column and remove the lower half of the upper clamp 53.
3 Withdraw the steering column assembly from the car, if necessary removing the other bolt and nut holding the coupling assembly to the lower column 9 so that the parts will pass through the grommet.

Replacement:

1 Slacken the locknut 23 on the impact clamp assembly and unscrew the socket screw 22 two complete turns, using an Allen key.
2 Set the front road wheels in the straight-ahead position and turn the steering wheel until the two spokes are level and the third spoke is vertical.
3 Replace the column assembly in the car holding it loosely in place by refitting the lower half of the upper

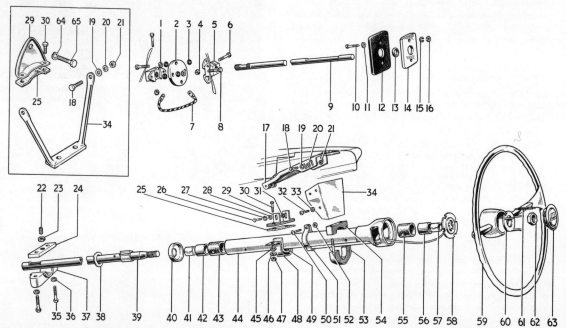

FIG 9:9 Steering column details, inset shows the bracket fitted to Herald 1200 models

Key to Figs 9:9, 9:10 and 9:12 1 Washer 2 Disc 3 Rubber washer 4 Nyloc nut 5 Adaptor 6 Pinch bolt 7 Earth cable 8 Bolt 9 Lower steering column 10 Bolt 11 Washer 12 Rubber seal 13 Washer 14 Retaining plate 15 Spring washer 16 Nut 17 Support bracket 18 Bolt 19 Spring washer 20 Washer 21 Nut 22 Socket screw 23 Nut 24 Clamp plate 25 Felt pad 26 Bolt 27 Spring washer 28 Washer 29 Bracket 30 Bolt 31 Nut 32 Screw 33 Washer 34 Bracket 35 Bolt 36 Spring washer 37 Clamp 38 Nylon washer 39 Upper inner steering column 40 End cap 41 Nylon bush 42 Steel bush 43 Rubber bush 44 Outer upper column 45 Washer 46 Spring washer 47 Nut 48 Lower outer column clamp 49 Felt pad 50 Screw 51 Cable trough clip 52 Nut 53 Upper clamp (lower half) 54 Upper clamp (upper half) 55 Rubber bush 56 Steel bush 57 Nylon bush 58 Horn contact ring 59 Steering wheel 60 Clip 61 Horn contact brush 62 Nut 63 Horn push 64 Spring washer 65 Bolt

clamp 53. Check that the steering wheel is correctly positioned and reconnect the coupling assembly to the steering unit pinion and the lower column 9, securing the coupling with the nuts and bolts.

4 Loosely replace the lower clamp parts. Slide the column assembly up or down until it is set at the desired height. **Do not set it at the bottom of its range of adjustment as the column will not be able to telescope.** Fully tighten the clamps 53 and 48.

5 Use an Allen key to tighten the screw 22 as tight as possible and then lock it with the locknut 23. Reconnect the electrical cables and clip them out of the way under the facia. It is advisable, though not essential, to jack up the front of the car and check that the steering moves freely and fully from lock to lock.

9:7 Servicing the steering column

Remove the assembly from the car as described in the previous section.

1 Remove the nut and bolt securing the coupling assembly to the lower column 9. The coupling need not be dismantled unless the parts are worn or the rubber washers defective.

2 Remove the cable trough 51. Take off the covers and remove the indicator and overdrive switches as shown in **FIG 9:11**. Prise out the horn push 63 and take out the brush 61.

3 Unscrew the bolts 35 and remove the two halves of the impact clamp 24 and 37. Withdraw the lower column 9 out from the bottom of the assembly. Remove the nylon washer 38 and draw the upper column 39 and steering wheel 59 assembly out through the top of the outer column 44.

4 Hold the column 39 in the padded jaws of a vice. Remove the nut 62 and clip 60 and then use an extractor No. S.3600 to remove the steering wheel from the column.

5 Take off the end cap 40. Press in the two protrusions on the rubber bush 43 so that they clear the holes in the outer column. Use a long rod to drive the bush assembly down and out of the outer column 44. Remove the metal insert 42 and nylon bush 41 from inside the rubber bush 43. Repeat the operation on the upper bush assembly.

Examine all the parts and renew any that are worn. Pay particular attention to the bush assemblies between the outer column and inner upper column as if these are worn they will be a source of looseness and rattles.

Reassemble the parts in the reverse order of dismantling. A sectioned view of the steering column bushes is shown in **FIG 9:12**. Fit them so that the metal reinforcing rings in the rubber bushes 43 and 55 are towards the lower end of the column. When refitting the steering wheel 59 to the upper column 39 ensure that the spokes align with the self-cancelling clip as shown in **FIG 9:11** and peen the nut 62 to ensure that it does not come loose in service. Take care not to push out the bushes when refitting the upper inner column through the outer column.

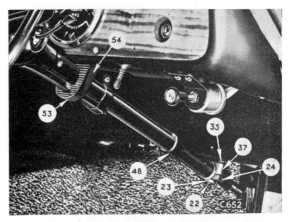

FIG 9:10 Steering column attachments, Herald 1200 models

FIG 9:11 Removing and replacing indicator switch and alignment of self-cancelling lugs with steering wheel spokes

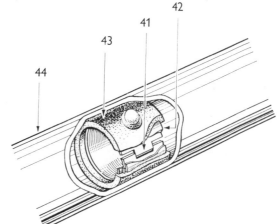

FIG 9:12 Steering column bush assembly

9:8 Fault diagnosis

(a) Wheel wobble

1 Unbalanced wheels and tyres
2 Slack steering connections
3 Incorrect steering geometry

(b) Wander

1 Check 2 and 3 in (a)
2 Damaged suspension or chassis
3 Uneven tyre pressures
4 Weak dampers or springs

(c) Heavy steering

1 Check 3 in (a)
2 Very low tyre pressures
3 Neglected lubrication

4 Wheels out of alignment
5 Steering unit incorrectly adjusted
6 Steering column bushes tight
7 Seized tie rod ends

(d) Lost motion

1 Loose steering wheel
2 Worn splines or loose bolts securing coupling
3 Worn steering coupling
4 Worn ball joints

CHAPTER 10

THE BRAKING SYSTEM

10:1 Description
10:2 Routine maintenance
10:3 The front disc brakes
10:4 Relining the rear brakes
10:5 Servicing the rear brakes

10:6 The handbrake
10:7 Removing a flexible hose
10:8 Bleeding the brakes
10:9 Fault diagnosis

10:1 Description

All the models covered by this manual are fitted with disc brakes to the front wheels. Earlier models of the Herald 1200, which are not covered by this manual, are fitted with expanding shoe drum brakes but these will not be dealt with here. The rear wheels on all models of Herald are fitted with drum brakes using one leading and one trailing shoe per brake. All four brakes are hydraulically operated using the foot brake but the handbrake lever acts only on the rear brakes through a mechanical linkage.

When the brake pedal is depressed it acts on the master cylinder where the hydraulic pressure is then generated. This hydraulic pressure is led to the wheel brakes through a system of metal pipelines and flexible hoses. The brake pipe layout and the connections for the 13/60 models are shown in **FIG 10:1**. The actual brake master cylinder is of exactly the same construction and design as the slave cylinder fitted to the clutch system. For this reason **refer to Chapter 5, Section 5:3, for all instructions on servicing the brake master cylinder.**

The front disc brakes use a caliper rigidly mounted on the suspension and acting on a disc rotating with the wheel hub. Friction pads are mounted in the caliper and these are pressed, simultaneously and with equal pressure, into contact with the sides of the brake disc by two pistons operated by the hydraulic pressure from the master cylinder. The pads are retracted when the pressure is released and wear in the pads is taken up automatically.

The rear brakes use a single piston and cylinder assembly on each brake. The piston moves one brake shoe out into contact with the brake drum and the reaction slides the cylinder housing in the brake backplate so that the cylinder presses the other brake shoe into contact with the drum. When the pressure is released the shoes are retracted by return springs. An adjuster is fitted to each rear brake so as to take up wear in the linings.

10:2 Routine maintenance

1 Regularly check the level of the fluid in the master cylinder. Wipe the top clean before removing the cap so that no dirt falls into the reservoir. If required, top up to the level marked by the arrow on the side of the reservoir, using only fresh Castrol Girling Crimson Clutch and Brake Fluid to specification SAE.70.R3 or a fluid which meets this specification. The level will drop steadily as the friction pads in the disc brakes wear, but any sudden drop should be investigated

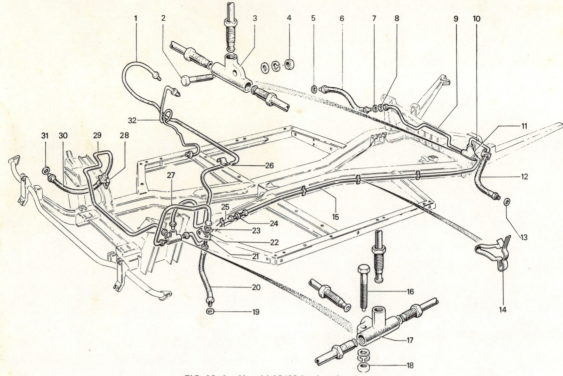

FIG 10:1 Herald 13/60 brake pipe layout

Key to Fig 10:1   1 Pipe—master cylinder to four-way connection (righthand steering)   2 Bolt—three-way piece attachment
3 Three-way piece   4 Nut—three-way piece attachment   5 Gasket—hose   6 Rear hose assembly
7 Shakeproof washer—hose attachment   8 Nut—hose attachment   9 Pipe—three-way to hose—righthand
10 Pipe—three-way to hose—lefthand   11 Three-way piece   12 Rear hose assembly   13 Gasket—hose
14 Clip—pipe to frame   15 Pipe—three-way to double end union   16 Bolt—four-way piece attachment   17 Four-way piece
18 Nut—four-way piece attachment   19 Gasket—hose   20 Hose—high pressure—front   21 Hose mounting bracket
22 Shakeproof washer—hose attachment   23 Nut—hose attachment   24 Double end union—connector   25 Pipe—four-way
to double end union   26 Clip—brake pipe attachment   27 Pipe—four-way to front hose—lefthand   28 Hose—mounting bracket
29 Pipe—four-way to front hose—righthand   30 Hose—high pressure—front   31 Gasket—hose   32 Pipe—clutch master
cylinder to slave cylinder

immediately as it may be caused by a leak in the hydraulic system.

2 Periodically adjust the rear brakes, which also automatically adjusts the handbrake. Jack up the rear of the car, leaving the handbrake off. Rotate the square headed adjuster (shown in **FIG 10:2**) on each brake fully in clockwise until it can be turned no more. Slacken back the adjusters a notch at a time until the wheels rotate without the brakes binding or dragging. **Do not confuse the resistance from the back axle with the drag caused by a binding brake.** Lower the car back to the ground and remove the jacks.

3 At 12,000 mile intervals pack grease into the secondary cable guides and compensator segment on the handbrake assembly.

Preventative maintenance:

Regularly examine the friction pads, rear brake linings and all pipelines. Renew any parts that are defective or doubtful. Apart from checking for leaks, dirt should be brushed and scraped off the metal pipelines, which should also be checked for corrosion or pitting. Renew suspect metal pipes as they may fail suddenly when they are most required during heavy braking. Protect the metal pipes either with thick grease or underseal.

Cleanliness is absolutely essential in all operations involving the hydraulic system. No precautions can be considered too stringent to ensure cleanliness. Lay parts out on clean sheets of paper as they are dismantled and never use dirty hydraulic fluid.

Use only hydraulic fluids which meet specification SAE.70.R3 as other fluids may attack the material of the seals causing them to swell and fail. It is advisable to discard any fluid that has been drained or bled from the hydraulic system unless it is perfectly clean. Never return fluid, however clean, that has just been bled or drained directly to the reservoir. Instead allow it to stand for at least 24 hours so that the minute air bubbles have all risen to the surface and dissipated. Store fluid in clean sealed containers so that it cannot absorb moisture from the air.

Dirt or gummy deposits in the system can be flushed out by first draining the system and then pumping through at least a quart of methylated spirits. It is recommended that the whole system be dismantled at three-yearly intervals and all the old seals and fluid discarded. This will also give the opportunity of examining the bores of the cylinders.

10:3 The front disc brakes

A sectioned view of the brake caliper assembly is shown in **FIG 10:3**.

Renewing the friction pads:

The friction material must not be allowed to wear completely away, as not only will the brake disc be damaged but some friction material is essential as heat insulation for the brake caliper.

1 Apply the handbrake and jack up the front of the car. Remove the front road wheels.
2 Remove the spring clips 9 and withdraw the retaining pins 10. Lift out the old pads 4 and the anti-squeal plates 5, noting the exact position of the anti-squeal plates. Fit new pads and never attempt to reline the old pads.
3 Use an airline and brush to clean out all dirt and dust from inside the caliper. Press the pistons 6 back into the cylinders. Fluid will be returned to the master cylinder reservoir during this operation so take care that it does not overflow. **Syphon excess fluid out of the reservoir before the level rises too far.**
4 Refit the anti-squeal plates and new friction pads in the reverse order of removal, securing them with the retaining pins and clips. Replace the road wheels and lower the car to the ground. Avoid heavy or prolonged braking until the new pads have become bedded-in.

Servicing the brake caliper:

Disconnect the flexible hose as instructed in **Section 10:7**. Remove and replace the caliper as detailed in **Chapter 8, Section 8:3**.

1 Remove the friction pads 4 and anti-squeal plate 5 as described just previously, then withdraw the pistons 6 from the caliper. If the pistons are difficult to withdraw, clamp one piston into place and temporarily reconnect the caliper to the hydraulic system. Apply pressure to the brake pedal until the free piston is ejected from the caliper. Service this side of the caliper and then remove the other piston by clamping the serviced piston and applying pressure.
2 Remove the dust cover 8 and extract the seal 7 from its recess in the bore. If a tool must be used to take out the seal 7, make sure that it is a blunt, soft one and take great care not to damage the bore of the cylinder.
3 **Do not separate the two halves of the caliper.** Wash all the parts in methylated spirits or hydraulic fluid. Do not use any other solvent as it will attack the rubber O-rings 1, causing them to fail. If these seals have failed then the caliper must be renewed.
4 Unless the old seals 7 and dust covers 8 are in excellent condition they should be discarded and new ones fitted. Wet the seals 7 in clean hydraulic fluid and refit them into their recesses, using only the fingers and taking great care to ensure that they are fully seated and not twisted. Refit the dust covers 8 into their recesses in the caliper.
5 Wet both the bore of the cylinder and the piston with hydraulic fluid. Press the piston back into the bore,

FIG 10:2 Rear brake adjuster and bleed nipple

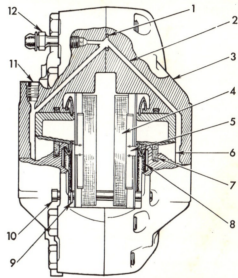

FIG 10:3 Sectioned front brake caliper assembly

Key to Fig 10:3   1 Rubber O-ring
2 Fluid transfer channels   3 Caliper body   4 Brake pad
5 Anti-squeal plate   6 Piston   7 Piston sealing ring
8 Dust cover   9 Retaining clip   10 Retaining pin
11 Flexible hose connection   12 Bleed nipple

closed end leading, taking great care that it enters the bore squarely and does not damage the seal 7. Secure the dust cover into its recess in the piston.
6 Refit the caliper and replace the anti-squeal plates and friction linings. Reconnect the flexible hose. Fill and bleed the brake system before replacing the road wheels.

The brake disc:

The disc should be renewed if it is cracked, distorted, scored or shows heavy burn marks. To change a brake disc first remove the front wheel hub assembly from the car and then separate the disc from the hub (see **Chapter 8, Section 8:3**).

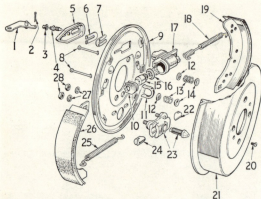

FIG 10:4 Rear drum brake details (lefthand side)

Key to Fig 10:4   1 Handbrake lever   2 Splitpin
3 Dust cap   4 Bleed nipple   5 Dust excluder
6 Retaining clip   7 Retaining clip   8 Steady pins
9 Backplate   10 Dust excluder   11 Clip
12 Steady pin cups 13 Springs   14 Steady pin cups
15 Piston 16 Seal 17 Wheel cylinder   18 Return spring
19 Brake shoe   20 Countersunk screw   21 Brake drum
22 Adjuster tappet   23 Adjuster wedge and body
24 Adjuster tappet 25 Return spring   26 Brake shoe
27 Shakeproof washers 28 Nuts

Refit the parts in the reverse order of removal. Set the correct hub end float and then mount a DTI (Dial Test Indicator) on the brake caliper so that the stylus of the DTI rests vertically on the outer working face of the disc. Push the hub firmly inwards to take up the end float and rotate it. The run out on the disc should not exceed .002 inch (.0508 mm). If the run out is excessive remove the disc from the hub and check that there are no small particles of dirt in between them. Refit the disc to the hub mating different securing holes and recheck the run out.

10:4 Relining the rear brakes

The details of the lefthand side rear brake are shown in **FIG 10:4**, and the correct assembly of the shoes and return springs of the righthand side rear brake in **FIG 10:5**.

Securely jack up the rear of the car, leaving the handbrake off. Remove the road wheels. Take out the two countersunk screws 20 and withdraw the brake drum 21. It will be easier to withdraw the drum if the brake adjuster is slackened right off. **If the linings are worn so much that the rivet heads are flush with the lining or the linings are contaminated with oil or grease, then the linings must be renewed.** Some linings are bonded to the shoes and these should be renewed before the shoe comes into contact with the drum. It is possible to rivet new linings onto the shoes but the average owner is unlikely to obtain a satisfactory result without previous practice. Do not attempt to remove oil or grease from badly contaminated linings as some will always remain to cause poor braking, so renew them instead.

1 Hold the steady pins 8 from the back of the backplate and use a pair of pliers to press in and turn through 90 degrees the steady pin cups 14. The cups will then come free off the T-headed pins and can be removed with the springs 13 and inner cups 12. Withdraw the pins 8 from the rear of the backplate.

2 Extract the splitpin 2 from the handbrake lever 1. Lever or pull the brake shoes 19 and 26 out of their abutment slots to relieve the tension on the springs. Once the tension has been relieved the springs can be disconnected and the shoes removed.

3 Use a stiff brush and airline to remove all dirt and dust from the brake and from inside the brake drum. If oil or grease has leaked into the brake wash it away with fuel. **Trace and cure the source of the oil before reassembling the brake.**

4 Take care to prevent oil or grease from contacting the new brake linings. Attach the return springs 18 and 25 to the front shoe and manoeuvre them back into position but with the shoe out of its slots and towards the centre of the brake. Attach the springs to the rear brake shoe which should be also out of its slots. Pull or lever the front shoe into its correct position and then pull and manoeuvre the rear shoe into position against the tension of the return springs and over the handbrake lever 1. A simple tool for pulling on the brake shoes is a length of cord with a wooden handle.

5 Fit a new splitpin 2 to the handbrake lever 1. Replace the steady pins 8, cups 12, springs 13 and cups 14 in the reverse order of removal. Tap the shoes along the slots so that they are concentric with the drum. Make sure that the adjuster is slackened right off and refit the brake drum.

6 Turn the adjuster clockwise until the shoes contact the drum and then centralize the shoes by heavily pumping the brake pedal. Adjust the rear brakes (**Section 8:3**) making sure that the brakes are not binding at all. Avoid heavy or prolonged braking until the linings are bedded in. The brakes will require adjusting sooner than normal because high-spots will be worn off and the full surface of the linings will only be in contact with the drum after the linings are bedded-in.

10:5 Servicing the rear brakes

The details of the rear brake assembly are shown in **FIG 10:4**. Remove the brake drum and brake shoes as

FIG 10:5 Arrangement of springs and shoes in the rear drum brake (righthand side)

described in the previous section. If it is necessary to remove the backplate 3 from the car then follow the instructions given in **Chapter 7, Section 7:5**.

Brake drum:

Check that the drum is not cracked by hanging it on a piece of wood through the centre hole and tapping it with a small metal object. If the note sounds flat then the drum probably has a crack somewhere. Deep scoring on the operating surface of the drum means that a new drum will have to be fitted. If the wear and scoring is only minor then the drum can be mounted on an arbor and the damage skimmed off in a lathe. Never mount a brake drum in a chuck as the pressure of the jaws is sufficient to distort the drum and prevent it from being concentric. Wash grease or oil off the drum with any suitable solvent except paraffin or white spirits, which leave a slow drying greasy film.

Brake adjuster:

Check that the threaded wedge screws freely along in the adjuster body. Withdraw the tappets 22 and 24 and screw the adjuster out of the body. If care is taken, the adjuster body can be cleaned out with a brush and fuel without removing the body from the backplate. Remove any corrosion from the threads of the wedge using a wire brush. Reassemble the adjuster in the reverse order of dismantling, using white zinc-based grease as lubricant. Make sure that the exposed threads of the wedge are well protected with grease.

The squared edges of the head sometimes become rounded off so that the adjuster cannot be turned with a spanner. If this occurs press a tightly fitting nut onto the squared head. If the nut slips it can be held in place with a small weld but the wedge cannot then be unscrewed from the body.

Wheel cylinder:

1 Remove the flexible hose (see **Section 10:7**). Disconnect the secondary handbrake cable from the lever on the brake and remove the rubber dust excluder 5.
2 Drive off the retaining plate as shown in **FIG 10:6**, then withdraw the wheel cylinder from the backplate as shown in **FIG 10:7**.

FIG 10:6 Removing the retaining plate from the rear wheel cylinder

FIG 10:7 Removing the rear wheel cylinder

3 Take off the spring clip 11 and remove the dust excluder 10. Grip the piston 15 with the fingers and withdraw it, complete with the seal 16, from the bore of the cylinder. Remove the seal from the piston and discard it. Renew the complete assembly if the bore of the cylinder is scored, worn or pitted.
4 The best solvents for washing the parts are either methylated spirits or hydraulic fluid. However, any solvent may be used on the metal parts, provided it is dried off completely and not allowed to contact the rubber seal or dust excluder.
5 Reassemble the cylinder using no tools but the fingers. Dip both the seal and piston into clean hydraulic fluid and refit them wet. Make sure that the seal is squarely in place and take great care not to bend back or damage its lips when refitting the piston to the cylinder.
6 Refit the wheel cylinder to the backplate in the reverse order of removal. After final reassembly the brake system must be bled.

10:6 The handbrake

The details of the handbrake are shown in **FIG 10:8** and the attachments of the secondary cable to the rear brakes are shown in **FIG 10:9**.

Handbrake adjustment:

Over a period of time the handbrake cables will stretch and cause excessive movement of the handbrake lever. Other possible causes of excessive movement must be checked before adjusting the cables. Adjust the rear brakes and check through the linkage for worn clevis pins or worn forks. Check that the bush 10 on which the relay lever pivots is not excessively worn. If the linkage is satisfactory check that the rear linings are not worn out. If everything else is satisfactory then adjust the cables as follows:

1 With the car on a ramp or stands, check that the relay lever 9 is set at the correct angle as shown in **FIG 10:10**. If the angle is incorrect, remove the front seats, carpets and combined handbrake lever gaiter and cover, so that the primary cable adjuster is exposed as shown in **FIG 10:11**. Slacken the locknut 39 and adjust the length of the cable 37 to

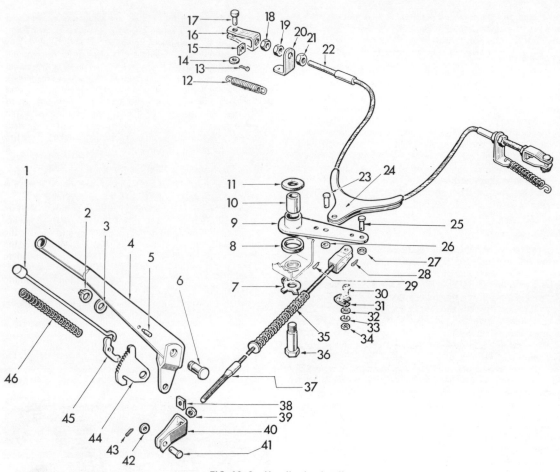

FIG 10:8 Handbrake details

Key to Figs 10:8, 10:9 and 10:10   1 Pawl release rod   2 Circlip   3 Plain washer   4 Handbrake lever
5 Pawl pivot pin   6 Pivot pin   7 Lockplate   8 Rubber seal   9 Relay lever   10 Bush   11 Felt seal
12 Pull-off spring   13 Splitpin   14 Plain washer   15 Square nut   16 Clevis   17 Clevis pin   18 Locknut
19 Adjusting nut   20 Adjustable spring anchor   21 Locknut   22 Secondary cable   23 Clevis pin
24 Compensator sector   25 Clevis pin   26 Plain washer   27 Plain washer   28 Splitpin   29 Splitpin
30 Clamp bolt   31 Clamp   32 Plain washer   33 Spring washer   34 Nut   35 Spring   36 Pivot bolt
37 Primary cable   38 Square nut   39 Locknut   40 Clevis   41 Clevis pin   42 Plain washer   43 Splitpin
44 Ratchet   45 Pawl   46 Pawl spring

FIG 10:9 Handbrake secondary cable attachments

set the relay lever at the correct angle. Tighten the locknut 39 and replace the trim parts and seats.

2 Withdraw the splitpins 13 and remove the washers 14 and clevis pins 17 which secure the clevis forks 16 to the handbrake levers on the rear brakes. Slacken the locknuts 18 and screw in the forks 16 by equal amounts on each end of the secondary cable 22, so as to shorten it and remove the slack. Screw both rear brake adjusters fully in to lock the rear brakes, and adjust the length of the cable so that the clevis pins 17 can just be refitted without having to pull or strain on the cable. Secure the clevis pins in place with the washers 14 and new splitpins 13.

3 Unscrew each adjuster a notch at a time until that road wheel rotates freely without the brake binding. Position the spring anchors 20 so that the springs 12 are giving a slight tension.

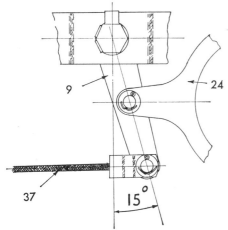

FIG 10:10 Correct angular position of the handbrake relay lever with the handbrake released

FIG 10:11 Handbrake primary cable adjuster

Renewing the primary cable:

1 Remove the front seats, carpets and cover to expose the handbrake lever as shown in **FIG 10:11**. Take off the circlip 2, plain washer 3 and withdraw the pivot pin 6 to free the assembly from the car.

2 Withdraw the clevis pin 41, after taking out the splitpin 43 and washer 42, so as to free the primary cable fork 40 from the handbrake lever 4. Slacken the locknut 39 and unscrew the fork assembly from the cable. From underneath the car, pull out the end of the cable through the hole in the floor.

3 Remove the splitpin 28, washer 27 and clevis pin 25 to free the rear end of the cable from the relay lever 9.

4 The cable is replaced in the reverse order of removal. It should be noted that the pawl 45 and ratchet 44 can easily be renewed if they are worn. After the handbrake has been adjusted, position the stop 31 so that the spring 35 is compressed by about 1 inch (25.4 mm) when the handbrake is in the off position.

Renewing the secondary cable:

1 Raise the car on stands or a ramp. Disconnect both clevis forks and tension springs from the rear brakes. Slacken the locknuts and remove all the nuts, spring anchors and clevis forks from the ends of the cable.

2 Free the tabs on the lockwasher 7 and remove the pivot bolt 36, allowing the relay lever assembly to drop down. Disconnect the compensator segment 24 from the relay lever by taking out the clevis pin 23. Pull the cables through and out of the cable guides arrowed in **FIG 10:12** and similarly remove it from the compensator segment.

3 The cable is replaced in the reverse order of removal. Grease the bush 10 of the relay lever. Pack the cable guides and the compensator segment with grease while the cable is still free from the wheel brakes, and slide the cable backwards and forwards so as to spread the grease evenly over the portion of cable that normally slides through the segment of guides. Adjust the cable length and the rear brakes after the cable has been reconnected.

10:7 Removing a flexible hose

If the flexible part of a hose is twisted then the hose is liable to fail prematurely, so use the correct method.

Unscrew the metal pipeline nut from its connection on the hose, holding the hose with a spanner on the adjacent hexagon. Still securing the hose, unscrew and remove the locknut holding the hose to its bracket. Withdraw the hose from its bracket. A spanner can then be used to unscrew the other end of the hose, leaving the whole length of the hose free to rotate without becoming twisted.

Replace a flexible hose in the reverse order of removal without straining the flexible portion.

10:8 Bleeding the brakes

This is only necessary when air has entered the hydraulic system, either because it has been dismantled or because the level has been allowed to drop so far in

FIG 10:12 Handbrake secondary cable guides

FIG 10:13 Bleeding the front brakes

the master cylinder reservoir that air has been drawn in. Air in the system makes the brake pedal operate with a spongy feel.

1. Fill up the master cylinder reservoir as full as possible with the correct grade of fresh, clean hydraulic fluid. Throughout the operation fluid will be pumped out of the system and the reservoir level will fall, so after every few strokes top up the reservoir again to prevent the level from falling so low that air is again drawn into the system.
2. Bleed the nipples in the order of decreasing pipe runs, that is, starting with the rear brake furthest from the master cylinder and ending on the front brake nearest the master cylinder.
3. Attach a length of $\frac{1}{4}$ inch (6.3 mm) bore plastic or rubber tubing to the brake nipple to be bled. Drop the free end of the tube into a clean glass container holding a little clean hydraulic fluid, as shown in **FIG 10:13**. Unscrew the bleed nipple a quarter to half a turn.
4. Have a second operator pump the brake pedal with full fast strokes, leaving a short pause between each stroke. At first a mixture of fluid and air will be ejected from the bleed tube, but carry on pumping until the fluid comes out air free. Tighten the bleed nipple on a down stroke. Repeat the bleeding operation on the remaining nipples.
5. If after bleeding the pedal still feels spongy or air is continuously ejected, then alter the technique slightly. Leave the nipple closed and have the second operator press down on the brake pedal. Open the nipple so that the fluid and air is forced out under higher pressure.

When the pedal has reached the end of its stroke, close the bleed nipple and allow the pedal to return under its own action. Repeat this method until all the air has been expelled.

Keep the reservoir constantly topped up and do not return fluid that has been bled through the system directly to the reservoir.

10:9 Fault diagnosis

(a) Spongy pedal

1. Air in the hydraulic system
2. Fluid leak in the hydraulic system
3. Gap between the underside of the linings and the shoes on the rear brakes

(b) Excessive pedal movement

1. Check 1 and 2 in (a)
2. Excessive lining or pad wear
3. Very low fluid level in the master cylinder reservoir

(c) Brakes grab or pull to one side

1. Wet or oily friction linings or pads
2. Cracked or distorted front brake disc
3. Cracked, scored or distorted rear brake drum
4. Worn out friction linings
5. Uneven tyre pressures
6. Seized wheel cylinder
7. Seized handbrake cable
8. Mixed linings of different grades
9. Broken shoe return spring
10. Defective suspension or steering

CHAPTER 11

THE ELECTRICAL SYSTEM

11:1 Description
11:2 The battery
11:3 The generator
11:4 The generator control box
11:5 The starter motor
11:6 The windscreen wipers
11:7 The fuses

11:8 The direction indicators
11:9 The headlamps
11:10 The horns
11:11 The fuel gauge and temperature gauge
11:12 Lighting circuits
11:13 Fault diagnosis

11:1 Description

All the models covered by this manual are fitted with a negative earth electrical system. Earlier models were fitted with positive earth systems, so care must be taken to ensure that the battery is connected the right way round. Standard models are not fitted with any items that are polarity sensitive but accessories containing diodes or transistors, such as radios, are polarity sensitive and may be irreparably damaged if incorrectly connected into the system.

The supply for the system is produced by a generator driven by a belt from the engine pulley. Electrical power is stored in a 12 volt lead/acid battery which is capable of giving out the heavy current required by the starter motor as well as providing power for the accessories and lights when the engine is not running. A control box regulates the voltage produced by the generator, depending on the demands of the system and the state of charge of the battery. The control box also has a cut-out, which isolates the generator from the electrical system when the generator is stopped or running too slowly to supply sufficient voltage. A warning light on the dash lights when the ignition is on but the generator is not charging.

A 12 volt test bulb or any working voltmeter may be used to carry out continuity checks, but high-grade moving coil instruments are essential when carrying out performance checks or adjusting components. Cheap and unreliable instruments are incapable of measuring to the accuracy required and will either mask faults or allow components to be incorrectly adjusted. For tracing wiring faults, Wiring Diagrams are shown in **Technical Data** at the end of this manual.

Detailed instructions for servicing the electrical equipment are given in this chapter but it is a waste of time and money to attempt to repair equipment which is seriously damaged either mechanically or electrically. Most items can be renewed on an exchange basis and in the long run will be found more economical and effective than trying to repair badly damaged items.

11:2 The battery

It is essential that the battery is always carefully and correctly maintained as, if it is allowed to deteriorate, difficulty will be experienced in starting and the performance of the whole electrical system will suffer.

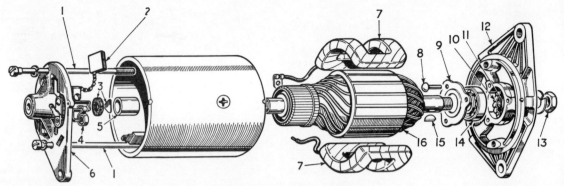

FIG 11:1 Generator details

Key to Fig 11:1   1 Bolts   2 Brush   3 Felt ring and aluminium sealing disc   4 Brush spring   5 Bearing bush
6 Commutator end bracket   7 Field coils   8 Rivet   9 Bearing retainer plate   10 Corrugated washer
11 Felt washer   12 Driving end bracket   13 Pulley retainer nut   14 Bearing   15 Woodruff key   16 Armature

Keep the top of the battery clean and dry as dampness or dirt can form an electrical leakage path from the battery positive terminal to the securing strap and surrounding metal parts. If the metal parts have corroded, either through galvanic action or acid spillage, then the battery should be removed and the acid neutralized with dilute ammonia or baking powder. Wash away the resultant mess with plenty of clean water and when the parts are dry paint them with anti-sulphuric paint. If the connectors or terminal posts are corroded then remove the connectors and wash them with dilute ammonia followed by clean water. Smear both the connectors and terminal posts with petroleum jelly before replacing the connectors. Make sure that the connectors are tight but do not over-tighten the securing screws.

At regular intervals, depending on temperature and amount of use, remove the battery vent caps and check the level of electrolyte. If required top up the electrolyte to just above the tops of the separators, using nothing but pure distilled water.

Avoid leaving the battery uncharged or standing idle for long periods. If the battery is stored it should be given monthly freshening-up charges to prevent the plates from sulphating. A lead/acid battery thrives better on being regularly nearly discharged and then fully charged again than it does on being kept fully charged. A weak battery may sometimes be partially restored by running it through a few cycles of discharge and charge.

Concentrated acid must never be added directly to the battery. Electrolyte of the correct specific gravity should only be added to replace spillage or leakage. If electrolyte is to be mixed use a suitable container, as heat is generated, and add the acid to the water. **Never under any circumstances add water to acid.**

The specific gravity of the electrolyte gives an accurate indication of the state of charge of the battery. Draw up sufficient electrolyte from the individual cells, using a hydrometer, to float the float clear of the sides, top and bottom of the hydrometer. Hold the instrument so that the reading is taken at eye level and note the reading on the float. If one cell differs radically from the others then it is possible that this cell is defective. Examine the electrolyte drawn up into the hydrometer and if it appears dirty or full of small specks then that cell is most likely defective.

The indications from the readings are as follows:

For climates below 32°C (90°F)

Cell fully charged   Specific gravity 1.270 to 1.290
Cell half-charged   Specific gravity 1.190 to 1.210
Cell discharged   Specific gravity 1.110 to 1.130
Use electrolyte of specific gravity 1.270 to replace spillage.

For climates above 32°C (90°F)

Cell fully charged   Specific gravity 1.210 to 1.230
Cell half-charged   Specific gravity 1.130 to 1.150
Cell discharged   Specific gravity 1.050 to 1.070
Use electrolyte of specific gravity 1.210 to replace spillage.

These figures are given assuming electrolyte temperature of 16°C (60°F). For accurate results the readings should be converted to standard by adding .002 for each 3°C (5°F) that the electrolyte temperature is above standard, and subtracting .002 from the reading for every 3°C (5°F) that the temperature of the electrolyte is below standard.

The individual cells may also be tested by using a heavy discharge tester across the inter-cell connections. A satisfactory cell should maintain a steady 1.2 to 1.7 volts for a period of 5 to 6 seconds. Any cell that drops below standard is probably defective but if all the cells appear sub-standard then charge the battery and repeat the test. **A heavy discharge test should not be carried out on a battery that is known to be low in charge.**

11:3 The generator

The generator details are shown in **FIG 11:1**.

Routine maintenance:

1 At regular intervals check that the driving belt is at the correct tension (see **Chapter 4, Section 4:4**) and examine it for fraying or other damage.
2 At 12,000 mile intervals, inject a few drops of engine oil through the hole in the cap of the commutator end bracket 6 so as to lubricate the bush assembly. Do not overlubricate or oil will find its way onto the brushgear and commutator.
3 At 24,000 mile intervals inspect the brushgear and commutator.

Testing in situ:

1 Check that the drive belt is at the correct tension and not slipping.
2 Disconnect the electrical leads from the D and F terminals on the generator and bridge the terminals with a short length of wire. Connect an accurate 0-20 voltmeter between the terminals on the generator and a good earth point on the car.
3 Start the engine and gradually increase its speed, noting the reading on the voltmeter. The reading should increase steadily and without fluctuation. **Do not allow the output to increase above 20 volts and do not race the engine.** If the maximum voltage obtained is only 1 volt then it is likely that the field coils are faulty, while faulty armature coils will limit the maximum voltage around 4 to 5 volts. If no reading is obtained then it is likely that the brushgear or commutator is defective.
4 Stop the engine and reconnect the cables to the generator, leaving the bridge wire in place. Disconnect the cables from the D and F terminals on the control box and repeat the test with the voltmeter connected between each cable in turn and the earth of the control box. In all cases the voltage readings should be exactly the same as when connected directly to the generator. This will check the continuity of the cables and the earthing of the control box.
5 Remove the bridge wire from between the generator terminals and correctly reconnect the cables.

Dismantling the generator:

1 Remove the generator by slackening all three mounting bolts and easing the driving belt off the pulley. Disconnect the cables from the terminals and remove the mounting bolts to free the generator from the engine.
2 Unscrew and remove the two through-bolts 1. Gently tap off the commutator end bracket 6 complete with the brushgear. The yoke can now be slid off the armature.
3 Normally the previous operation dismantles the generator sufficiently for most servicing operations. Remove the nut 13 and withdraw the driving pulley from the armature shaft. Extract the Woodruffe key 15 from the shaft. Use a support under the retainer plate 9 and press the shaft out of the bearing. **Do not attempt to remove the field coils or their polepieces.**

The generator is reassembled in the reverse order of dismantling. The brushes should be held up as shown in **FIG 11:2** when replacing the commutator end bracket, otherwise they will catch on the edge of the commutator and become chipped or damaged.

Servicing the brushgear:

Remove the commutator end bracket. Renew the brushes if they are worn shorter than $\frac{11}{32}$ inch (.8 mm) or if they are close to this limit. Check that the brushes move freely in their holders by holding up the spring and gently pulling on the flexible connectors. If the brushes stick, remove them and polish their sides on a flat smooth file. Clean out the holders with a fuel-moistened piece of cloth. Replace the brushes in their original positions so that the bedding is not disturbed and the brushes still mate to the commutator. New brushes may be lightly

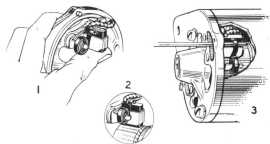

FIG 11:2 Fitting commutator end bracket

Key to Fig 11:2 1 Method of trapping brush in raised position with spring   2 Normal working position
3 Method of releasing brush on to commutator

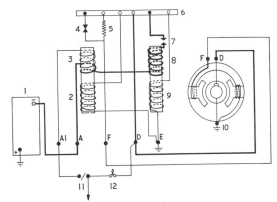

FIG 11:3 Generating system circuit

Key to Fig 11:3 1 Battery 2 Voltage regulator relay coil
3 Split series coil 4 Voltage regulator contacts 5 Resistor
6 Main frame 7 Cut-out contacts 8 Series winding
9 Cut-out relay coil 10 Generator 11 Ignition switch
12 Ignition warning lamp   Nos. 2 to 9 are incorporated in the control box

bedded-in by wrapping the commutator with fine glasspaper and rotating it between the brushes.

Use a spring balance to check the tension of the springs. With good brushes and in the fitted position the spring tension should lie between 22 to 25 oz (.62 to .71 kg) but renew the springs if their tension is less then 15 oz.

Servicing the commutator:

Normally wiping the commutator with a fuel-moistened cloth is all that should be required. The commutator should then have a dark polished surface. Light score marks can be removed by polishing it with a strip of fine glasspaper (do not use emerycloth as this will leave particles embedded in the copper). If the scoring or damage is deeper then it should be turned off in a lathe to a depth just sufficient to remove the damage. Use a very sharp tool and the highest speed possible. The best finish is obtained by taking a light final cut using a diamond tipped tool, but polishing with very fine glasspaper will leave a sufficiently good finish.

Grind the sides of a hacksaw blade until it is the thickness of the insulation slots. Use this tool to squarely undercut the insulation to a depth of $\frac{1}{32}$ inch (.8 mm).

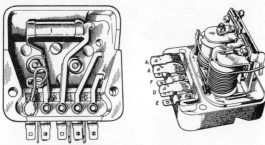

FIG 11:4 The control box

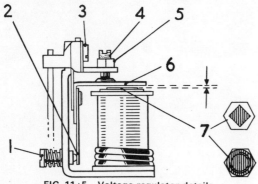

FIG 11:5 Voltage regulator details

Key to Fig 11:5
2 Armature tension spring
4 Fixed contact adjustment screw
7 Core face and shim
1 Voltage adjusting screw
3 Armature securing screws
5 Locknut 6 Armature

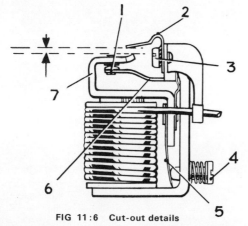

FIG 11:6 Cut-out details

Key to Fig 11:6 1 Follow through .010 to .020 inch (.254 to .508 mm) 2 Stop arm 3 Armature securing screws 4 Cut-out adjusting screw 5 Armature tension spring 6 Fixed contact blade 7 Armature tongue and moving contact

The armature:

Specialized equipment is required to check the armature coils. Individual burned segments on the commutator are an indication that there is a fault in some of the coils. Check the armature for loose laminations, score marks on the laminations which indicate either a bent shaft or loose polepieces in the yoke. Also check it for signs of overheating or other obvious defects. Renew the armature if it is defective and never try to machine it or straighten a bent shaft.

The field coils:

Leave the field coils in the yoke and use an ohmmeter to measure the electrical resistance between the F terminal and the yoke. If an ohmmeter is not available use an ammeter and 12 volt supply connected in series. The reading should be approximately 6 ohms (2 amps on a 12 volt supply). If the resistance is very high and the current either very low or nil then there is an open circuit in the coils. Conversely very low resistance or high current indicates a short circuit. If the field coils are defective their renewal should be left to a garage, as a special wheel screwdriver is essential for tightening and slackening the screws that hold the polepieces. If the screws can be moved using an ordinary screwdriver then they are much too loose and there is a danger of the polepieces hitting the armature.

Bearing bush:

This must be renewed if it is so worn that there is excessive sideways movement on the armature shaft.

1 Screw a $\frac{5}{8}$ inch tap partly into the old bush 5 and withdraw the bush by pulling on the tap. Remove the retainer and felt ring 3. Either renew the parts 3, or wash the felt ring in clean fuel and when it is dry soak it in engine oil. Squeeze out the surplus oil and refit the felt ring and sealing disc.

2 Soak the new bush in engine oil for twenty-four hours. The period can be reduced by heating the oil to the temperature of boiling water for two hours and then allowing the oil and bush to cool together.

3 Use a stepped mandrel whose highly-polished spigot is of the same diameter as the armature shaft. Press the bush back into position so that the bearing bush is flush with the inner face of the bracket. This method will ensure that the bush is of the correct diameter and finish. **Do not ream or bore the bush as this will ruin the porosity of the material.**

Ballbearing:

Renew this if it is worn or runs noisily.

1 Completely dismantle the generator, except for removing the field coils. Carefully drill off the heads of the rivets 8 then use a suitable pin punch to drive out the rivet stems. Take off the retaining plate 9, press out the old bearing 14 and remove the corrugated washer 10 and felt washer 11.

2 Either clean or renew the felt washer. Refit the felt washer and corrugated washer. Pack the new bearing with Energrease RBB.3 or equivalent high melting point grease and press it back into position. Secure the retaining plate 9 back in place with new rivets 8 and reassemble the generator.

11:4 The generator control box

The charging circuit is shown in **FIG 11:3** and the control box is shown in **FIG 11:4**. **The use of high-grade instruments is absolutely essential when checking or adjusting the control box.**

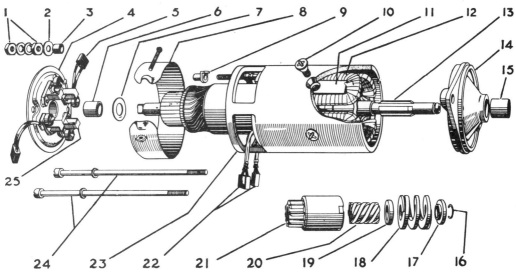

FIG 11:7 Components of Lucas M.35G starter motor

Key to Fig 11:7   1 Terminal nuts and washers   2 Insulating washer   3 Insulating bush   4 End plate
5 Brush   6 Bush   7 Thrust washer   8 Cover band   9 Insulating bush   10 Pole securing screw
11 Polepiece   12 Field coil   13 Shaft   14 End bracket   15 Bush   16 Jump ring   17 Retainer
18 Main spring   19 Thrust washer   20 Sleeve   21 Pinion and barrel assembly   22 Brushes   23 Yoke
24 Through-bolts   25 Brush box

Before making any adjustments on the control box, check the following points to ensure that the fault does not lie outside the unit.
1 Test the output of the generator and the cables joining the generator to the control box, as described in **Section 11:3**.
2 Check that the battery is satisfactory and capable of holding a charge, also that the battery connections are clean and tight.
3 Check the earth points, especially the earth point for the control box.
4 If the main symptom is that the battery is flat check that the car is not just being used for short mileage journeys where the generator has not sufficient time to recharge the battery after use of the starter.

Cleaning the points:

After a long period of service dirt may build up on the contact points, causing them to have high resistance and making the output fluctuate. After cleaning the points wipe away loose dirt and filings using a piece of cloth moistened with methylated spirits.

Regulator contacts   Use fine carborundum stone or fine silicone carbide paper.
Cut-out contacts   Use only a strip of fine glasspaper, **never carborundum, emery or silicone carbide.**

Voltage regulator—electrical setting:

The voltage regulator details are shown in **FIG 11:5**. **The checks and adjustment should be completed within 30 seconds of starting engine, otherwise heating of the coils will cause false settings to be made.**

1 Remove the cover and place a thin piece of cardboard between the armature tongue and the core face on the coil of the cut-out (see **FIG 11:6**) so as to prevent the cut-out from operating.
2 Connect a first-grade 0-20 voltmeter between the terminal D on the control box and a good earth point. The warning light cable can be disconnected from its terminal on the control box and the voltmeter attached to this terminal, as it is directly connected to the terminal D.
3 Start the engine and slowly raise its speed until the generator is turning at 3000 rev/min. At this speed the reading on the voltmeter should be steady and within the following limits:

Ambient temperature	Voltage reading
10°C (50°F)	16.1 to 16.7
20°C (68°F)	16.0 to 16.6
30°C (86°F)	15.9 to 16.5
40°C (104°F)	15.8 to 16.4

If the readings are unsteady then clean the points as instructed and repeat the test. If the readings still fluctuate then the unit is internally defective and must be renewed.

4 Provided that the readings are steady but outside the limits then they can be adjusted. Stop the engine and allow the coils to cool if the engine has been running for more than 30 seconds. With the engine running at the correct speed turn the voltage adjusting screw 1 (see **FIG 11:5**) clockwise to raise the voltage or anticlockwise to lower the voltage. Turn the screw by only small amounts and aim at the middle of the range of limits.
5 When the adjustment is satisfactory remove the cardboard from the cut-out, after stopping the engine.

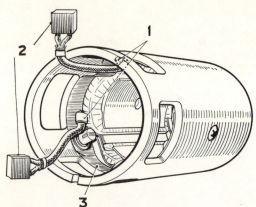

FIG 11:8 Yoke and field coil brush connections

Key to Fig 11:8   1 Field coil connections   2 Brushes
3 Yoke

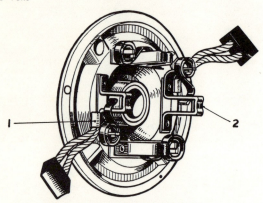

FIG 11:9 Commutator end bracket

Key to Fig 11:9   1 Brush connections   2 Brush boxes

Cut-out electrical setting:

If, after setting the voltage regulator, the system does not charge correctly then refer to **FIG 11:6** and test and set the cut-out. **Tests and adjustments must be completed within 30 seconds of starting the engine, otherwise heating of the coils will produce spurious readings.**

1 Remove the cover and connect a voltmeter between the D terminal and earth, as for testing the voltage regulator.
2 Start the engine and gradually increase its speed until the cut-out points are seen to close. This should occur at a voltmeter reading of 12.7 to 13.3 volts.
3 If the reading is outside the limits, adjust it by turning the adjusting screw 4 a fraction of a turn at a time in the required direction and testing each adjustment. Turning the screw clockwise will raise the voltage setting. If the cut-out does not operate then it is likely that there is a short-circuit in the unit and it should be removed for further examination or renewal.

Voltage regulator—mechanical setting:

The mechanical settings of the control box are accurately set on manufacture and should only require resetting if the unit has been dismantled. Before carrying out any mechanical settings the unit must be isolated from the battery. Refer to **FIG 11:5**.

1 Slacken the locknut 5 and unscrew the fixed contact 4 so that it is well clear of the moving armature contact. Slacken the two armature securing screws 3, and undo the adjusting screw 1 until it is well clear of the armature spring 2.
2 Examine the face of the core 7. If a round copper separator is used a .015 inch (.38 mm) feeler gauge is required to set the correct air gap, while if a square separator is fitted then a .021 inch (.53 mm) feeler gauge is required.
3 Insert the correct gauge between the core face and the armature so that it covers the core face, taking great care not to damage or peel off the copper separator. Press the armature squarely down onto the gauge and retighten the securing screws 3.
4 Leave the setting gauge in place and screw in the fixed contact 4 until it just touches the moving contact. Tighten the locknut 5 to hold the fixed contact in place. Remove the gauge and reset the electrical setting of the regulator.

Cut-out mechanical setting:

This is factory set and should only need adjusting if the unit has been dismantled. Refer to **FIG 11:6**.

1 Slacken the adjusting screw 4 until it is well clear of the armature spring 5. Slacken the two armature securing screws 3. Press the armature squarely down onto the core face, without any gauge in between, and tighten the securing screws 3 in this position.
2 Still holding the armature down, bend the stop arm 2 until the gap between it and the armature tongue 7, shown between the arrows, is .032 inch .(81 mm)
3 Bend the fixed contact blade 6 so that it is deflected by .015 inch (.38 mm) when the armature is pressed down against the core face.
4 Reset the electrical adjustment and replace the cover.

11:5 The starter motor

The starter motor details are shown in **FIG 11:7**. It should be noted that the starter motor is of very similar construction to the generator, though there are windows in the yoke, covered by the band 8, through which the brushgear can be inspected, and the wiring is much thicker so as to take the heavy currents.

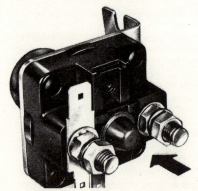

FIG 11:10 Starter solenoid

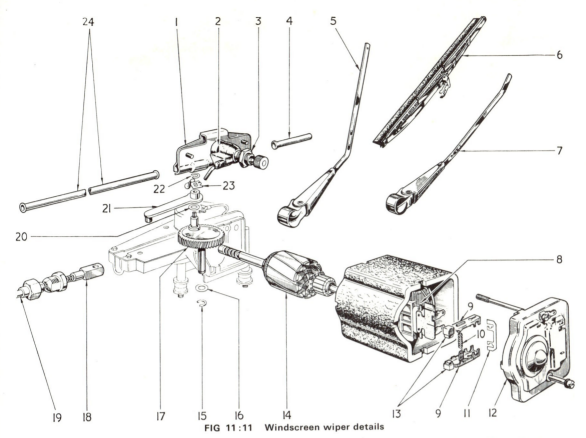

FIG 11:11 Windscreen wiper details

Key to Fig 11:11 1 Wheel box 2 Jet and bush assembly 3 Nut 4 Rigid tubing—righthand side 5 Wiper arm
6 Blade 7 Wiper arm 8 Field coil assembly 9 Brushgear 10 Tension spring and retainers 11 Brushgear retainer
12 End cover 13 Brushes 14 Armature 15 Circlip 16 Washer 17 Final drive wheel 18 Cable rack
19 Rigid tubing—lefthand side 20 Spacer 21 Connecting rod 22 Circlip 23 Parking switch contact
24 Rigid tubing—centre section

Removing and replacing the starter motor:

Disconnect the battery and then disconnect the cable from the starter motor terminal. Remove the two bolts securing the motor, withdraw it from the clutch housing and lift it upwards out of the car. Collect any shims and packing pieces fitted between the motor and its mounting face.

Before refitting the starter motor, accurately measure the distance between the pinion side of the flywheel ring gear and the starter motor mounting face, and measure the distance between the end of the pinion and the mounting face on the starter motor. Select packing pieces and shims to make up a pack of the thickness to ensure that there is a clearance of $\frac{3}{32}$ to $\frac{5}{32}$ inch between the starter pinion and the flywheel ring gear when the motor is refitted and out of mesh. Refit the starter motor in the reverse order of removal, leaving the battery connections until last.

Dismantling the starter motor:

The brush connections in the yoke are shown in **FIG 11:8** and the commutator end bracket is shown in **FIG 11:9**.

1 Remove the cover band 8. Lift up the springs and withdraw the two brushes connected to the yoke from their brush boxes. Note the position and direction of the brushes so that they can be replaced in exactly the same positions.
2 Remove the two through-bolts 24 and ease off the end plate 4, after removing the terminal nuts, washers and bush 1, 2 and 3. Withdraw the armature complete

FIG 11:12 Location of windscreen wiper motor on Herald 1200

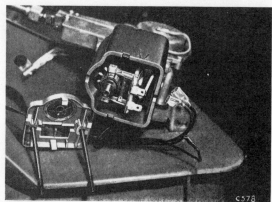

FIG 11:13 Windscreen wiper motor end cover removed

with end bracket 14 and the starter drive assembly. This is sufficient dismantling for most servicing operations.

3 If the pinion drive or bush 15 require servicing then use a press and suitable adaptors to compress the main spring, and move the retainer 17 off the jump ring 16. Prise out the jump ring and remove the pinion drive parts from the shaft 13. The end plate 14 can then be removed from the shaft.

The starter motor is reassembled in the reverse order of dismantling, refitting the commutator end bracket by a method similar to the one shown in **FIG 11:2**.

Testing the starter motor:

If the starter motor fails to operate when fitted to the car then check as follows:

1 Check that the battery is fully charged and satisfactory. Make sure that the battery connections are clean and tight.
2 Switch on the lights and operate the starter control. If the lights dim then current is reaching the starter and it is possible that the starter is jammed in mesh. Either rock the car backwards and forwards in gear, or rotate the starter shaft using a spanner on the squared end. If these methods fail to unjam the starter then it must be removed for further examination. If the starter jams often, either the teeth on the flywheel ring gear and pinion are worn or the main spring is broken, though dirt on the screwed sleeve can also cause it to jam.
3 The lights remaining bright shows that the motor is taking no current. Press the rubber covered button on the solenoid, shown in **FIG 11:10**, and if the starter now operates then the starter switch and its associated wiring are faulty. If the starter does not operate use an old pair of pliers, or thick rod, and short across the starter solenoid terminals. If the starter motor now operates, the solenoid is defective and, since it is a sealed unit, it must be renewed. If no fault is found then the starter motor must be removed for further examination.

A torque measuring rig, high current ammeter and tachometer are required to test the starter motor performance fully and the figures are given in **Technical Data** at the end of this manual. However, the motor can be clamped in a vice so that a heavy duty cable from a 12 volt battery negative terminal is held to the yoke. Connect another heavy-duty cable between the positive terminal of the battery and the starter motor terminal. The motor should turn freely and run at high speed. At the same time the brush gear can be examined for excessive sparking or movement.

Brushgear:

Check that the brushes move freely in their brush boxes. Polish their sides on a fine file and clean the brushboxes with a petrol moistened rag if the brushes stick. Renew the brushes if they are worn to less than $\frac{5}{16}$ inch (8 mm) and renew the springs if their tension fitted is less than the correct limits of 32 to 40 oz (.9 to 1.1 kg). New brushes are preformed and require no bedding-in.

Commutator and armature:

These are renovated and checked in exactly the same manner as the equivalent parts fitted to the generator (see **Section 11:3**). **Do not undercut the insulation on the commutator.**

Armature shaft bushes:

These are renewed in exactly the same manner as the bearing bush fitted to the generator (see **Section 11:3**).

The pinion drive:

This can be removed as instructed earlier, and it should be noted that it can be removed without dismantling the rest of the starter motor. If the main spring 18 is broken or cracked the parts can be removed by hand pressure and without the use of a press.

Check the spring for cracks. Renew the sleeve 20 and pinion and barrel assembly 21 as a set if either are worn. Degrease the parts and reassemble them dry in the reverse order of dismantling. If a press is not available, select a socket or piece of tubing which is a good slide fit on the armature shaft. Reassemble the parts and hold the jump ring in place on the bevelled end of the shaft, using the socket. Give the end of the socket a sharp rap with a hammer to drive the jump ring into position. Do not lubricate the pinion drive as grease or oil will pick up dirt and cause the drive to stick.

11:6 The windscreen wipers

The details of the windscreen wiper mechanism are shown in **FIG 11:11** and the location of the wiper motor on Herald 1200 models is shown in **FIG 11:12**.

Wiper arms and blades:

Renew the blades 6 at yearly intervals or when they no longer give a clean sweep. The blades are secured to the arms 5 and 7 by a spring clip. Use a screwdriver pressed up along the arm and under the clip to free the blades from the arms.

The arms 5 and 7 fit onto splines on the wheelbox spindles and are held in place by spring clips which fit under the splined end of the spindles. Use a screwdriver to lift the clip free and lever the arms off the spindles.

When replacing the arms switch on the ignition and the wipers. Switch off the wipers so that they stop in their parked positions. This parked position can be altered by slackening the screws holding the gearbox cover on the motor and rotating the domed cover until the wipers stop in the required position. Tighten the cover securing screws after adjustment. Final accurate positioning of the arms is by pushing them on the required splines of the spindle.

Occasionally lubricate the rubber bushes around the spindles with a few drops of glycerine.

The cable rack:

To remove the cable rack it is necessary to remove the motor.

1 Remove the wiper arms from the wheelbox spindles.
2 Disconnect the battery and the leads to the wiper box.
3 Unscrew the large nut securing the tubing 19 to the motor and remove the three bolts securing the motor, or its bracket, to the car. Remove the motor and draw out the cable rack 18 with it.

The cable rack can be freed from the motor, either with the motor in position or removed from the car, by taking off the gearbox cover after having carefully noted the position of the domed park switch. Remove the circlip 22 and the parking switch contact 23. Lift out the connecting rod 21, collecting the spacer 20 from underneath it.

The cable rack is replaced in the reverse order of dismantling, but before it is fully replaced it should be fitted back through the tubing and a spring balance used to withdraw it. The maximum load required should not exceed 6 lb (2.7 kg). If this is exceeded then check the tubing for dents or kinks and the wheelboxes for damage or misalignment with the tubes. Pack the cable rack with grease before finally refitting it.

Testing the motor:

Disconnect the cable rack assembly from the motor and connect an ammeter in series into the motor electrical circuit. Switch on the motor and time the cycles. The motor should operate between 44 to 48 cycles/min and run at a current of 2.7 to 3.4 amps.

Motor takes no or abnormally low current:

Check through the wiring using either a voltmeter or 12 volt test bulb to see if power is reaching as far as the motor or to trace the defective section of the wiring. If power is reaching the motor then remove the through-bolts and withdraw the end cover 12. The motor will then appear as shown in **FIG 11:13**. Check that the brushes are bearing on the commutator and that the brush tension is between 125 and 140 grammes. Renew the brushes if they are excessively worn and renew the spring 10 if the brush tension is low. Make sure that the brushgear 9 moves freely on its pivots. Clean the commutator with a petrol moistened piece of cloth. If the motor still does not function, it will have to be removed and dismantled for further examination.

Motor takes a high current:

The motor will stall at a current of 13 to 15 amps. If the motor runs freely with the cable rack disconnected then check the cable rack and wheelboxes for excessive stiffness. Check that the armature shaft bearings are free to move in their holders otherwise misalignment of the

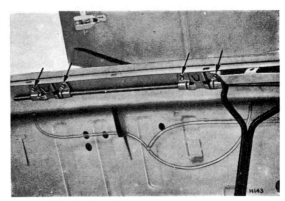

FIG 11:14 Wheelbox attachment screws

bearings may cause excessive stiffness. Check that the end float of the armature lies between .008 and .012 inch (.203 to .305 mm) and adjust it if necessary using the screw and locknut on the side of the brushgear. Examine the brushgear and clean the commutator to remove any dirt or carbon particles that may be shorting it. If it is suspected that the armature is faulty then use a substitute satisfactory armature. The field coils should have a resistance of 8 to 9.5 ohms giving a current of $1\frac{1}{2}$ to $1\frac{1}{4}$ amps when connected across a 12 volt supply.

Dismantling the motor:

1 Remove the motor and cable rack from the car. Disconnect the cable rack from the motor.
2 Remove the end plate 12 and take out the brushgear after removing the retainer 11.
3 Remove the body and field coils from the gearbox. The red earth lead is sufficiently long to allow this.
4 Remove the armature. Take off the circlip 15 and washer 16. Use a smooth file to remove any burrs from the final drive shaft and then lift the final gear 17 out of the gearbox.
5 Mark the position of the field coils in relation to the body and remove them by undoing the two securing screws.

The motor is reassembled in the reverse order of dismantling but noting the following points.

1 Lubricate the armature and final drive bearings with Oilene BBB or engine oil.
2 Set the screw and locknut on the side of the gearbox to give the armature an end float of .008 to .012 inch.
3 If the gearbox has been cleaned out, pack it with 25 to 35 cc of Ragosine Listate grease to refill it.

Wheelboxes:

1 Remove the wiper arms 5 and 7 then withdraw the cable rack 18, as described earlier in this section.
2 From outside the car, remove the nuts 3 and rubber bushes that secure the wheelboxes in place.
3 Working inside the car and behind the facia panel, disconnect the windscreen washer tubes from the wheel boxes. Remove the screws arrowed in **FIG 11:14** and withdraw the wheelboxes from the car.

The wheelboxes are replaced in the reverse order of removal, but take care to align them with the tubing so that the cable rack has a smooth run.

FIG 11:15 Herald 13/60 line fuse

FIG 11:16 Headlamp beam adjustment screws

11:7 The fuses

An in-line fuse is fitted to protect the headlamp flasher circuit on Herald 13/60 models. The fuse unit is shown in **FIG 11:15** and the parts of the unit are held together by a bayonet-type fitting. If the fuse blows it should be replaced with the correct 25 amp rated (pink colour coded) fuse. If this fuse blows when the headlamps are flashed the circuit should be checked and the fault rectified before fitting another fuse.

Apart from this no other circuits on any of these models are fuse protected.

11:8 The direction indicators

A flasher unit is plugged into a socket under the facia. The unit is sealed and cannot be rectified or adjusted once it is defective. The unit is also delicate and will suffer from careless handling or plugging in when the circuit is live.

A warning light is fitted to the dashboard to indicate when the direction indicators are operating. This light will flash at the same rate as the indicator lights.

Faulty operation:

1 Check all the bulbs as if one bulb has blown then the flash rate will be altered. At the same time check that the lamps are properly earthed as sometimes a little corrosion forms so that there is a high resistance and the bulbs will not operate.
2 Remove the flasher unit from its socket and use a voltmeter or test bulb to check that battery voltage reaches the B terminal in the socket. If battery voltage does not reach the socket when the ignition is switched on, then trace back through the wiring until the fault is found.
3 Connect the B and L terminals together with a piece of wire. Switch on the ignition and operate the direction indicator switch in both directions. If, when the switch is selected, the appropriate lights stay on continuously then the flasher unit is defective and must be renewed. If the lights do not come on then the switch or the wiring beyond the socket is defective.

11:9 The headlamps

The majority of headlamps will be fitted with sealed units where the filaments are built into the reflector and lens so that they form a single assembly. Any defect, such as a burnt out filament or cracked lens will necessitate renewing the complete unit but normally it will be found that they last longer and give better light than the prefocus bulb fitted into a separate reflector and lens unit that is required in some countries.

The rim and rubber sealing can be removed after taking out the screw securing them. The leadlamp will then appear as shown in **FIG 11:16. To remove the headlight do not turn the adjusting screws shown.** Instead, lightly press in the unit and turn it anticlockwise so that the adjusting screw heads will pass through the larger holes.

Beam setting:

This is altered by turning the screws shown in **FIG 11:16**. It is inadvisable to attempt to set the beams without specialized equipment to ensure the accuracy of the settings, especially as in some countries lighting regulations are very stringent.

11:10 The horns

The windtone type of horns fitted to the car do not alter in pitch but if they are out of adjustment they will sound rough and take excessive current.

Before carrying out any adjustments to the horns check that the battery is fully charged, the circuit is satisfactory, the horn mounting bolts are tight and that they are not fouling on any adjacent structure.

If a horn is defective it cannot be dismantled and must be renewed. The horn adjusting screw is shown in **FIG 11:17. Do not slacken or alter the central slotted core or its locknut.**

1 Disconnect both horns from the circuit, taking care to prevent the cables from earthing onto metal parts. Connect an accurate ammeter into series with the horn to be tested and connect these into the circuit. Press the horn push and adjust the horn to its best performance with the minimum current. Turning the adjusting screw clockwise will increase the current and turning it anticlockwise will decrease the current.
2 If an ammeter is not available unscrew the adjusting screw until the horn just ceases to sound and then

turn the screw back in one quarter of a turn. This will provide an adequate setting.

3 Repeat the setting procedure on the other horn and then connect them back into the circuit correctly.

11:11 The fuel gauge and temperature gauge

On most models these use a stabilized 10 volts from a bi-metallic voltage stabilizer unit. On some models the fuel contents gauge may be run directly off the battery. The type of system is easily checked by observing the behaviour of the needle. If, as soon as the ignition is switched on, the needle flicks to its mark then the system uses battery voltage. If the needle slowly moves to its position and does not fluctuate with the movement of the car then the system uses the supply from a voltage stabilizer.

Special equipment is required to test the correct operation of the units so the best check for a suspect unit is substituting one of known satisfactory performance. The wiring should be carefully checked through for faulty insulation, broken wires and loose or poor connections.

Tank unit:

The position of the unit for cars is shown in **FIG 11:18**. The tank unit for estate cars is shown in **FIG 2:1** of **Chapter 2. Before removing the unit make sure that the level of the fuel is below the tank unit.** Pull back the rubber gaiter as shown and mark the vertical on both the tank and the unit to ensure that the unit will be correctly replaced the right way up. Remove the six securing screws and withdraw the unit from the tank, taking care not to bend the float arm. Scrape off the old cork seal and all traces of sealing compound.

Replace the unit in the reverse order of removal, using a new cork seal and smearing the jointing faces liberally with jointing compound.

11:12 Lighting circuits

Lamps give insufficient light:

Check that the battery is fully charged and that the connectors are clean and on tightly. If necessary recharge the battery on a trickle charger until it gases freely.

Have the settings of the beam checked. If the bulbs or reflectors have darkened with age then renew them.

On a long journey dirt can build up and dry on the headlamp lenses unnoticed, gradually cutting down the light. At stops wipe the lenses clean with a damp cloth. This also applies to rear lights which can become partially obscured by mud and dirt.

Bulbs burn out frequently:

If this is accompanied by a need for frequent topping up of the battery and high hydrometer readings, check the charging rate. Normally this should be 3 to 4 amps with all accessories switched off. If the reading is regularly high then the voltage regulator requires checking and setting.

Lamps light when switched on but gradually fade:

This fault will most likely be accompanied by starting troubles. Check the battery as it is incapable of supplying

FIG 11:17 Adjusting the horn

FIG 11:18 Fuel tank unit location

current for any length of time. Also use an ammeter to check the charging rate as this may be low and preventing the battery from becoming recharged.

Lamp brilliance varies with engine speed:

Check the condition of the battery. If difficulty in starting is also experienced then it is likely that the battery is defective. If the battery is satisfactory, clean and securely replace the battery connections. Check through the wiring system as defective or perished cables can also be a cause.

11:13 Fault diagnosis

(a) Battery discharged

1 Terminal connectors loose or dirty
2 Short circuit in electrical system
3 Generator not charging
4 Control box defective or requires adjustment
5 Battery internally defective

(b) Insufficient charging current
1 Check 1 and 4 in (a)
2 Drive belt broken or slipping

(c) Battery overcharging
1 Check 4 in (a)

(d) Battery will not hold charge
1 Low electrolyte level
2 Battery plates sulphated or plate separators ineffective
3 Electrolyte leakage from cracked casing or top sealing compound

(e) Generator output low or nil
1 Check 4 in (a) and 2 in (b)
2 Worn bearings, loose polepieces or bent armature shaft
3 Armature or field coils burned, shorted or broken
4 Commutator burned, worn or shorted
5 Brushes sticking or excessively worn, weak or broken springs
6 Insulation standing proud between commutator segments

(f) Starter motor lacks power or will not operate
1 Battery discharged
2 Starter pinion jammed in mesh
3 Defective starter switch or starter solenoid
4 Brushes worn or sticking, weak or broken springs
5 Defective field coil or armature windings
6 Commutator worn or dirty
7 Starter shaft bent, polepieces loose or worn bushes
8 Engine abnormally stiff

(g) Starter motor runs but does not turn engine
1 Pinion sticking on screwed sleeve
2 Broken off or worn out teeth on pinion or flywheel ring gear

(h) Starter motor rough or noisy
1 Check 7 in (f) and 2 in (g)
2 Mounting bolts loose
3 Insufficient packing between motor and mounting face
4 Main spring weak or broken

(j) Lamps inoperative or erratic
1 Battery low in charge
2 Bulbs burned out
3 Faulty earth on lamps or battery
4 Faulty switch
5 Loose or broken wiring connections
6 Insulation damaged on wiring causing intermittent shorts

(k) Wiper motor sluggish taking high current
1 Faulty armature or field coil windings
2 Defective armature bearings
3 Insufficient armature end float
4 Wheelbox spindle binding
5 Cable rack defective or tight in housing

(l) Wiper motor operates but does not drive arms
1 Wheelbox gear and spindle worn
2 Cable rack faulty
3 Gearbox components badly worn

CHAPTER 12

THE BODYWORK

12:1 Bodywork repairs
12:2 Seats and seat belts
12:3 The doors
12:4 The windscreen

12:5 The bonnet
12:6 The tail gate (estate cars only)
12:7 Facia components
12:8 The heater

12:1 Bodywork repairs

All the models use a chassis onto which the bodywork is mounted. The body is divided into sub-sections and a number of these sub-sections can be further dismantled into panels. As a result of this method of construction damaged panels can be removed and replaced with new panels and this will quite often be found to be cheaper than having a skilled panel beater to dress out the damage.

Minor dents can still pose a problem. It is not advisable for the average owner to attempt to beat out the dents, as incautious or excessive hammering will stretch the metal and make things worse instead of better. Filling minor dents and scratches is probably the best method of restoring the surface. The touching-up of paintwork is well within the powers of most owners, particularly as self-spraying cans of paint are now readily available in the correct matching colours for most models. Paint fades and changes colour with age so although touching-up paint is an exact match for brand new paint, it will not be an exact match after the car has been in use for some time. For this reason it may be better to spray a whole wing or panel rather than to try to touch-up a small area.

Before spraying it is essential to remove all traces of wax polish with white spirits. Even more drastic treatment will be required if silicone-based polishes have been used. Mask off surrounding areas with newspaper and masking tape to prevent spray dust from settling on them, and spray in the cleanest and most dust free conditions available. Lightly scuff the area to be sprayed. Use a primer surfacer or paste stopper according to the amount of filling required and, when it is dry, rub it down with 400 grade 'Wet or Dry' paper, using plenty of water as a lubricant and cleaner. Spend plenty of time and patience in obtaining the best surface possible, using more coats of filler if required. Small blemishes which are hardly noticeable on the matt surface will stand out glaringly in the final polished surface.

Apply the final coat evenly to a complete panel, but more lightly around the edges if only part of a panel is being sprayed. Use two thin coats, rubbing down between each coat, rather than apply one thick coat which may run.

When the paint is hard and dry, use a cutting compound to remove spray dust, and lightly polish the surface. Leave the car for at least a week before applying wax polish.

FIG 12:1 Front seat adjustments

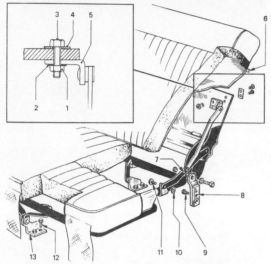

FIG 12:2 Estate car rear seat details

Key to Fig 12:2 1 Nut 2 Shakeproof washer
3 Setscrew 4 Plate washer 5 Squab bracket
6 Squab shoot bolt 7 Squab link arm 8 Squab pivot
bracket 9 Setscrew 10 "Salter" clip
11 Stud—link arm 12 Bolt 13 Cushion brackets

12:2 Seats and seat belts

Seat belts:

All the models are fitted with strong points to secure a three point fixing seat belt for each of the front seats. Two eye bolts are fitted on the floor behind each front seat for the latched hooks on the belt. On the convertible models the third strong point is behind the rear side trim and on the wheel arch, the belt passing through a slot in the trim panel. On all other models the third point is through the veneered capping strip on the rear waist rail. The third fixing uses a chromium-headed bolt and then a corrugated washer and spacer under the belt tab.

If reel or inertia-type seat belts are to be fitted it is best to leave the work to a competent garage, thus ensuring the security and correct positioning of the reel.

Front seats:

All front seats are adjustable for leg reach, using the lever on the front of each seat to release the catch. The height of the front of the seats can be set to two positions by fitting them either in the **A** or in the **B** positions shown in **FIG 12:1**. The driver's seat is also adjustable for rake by turning the blocks **C** to one of the four different positions.

Remove the seats by sliding them fully to the rear of their adjustment and taking out the bolt that secures each of the slide rails to the floor. Slide the seat fully forward and similarly remove the two bolts that secure the rear of the rails to the floor. The seat and rails can then be lifted out of the car.

Rear seats:

On the convertible the rear seat is secured to the car by six rivets along the top (use a No. 30 drill to remove them) and two Acme screws on either side.

On saloons the rear seat is held in place by two sets of nuts, bolts and washers, which are accessible from the luggage compartment.

The details of the rear seat on estate car models are shown in **FIG 12:2**.

1 Remove the four screws securing the cushion apron to the floor heelboard. Take out the eight bolts 12 securing the brackets 13 to the floor. Disconnect the link arms 7 by removing the two Salter clips 10 and studs 11. The seat cushion assembly can then be lifted out of the car.

2 Release the locking bolts 6 and disconnect the squab bracket 5 from the closing board (shown in inset). Remove the four screws 9 securing the squab pivot brackets 8 to the car, and lift out the rear squab collecting the rubber seal.

The seat is replaced in the reverse order of removal. Leave the bolts 9 slack and tighten them when the squab is upright and the bolts 6 are locked in the wheel arch retainers. Lower the seat and adjust the brackets on the **B** post to align with the bolts 6.

12:3 The doors

The door details are shown in **FIG 12:3** and the attachments of the components in **FIG 12:4**. Whenever parts are removed they should be adequately greased over their moving surfaces before replacement. At monthly intervals inject a few drops of oil into key slots and the latch slot.

Door trim panel:

Remove the interior handles by pressing the escutcheons 40 firmly against the trim panel and then using a thin tool to press out the securing pins 41. The handles 42 and 43 together with their escutcheons can then be removed. Use a blunt screwdriver between the edges of the panel and the door to lever out the spring clips that retain the panel in place. Remove and store the springs 47.

Replace the panel in the reverse order of removal.

Door assembly:

Remove the rivet securing the check arm 32 to the **A** post. Support the door and remove the three bolts securing each hinge 31 and 38 to the **A** post and lift off the door.

Replace the door in the reverse order of removal. Some adjustment is allowed in the mounting holes so that the

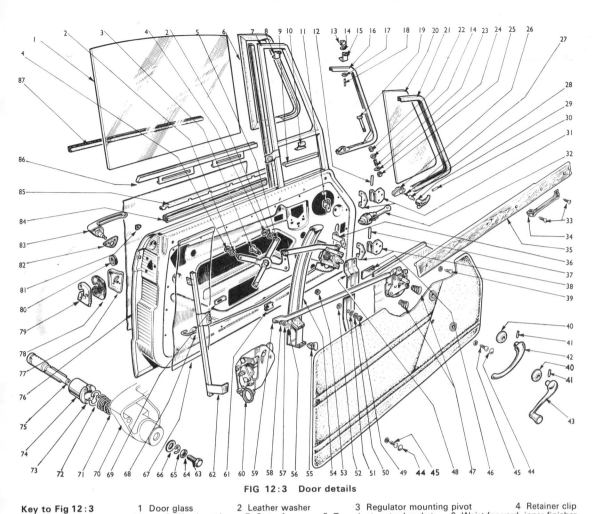

FIG 12:3 Door details

Key to Fig 12:3   1 Door glass   2 Leather washer   3 Regulator mounting pivot   4 Retainer clip
5 Window regulator assembly   6 Weatherstrip   7 Outer frame   8 Top pivot, outer bracket   9 Waist forward, inner finisher
10 Catch plate   11 Vent support bracket   12 Door hinge pin   13 Thick washer   14 Thin washer
15 Top pivot, inner bracket   16 Inner frame assembly   17 Thin washer   18 Semi-tubular rivet
19 Bottom pivot shaft assembly   20 Vent glass   21 Glazing strip   22 Spacing piece   23 Spring
24 Tab washer   25 Nut   26 Bracket assembly handle   27 Spring   28 Push button   29 Locking handle
30 Locking pin   31 Door hinge   32 Door check link assembly   33 Screw   34 Door pull handle
35 Capping veneer   36 Vent support assembly bracket   37 Door hinge pin   38 Door hinge   39 Capping veneer screw
40 Inside handle escutcheon   41 Handle fixing pin   42 Remote control handle   43 Window regulator handle
44 Door trim cap   45 Door trim screw   46 Felt pad   47 Regulator spring   48 Regulator pivot reinforcement
49 Nut   50 Lock washer   51 Plain washer   52 Plain washer (thin)   53 Special washer   54 Anti-drum stiffener assembly
55 Trim panel to door clip   56 Clip   57 Waved washer   58 Plain washer   59 Remote control mechanism
60 Cam lock assembly   61 Tie rod attachment clip   62 Glass assembly channel   63 Lock adjusting bolt
64 Lock adjusting nut   65 E-clip securing push button in handle   66 Rubber washer   67 Weather curtain
68 Bottom glass channel tie rod   69 Window regulator stop bracket   70 Door handle body, outside   71 Button return spring
72 E-clip, locking handle only   73 Locator plunger   74 Push button, locking handle only   75 Locking barrel (plunger),
locking handle only   76 Door assembly   77 Dove tail cam lock plate   78 Rubber sealing cam lock striker
79 Cam lock striker assembly   80 Rubber grommet   81 Small seating washer   82 Large seating washer
83 Outside door handle assembly   84 Door inner sealing strip, waist   85 Door outer sealing strip, waist
86 Window regulator channel assembly   87 Glazing channel strip

door can be positioned accurately. Slackening the bolts that secure the hinges to the door will allow the door to be positioned in line with the body.

Weatherstrip:

Both the inner weatherstrip 85 and outer weatherstrip 87 can be removed with the window glass in the fully down position by pressing the retaining clips downwards with a screwdriver.

To refit the weatherstrips, a tool as shown in **FIG 12:5** is required to pull the clips back onto the flanges. The inner weatherstrip can be refitted with the glass in the fully down position, but to refit the outer weatherstrip the stiffener 54 will have to be removed and the glass lowered as far as possible. The stiffener is held in place

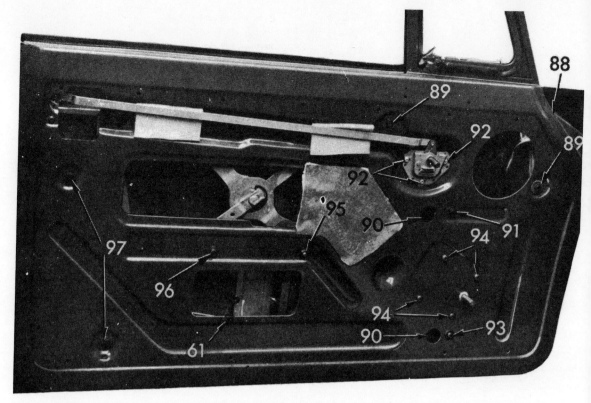

FIG 12:4 Door component attachments

by two cross-headed screws located below the bracket on the underside of the door.

Window regulator mechanism:

Remove the door trim panel, leaving the glass partly down. If need be loosely refit the winding handle 43 and position the glass so that the operating arms are accessible through the large aperture in the inner panel. Remove the clips 4 and the leather washer 2 and spring the regulator arms free from the glass channel 86. Lift the glass up to its highest position and hold it there using a soft wedge. Remove the nut 49, spring washer 50, pivot 3 and double coil spring washer 55 which secure the regulator arms to the inner panel. Remove the bolts 89 and cross-headed screws 90 (two of each, accessible through the circular holes in the inner panel). Remove the screw 88 and lift the quarter light ventilator assembly approximately 2 inch (50 mm). Take out the four cross-headed screws 94 and manoeuvre the unit out of the door.

Refit the assembly in the reverse order of removal but make sure that the screw 90 also holds the front end of the tension wire 68.

Door glass:

1 Remove the door trim and, with the handle loosely attached, wind the glass fully closed. Remove the rubber grommet 80 and unscrew the now exposed bolt and washer.

2 Remove the two bolts 97. Pull the lower end of the glass run channel 62 away from the tension wire 68, lower the channel into the bottom of the door and remove the channel through the lower aperture in the inner panel.

3 Wind down the glass until the regulator arms are accessible. Remove the clips 4 and leather washers 2 and spring the regulator arms out of the glass channel 86.

4 Remove the weatherstrips. Take out the two bolts 89 and two screws 90, accessible through the circular apertures in the inner panel. Remove the screw 88. The quarter light ventilator can now be removed from the door. If the window glass only is to be removed lift the quarter light 2 inches up, and manoeuvre the glass out of the door, taking care not to damage the polythene sheet of the water deflector.

Replace the glass and parts in the reverse order of removal. When fitting back the glass, fold the deflector flat against the inner side of the glass. If the deflector and glass channel have been removed from the glass, make sure that the 3.75 inch (95 mm) leg of the channel faces forwards and that the front end of the channel is .75 inch (19 mm) from the front corner of the glass.

Dismantling quarter light:

Free the tag on the washer 24 and remove the nut 25, washer 14 and spring 23. Remove the rivet 18 and spacer 13 from the upper pivot. Remove the vent from the frame

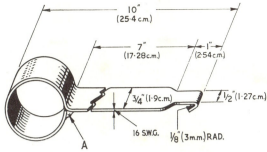

FIG 12:5 Tool for refitting weatherstrips to door

FIG 12:6 Fitting windscreen

by pushing the upper edge of the vent outwards. Use a suitable pin punch to remove the pin 30 and the handle 29 and push button 28 can then be removed.

Reassemble the parts in the reverse order of dismantling.

Remote control unit:

Remove the trim panel. Refit the interior handle and keep it in the door open position. Free the link arm from the lock by removing the spring clip 56 and waved washer 57. Take out the three screws 92 and remove the unit from the car.

Replace the unit in the reverse order of removal but leaving three screws 92 slack. Slide the remote control unit towards the lock until the lock lever comes in contact with its stop, and fully tighten the securing screws in this position.

Door lock:

Remove the door trim. Remove the glass run channel as detailed in operations 1 and 2 in 'Door glass'. Disconnect the remote control link arm from the lock. Take out the three countersunk screws securing the lock and dovetail to the end of the door, and the cross-headed screw securing the lock by the door aperture. Remove the lock through the larger rectangular aperture. Do not force the lock out. If required the lower edge of the aperture may be cut away slightly to allow the lock to be removed.

Refit the lock in the reverse order or removal.

Exterior door handle:

One of the bolts securing the handle is accessible just by the lock dovetail plate but the trim panel must be removed and the glass wound right up to gain access to the other bolt. When refitting the handle, the adjusting bolt 63 should be set so that there is a $\frac{1}{16}$ inch (1.6 mm) gap between it and the lock lever in the button free position.

12:4 The windscreen

Before removing or replacing the windscreen remove the windscreen wiper arms. The instructions for removing and refitting the windscreen apply equally to the back light and the quarter lights, though there is no moulding fitted to the quarter lights and that part of the instructions can be ignored.

To remove the glass, use a blunt screwdriver or wedge of wood to break the seal between the rubber weatherstrip and the flange on the body. Keep the tool firmly pressed under the lip of the weatherstrip to avoid damaging the paint as the tool is worked around the weatherstrip. Apply firm hand pressure at the lower corners of the glass from the inside of the car to push the glass out, and have an assistant outside the car to take the glass as it comes free.

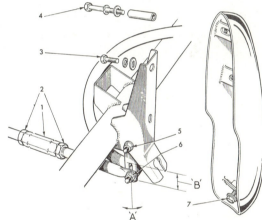

FIG 12:7 Herald 1200 bonnet adjustment points

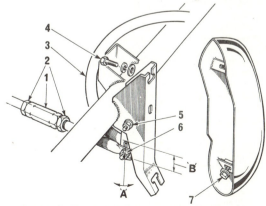

FIG 12:8 Herald 13/60 bonnet adjustment points

FIG 12:9 Bonnet height adjusters

FIG 12:10 Engine bay valance attachments

protruding freely from the top centre of the weatherstrip. Lubricate the aperture flange with soap solution and lay the glass and weatherstrip assembly into position on the outside of the car with the ends of the cord passed in through the aperture. While an assistant firmly presses the glass into place, pull out the cord as shown in **FIG 12:6** so that the lip of the weatherstrip is drawn over the flange. It may be necessary to use a rubber hammer to drive the windscreen fully into place.

4 With the cord completely removed, inject sealant between the weatherstrip and flange, wiping away surplus sealant with a cloth moistened in petrol or white spirits.

12:5 The bonnet

The adjustment points for the Herald 1200 are shown in **FIG 12:7** and the equivalent points on the Herald 13/60 are shown in **FIG 12:8**. The points for adjusting the height of the bonnet at the rear are shown in **FIG 12:9**.

Removal:

Disconnect the bonnet stay from the suspension unit. Take off the overriders by removing the bolts 3, 4 and 7. Support the bonnet and remove the bolts 5 and 6. The bonnet can then be lifted off the car. Before removing the bonnet disconnect the electrical cables at their snap connectors at the top centre of the grille. Label the cables if the colours have faded or there may be doubt on their correct connections.

Replace the bonnet in the reverse order of removal, adjusting it to fit as required.

Horizontal adjustment:

The gap between the rear of the bonnet and the scuttle should be an even $\frac{3}{16}$ inch (5 mm). Slacken the locknuts 2 and rotate the sleeve nut 1 as required.

Vertical adjustment:

With the bolts 5 and 6 just slack, raise or lower the bonnet at the front until the rear edge of the bonnet is parallel to the edge of the door. Fully tighten the bolts when the bonnet is in the correct position.

Height:

Slacken the locknut 1 and raise or lower the rubber buffer until the rear of the bonnet is at the correct height. Tighten the locknut in this position and adjust the position of the catch plate 3 to match.

The attachment points of the engine bay valances are shown in **FIG 12:10**.

12:6 The tail gate (estate cars only)

The details of the tail gate fitted to estate car models are shown in **FIG 12:11**.

Removal:

1 Remove the number plate and trim panel. Disconnect the cables from the number plate illumination lamp and withdraw the cables from the tail gate.

If the glass has been broken it is essential to remove all the particles of glass. For the windscreen the demister ducts should be removed and cleaned out, otherwise particles of glass may be blown out when the heater is operated. If glass has broken it is most advisable to obtain a new weatherstrip with the replacement glass, as the old weatherstrip is sealed to both the glass and aperture and it will most likely be damaged on removal.

1 Refit the weatherstrip around the glass and inject sealant between the weatherstrip and the glass. If applicable, refit the mouldings by pressing them back into their slot in the weatherstrip. Slide the coverplates into place so that they cover the junctions of the two mouldings. Remove surplus sealant using a piece of cloth dampened in petrol or white spirits, but do not use so much solvent that it seeps into the join.

2 Remove old sealant from around the glass aperture, again using petrol or white spirits. Check that the flange is true. Dress out any dents using a hammer and block. Any protrusions should be filed smooth with the rest of the flange, otherwise they may cause the new glass to fracture after fitting.

3 Insert a long length of thick cord all the way around the channel in the weatherstrip, leaving the ends

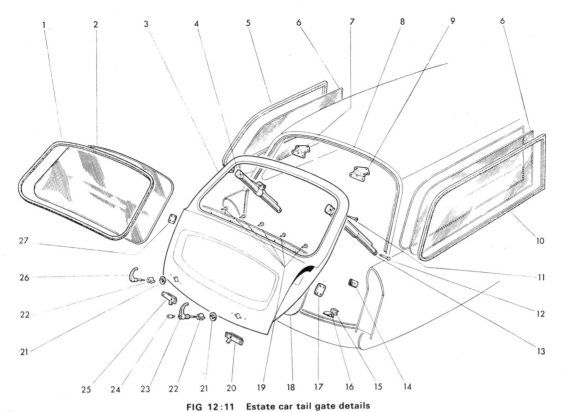

FIG 12:11 Estate car tail gate details

Key to Fig 12:11 1 Weatherstrip 2 Rear door glass 3 Rear door assembly 4 Lefthand spring stay assembly
5 Lefthand weatherstrip 6 Quarterlight glass 7 Hinge 8 Rear door sealing rubber 9 Hinge
10 Righthand weatherstrip 11 Upper pivot bolt 12 Lower pivot bolt 13 Righthand spring stay assembly
14 Rubber dovetail block 15 Catch plate 16 Protection plate 17 Rubbing plate dovetail 18 Rear door trim pad
19 Trim buttons 20 Righthand budget lock 21 Seating washer 22 Door handle escutcheon 23 Righthand locking
door handle 24 Locking barrel 25 Lefthand budget lock 26 Non-locking door handle 27 Rubbing plate dovetail

2 Taking great care, remove the upper pivot bolts 11 from the support stays 13. The righthand stay is in three parts which will fly apart when released.

3 Have an assistant support the weight of the tail gate in the open position, and remove the three screws securing each hinge 7 and 9. The tail gate can then be removed.

The locks can be removed after taking off the nuts securing the handles and then withdrawing the handles.

Refit the tail gate in the reverse order of removal.

12:7 Facia components

The components of the Herald 1200 facia are shown in **FIG 12:12** and the parts for the Herald 13/60 are shown in **FIGS 12:13** and **12:14**.

Removing the 1200 facia:

Refer to **FIG 12:12**.

1 Disconnect the battery. Release the clips securing the wiring loom to the bulkhead and disconnect all the wires from the back of the instrument panel, unplugging warning lights and panel lights as required. Unscrew the speedometer drive cable from the back of the instrument. Disconnect the earth cable from the back of the speedometer.

2 Disconnect the demister hoses from the ducts. Disconnect the plastic pipes from the windscreen washer pump. Remove the steering column assembly as detailed in **Chapter 9, Section 9:6**. Disconnect the heater controls and the choke cable.

3 Free the bracket 1 from the bulkhead by taking out the two securing screws. Remove the seven screws securing the top of the facia to the lower windscreen rail, and, if fitted, the screw securing the ashtray bracket 11 to the facia support bracket.

4 Take out the four bolts 21 (two a side) securing the reinforcement rail 16 to the dash sides and carefully withdraw the assembly, making sure that there are no connections left.

Replace the assembly in the reverse order of removal and carry out a careful road test to ensure that all the instruments and controls operate correctly.

Removing 13/60 facia:

1 Carry out the operations 1 and 2 as detailed in removing the 1200 facia.

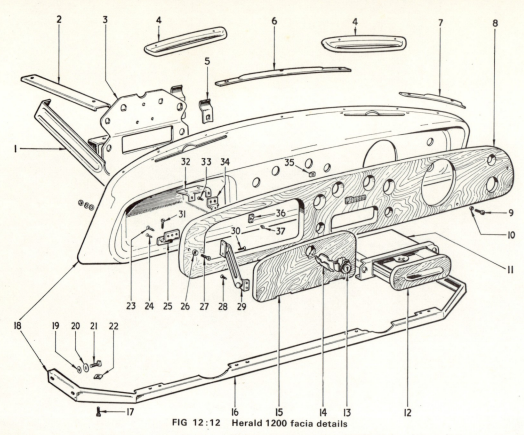

FIG 12:12 Herald 1200 facia details

Key to Fig 12:12   1 Bracket   2 Bracket*   3 Reinforcement plate*   4 Cover   5 Bracket*   6 Finisher
7 Finisher   8 Veneered panel   9 Screw   10 Cup washer   11 Bracket   12 Ash tray   13 Lock
14 Finger pull   15 Lid   16 Reinforcement rail   17 Screw   18 Facia panel assembly   19 Washer
20 Washer   21 Bolt   22 Spirefix   23 Screw   24 Screw   25 Hinge   26 Cup washer   27 Screw
28 Screw   29 Check link   30 Screw   31 Screw   32 Bracket   33 Screw   34 Striker   35 Spirefix*
36 Buffer bracket   37 Buffer rubber
Not fitted to models covered by this manual

2 Refer to **FIGS 12:13** and **12:14**. Remove the two screws 44 securing the support 45 to the bulkhead and also remove the screw 51 securing the choke control bracket 54 to the bulkhead.

3 Remove the seven screws 32 securing the facia top and finishers to the windscreen lower rail. Take out the four screws (two a side) securing the facia rail to the dash sides. Carefully withdraw the facia assembly, disconnecting any cables or connections which were not accessible before.

Replace the facia in the reverse order of removal and carry out a road test to check the correct operation of the controls and instruments. The connections behind the facia for both the 13/60 and 1200 models are shown in **Technical Data**.

Instruments and switches:

The instruments are secured to the facia by bridge pieces and knurled nuts, accessible from behind the instrument panel. Switches and controls are secured by chromium-plated threaded bezels which are accessible from the front of the panel. Some knobs which are too large to pass through the panel are held to the spindle by a spring loaded plunger passing into a hole in the side of the knob. Use a thin piece of rod to press in the plunger until the knob can be pulled off.

Veneer panel:

This can be removed after the facia assembly has been taken out of the car and all the instruments and switches have been removed.

12:8 The heater

The heater details are shown in **FIG 12:15**. The actual water hose arrangement for the Herald 1200 model is shown in **FIG 12:16** and that for the 13/60 is shown in **FIG 12:17**. Some models may be fitted with Delaney Gallay heaters in which case the water valve and blower motor mountings are as shown in **FIG 12:18**.

Removing heater:

1 Disconnect the battery and drain the cooling system. Remove the rubber water hoses. Take out the screw 10. Release the heater control cable 5 from the water valve 26, and disconnect the electrical cables from the blower motor 12.

2 Working inside the car, remove the dash millboard and disconnect the distribution control cable 3 from

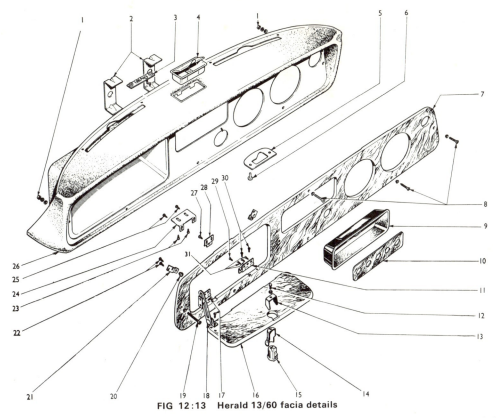

FIG 12:13 Herald 13/60 facia details

Key to Fig 12:13 1 Panel attachment nut 2 Switch panel, saddle bracket 3 Light switch facia 4 Ash tray
5 Light switch coverplate 6 Light switch nylon stud 7 Veneered panel 8 Screw panel attachment 9 Switch panel
10 Finisher plate 11 Glove box hinge 12 Lock clamp screw 13 Lock clamp 14 Finger pull 15 Glove box lock
16 Glove box lid 17 Link attachment screw 18 Check link 19 Facia attachment screw 20 Rubber buffer
21 Buffer bracket 22 Bracket attachment screw 23 Tie bracket screw 24 Tie bracket 25 Tie bracket screw
26 Trimmed facia 27 Striker bracket screw 28 Striker bracket 29 Hinge to lid screw 30 Hinge to panel screw
31 Hinge to lid screw

the lever on the distribution box 22. Remove the two sets of nuts and washers 21.

3 Lift the heater unit from the bulkhead, if necessary disconnecting the choke cable from the carburetter so as to make the task easier.

Refit the heater unit in the reverse order of removal. Before refitting the unit apply a liberal coating of Seelastik SR.51 to the contact faces of the rubber seals 7 and 19. Adjust the heater control cables as described later.

Air distribution box:

The distribution box can be removed after disconnecting the control cable 3, pulling off the demister hoses 6 and removing the nuts and washers 21. The demister ducts 2 can be removed, after pulling off the hoses 6, by taking out the screws at the extremities of the demister vent finisher on top of the facia.

Air distribution:

The control knob 1 sets the distribution of the air between the car and demisting the windscreen. With the knob fully pressed in all the air is sent into the car, and with the knob fully out all the air is sent to the demister ducts. Intermediate positions of the knob produce a varied distribution between the car and windscreen.

The cable 3 outer casing is secured to the distribution box casing by a clip and bolt. The inner cable is secured to a lever on the flap by a trunnion and securing bolt. Slacken both bolts to free the cable from the distribution box.

When refitting the cable 3, slide it into place with the securing bolts loose. Push the control knob fully in and move the flap lever fully forwards. Tighten the securing bolts in this position.

Temperature control:

The control knob 4 moves a lever on the water valve 26 through the cable 5. When the valve is in the shut position no hot water from the engine passes through the heater and the air passing through the heater is not warmed but comes out cold. As the control knob is pulled out, the lever on the water valve moves gradually, opening the valve and allowing hot water from the engine to pass through the heater. Some degree of temperature control is obtainable by allowing more or less hot water to flow through the heater, using intermediate positions of the control knob.

The outer casing of the cable 5 is secured to the water valve by a clip and bolt while the inner cable is secured

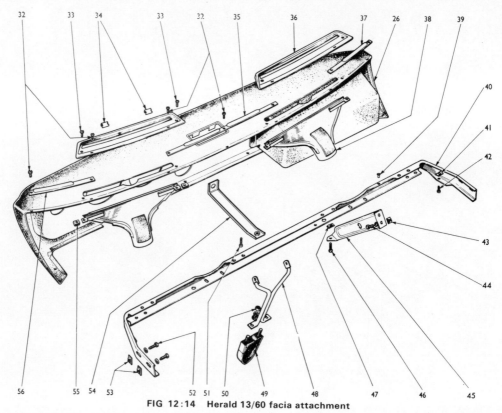

FIG 12:14 Herald 13/60 facia attachment

Key to Fig 12:14 32 Facia attachment screw 33 Demister finisher attachment screw 34 Demister finisher attachment clips 35 Centre top edge finisher 36 Demister vent finisher 37 Lefthand top edge finisher 38 Demister vent 39 Pop rivet 40 Facia rail 41 Fix nut 42 Facia to rail screw 43 Fix nut 44 Bracket to bulkhead screw 45 Support bracket 46 Bracket to facia screw 47 Fix nut 48 Steering column support bracket 49 Steering column clamp 50 Nut 51 Choke bracket attachment screw 52 Facia rail to dash side bolts 53 Fix nuts 54 Choke support bracket 55 Fix nuts 56 Righthand top edge finisher

to the lever by a trunnion and bolt. Both types of water valve should be set with their levers moved fully clockwise and the control knob in the fully in position.

On the Delaney Gallay type of water valve, shown in **FIG 12:18**, the shut-off adjusting screw 4 is set by the manufacturers. It may be reset by slackening the bolts securing the cable, turning the lever 3 fully clockwise, and turning the adjusting screw 4 down onto its stop. Resecure the cable with the control knob fully in.

If the water valve on either make of heater fails, then it must be renewed, as they are both sealed assemblies and cannot be rectified.

Blower:

A blower, controlled by an electrical switch, is fitted to augment the airflow through the heater when the car is stationary or travelling slowly. The motor is secured to the heater unit as shown in **FIG 12:15** or **FIG 12:18**, depending on make. The impeller on the Smiths system is secured to the motor spindle by a contracting collet and nut, where slackening the nut will ease the collet. On the Delaney Gallay motor the impeller is secured to the spindle by a clip.

Neither make of motor can be serviced and if they are defective then they must be renewed.

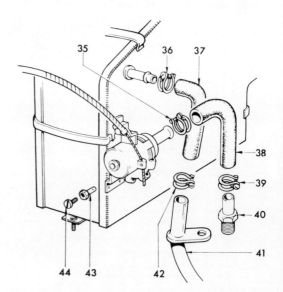

FIG 12:16 Heater water hoses for Herald 1200 models

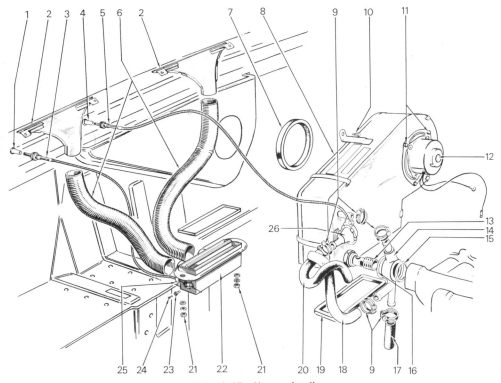

FIG 12:15 Heater details

Key to Figs 12:15, 12:16 and 12:17   1 Control knob   2 Demister duct   3 Air distribution control cable
4 Control knob   5 Temperature control cable   6 Demister hoses   7 Sealing rubber   8 Heater unit   9 Hose clips
10 Spire screw   11 Blower motor attachment screws   12 Heater blower   13 Banjo bolt   14 Adaptor   15 Washer
16 Washer   17 Bottom hose   18 Adaptor/heater unit hose   19 Seal   20 Adaptor/water valve hose   21 Nuts
22 Air distribution box   23 Trunnion   24 Securing bolt   25 Securing bracket   26 Water valve   27 Hose clip
28 Water hose   29 Hose clip   30 Water pipe   31 Adaptor   32 Hose clip   33 Water hose   34 Hose clip
35 Hose clip   36 Hose clip   37 Water hose   38 Water hose   39 Hose clip   40 Adaptor   41 Water pipe
42 Hose clip   43 Water valve trunnion   44 Trunnion screw   45 Hose clip   46 Water hose   47 Water hose
48 Water pipe manifold   49 Hose clip   50 Hose clip   51 Hose clip

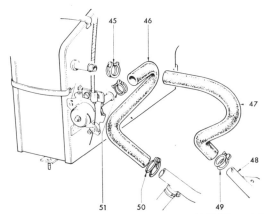

FIG 12:17 Heater water hoses for Herald 13/60 models

FIG 12:18 Delaney Gallay heater unit

THA/2

NOTES

APPENDIX

TECHNICAL DATA
    Engine   Fuel system   Ignition system   Cooling system
    Clutch   Gearbox   Rear axle and rear suspension
    Front suspension and steering   Brakes   Electrical
    Weights and dimensions   Capacities   Wheels and tyres
    Torque wrench settings

SPECIAL TOOLS

WIRING DIAGRAMS
    FIG 13:1   Herald 1200 wiring diagram
    FIG 13:2   Herald 1200 facia connections
    FIG 13:3   Herald 13/60 wiring diagram
    FIG 13:4   Herald 13/60 facia connections

RUNNING-IN

STANDARD MEASURE AND METRIC EQUIVALENTS

FRACTIONAL AND METRIC EQUIVALENTS

HINTS ON MAINTENANCE AND OVERHAUL

GLOSSARY OF TERMS

INDEX

NOTES

TECHNICAL DATA

Dimensions are given in inches; figures in brackets are in millimetres

ENGINE

Type	4 cylinder, OHV, water cooled
Compression ratio:	
1200 models:*	
GD–HE	8.5:1
GA–LE	6.8:1
13/60 models:*	
GE–HE	8.5:1
GE–LE	7.5:1
*Engine serial numbers given	
Cubic capacity:	
1200	1147 cc (70 cu in)
13/60	1296 cc (79.2 cu in)
Nominal bore:	
1200	2.728 (69.3)
13/60	2.900 (73.7)
Stroke	2.992 (76.0)
Firing order	1–3–4–2
Crankshaft:	
End float	.004 to .008 (.102 to .203)
Thrust washers:	
Standard	.091 to .093 (2.31 to 2.36)
Oversize	.096 to .098 (2.44 to 2.49)
Main journal diameter	2.0005 to 2.001 (50.81 to 50.83)
Undersize grinding limit	—.040 (—1.02)
Undersize bearings	—.010, —.020, —.030, —.040 (—.254, —.508, —.762, —1.02)
Crankpin diameter	1.6250 to 1.6255 (41.27 to 41.28)
Undersize grinding limit	—.030 (—.762)
Undersize bearings	—.010, —.020, —.030 (—.254, —.508, —.762)
Pistons:	
Oversizes available	+.010, +.020, +.030
Piston and bore grades:	

Herald 1200:

Grade	F inch	mm	G inch	mm	H inch	mm	Make
Cylinder bore	2.7283 / 2.7280	69.3 / 69.29	2.7287 / 2.7284	69.31 / 69.30	2.7291 / 2.7288	69.32 / 69.31	—
Piston top dia.	2.7254 / 2.7250	69.22 / 69.21	2.7258 / 2.7254	69.235 / 69.22	2.7262 / 2.7258	69.24 / 69.23	Automotive Engineering Co. Ltd.
Piston bottom dia.	2.7272 / 2.7268	69.27 / 69.26	2.7276 / 2.7272	69.28 / 69.27	2.7280 / 2.7276	69.3 / 69.28	
Piston top dia.	2.7120 / 2.7090	68.88 / 68.81	2.7120 / 2.7090	68.88 / 68.81	2.7120 / 2.7090	68.88 / 68.81	British Piston Ring Co. Ltd.
Piston bottom dia.	2.7271 / 2.7268	69.22 / 69.26	2.7275 / 2.7272	69.31 / 69.29	2.7279 / 2.7276	69.28 / 69.31	
Piston top dia.	2.7245 / 2.7242	69.30 / 69.20	2.7249 / 2.7246	69.21 / 69.27	2.7253 / 2.7250	69.22 / 69.21	Wellworthy
Piston bottom dia.	2.7271 / 2.7268	69.36 / 69.26	2.7275 / 2.7272	69.278 / 69.27	2.7279 / 2.7276	69.288 / 69.281	

Herald 13/60:

Cylinder bore ..	2.900	73.66	2.9005	73.67	—	—	—
	2.899	73.64	2.9001	73.66	—	—	
Piston top dia...	2.880	73.15	2.880	73.15	—	—	Brico Co. Ltd.
	2.875	73.03	2.875	73.03	—	—	
Piston bottom dia.	2.8981	73.61	2.8987	73.62	—	—	
	2.8976	73.59	2.8982	73.617	—	—	
Piston top dia...	2.8799	73.15	2.8799	73.15	—	—	Hepworth
	2.8752	73.03	2.8752	73.03	—	—	Co. Ltd.
Piston bottom dia.	2.8981	73.61	2.8987	63.627	—	—	
	2.8976	73.59	2.8983	73.617	—	—	

Piston rings:
- Oversizes available .. .. +.010, +.020, +.030
- Top ring .. .. Chromium plated compression ring
- Middle ring .. .. Taper-faced compression ring
- Bottom ring .. .. Oil control ring
- Ring gaps (fitted):
  - 1200 .. .. .008 to .013 (.20 to .33)
  - 1300 .. .. .012 to .022 (.30 to .85)
- 1200 ring width:
  - Compression .. .. .. .077 to .078 (1.97 to 1.99)
  - Oil control .. .. .. .1540 to .1560 (3.90 to 3.96)
- 13/60 ring widths:
  - Compression .. .. .. .0625 to .0620 (1.587 to 1.575)
  - Oil control .. .. .. .1540 to .1560 (3.90 to 3.96)

Piston ring grooves:
- 1200 compression ring .. .. .. .0807 to .0797
- 1200 oil control ring .. .. .. .158 to .157 (4.01 to 3.99)
- 13/60 compression ring .. .. .. .0650 to .0640 (1.65 to 1.625)
- 13/60 oil control ring .. .. .. .1588 to .1578 (4.01 to 3.99)

Camshaft:
- Bearings .. .. Renewable steel-backed
- Journal diameter .. .. .. 1.9654 to 1.9649 (49.92 to 49.91)
- Bore in block .. .. .. 1.9695 to 1.9680 (50.025 to 49.98)

Flywheel:
- Maximum run-out .. .. .. .002 (.051) at 3 inch (76.2 mm) radius
- Maximum eccentricity .. .. .. .004 (.10) when mounted on crankshaft

Valves:
- Head diameter:
  - All inlet valves .. .. 1.308 to 1.304 (33.22 to 33.12)
  - 1200 exhaust valve .. .. .. 1.182 to 1.148 (29.26 to 29.16)
  - 13/60 exhaust valve .. .. .. 1.172 to 1.168 (29.76 to 29.66)
- Stem diameter:
  - 1200 inlet valve .. .. .. .311 to .310 (7.89 to 7.87)
  - 1200 exhaust valve .. .. .. .309 to .308 (7.85 to 7.82)
  - 13/60 inlet valve .. .. .. .3112 to .310 (7.90 to 7.87)
  - 13/60 exhaust valve .. .. .. .310 to .3105 (7.874 to 7.887)

Valve guides:
- Length:
  - 1200 .. .. 2.25 (57.15)
  - 13/60 .. .. 2.0625 (52.387)
- Bore .. .. .313 to .312 (7.95 to 7.92)
- Outside diameter .. .. .. .502 to .501 (12.75 to 12.72)
- Protrusion above cylinder head top face .. .. .749 to .751 (19.025 to 19.075)

Valve springs:
- Fitted length 1.36 (34.54)
- Fitted load .. .. 27 to 30 lb (12.25 to 13.61 kg)
- Number of coils .. .. $7\frac{1}{4}$

Valve timing:
- Inlet valve opens .. .. 18 deg BTDC
- Inlet valve closes .. .. 58 deg ABDC
- Exhaust valve opens .. .. 58 deg BBDC
- Exhaust valve closes .. .. 18 deg ATDC

Cam followers:
- Diameter .. .. .800 to .7996 (20.32 to 20.294)
- Bore in block .. .. .8002 to .8009 (20.354 to 20.343)

Rocker clearance:
- Valve timing only .. .. .040 (1.0)
- Standard .. .. .010 (.25) cold

Lubrication:
- Oil filter .. .. Renewable fullflow (sealed unit)
- Oil pressure .. .. 40 to 60 lb/sq in (2.8 to 4.2 kg/sq cm) at 2000 rev/min
- Oil pump .. .. Hobourn Eaton double eccentric rotor
  - Clearance between rotors .. .. .010 (.254) maximum
  - Clearance between outer rotor and body .. .0075 (.19) maximum
  - Rotor end float .. .. Lap if greater than .004 (.10) and oil pressure is affected
- Relief valve spring:
  - Free length 1.54 (39.11)
  - Fitted length 1.25 (31.75)
  - Load at fitted length .. .. .. 14.5 lb (6.58 kg)

Performance data:
- 1200 maximum bhp:
  - High compression .. .. 48 bhp at 5200 rev/min
  - Low compression .. .. 43 bhp at 4750 rev/min
- 13/60 maximum bhp:
  - High compression .. .. 61 bhp at 5000 rev/min
  - Low compression .. .. 54 bhp at 5200 rev/min
- 1200 maximum torque:
  - High compression .. .. 740 lb in (8.517 kg m) at 2500 rev/min
  - Low compression .. .. 675 lb in (7.763 kg m) at 2250 rev/min
- 13/60 maximum torque:
  - High compression .. .. 875 lb in (10.32 kg m) at 3000 rev/min
  - Low compression .. .. 800 lb in (8.4 kg m) at 3000 rev/min

FUEL SYSTEM

Fuel pump:
- Type .. .. AC mechanically driven
- Pressure .. .. 1.5 to 2.5 lb/sq in (.1 to .18 kg/sq cm)

Carburetter:
- Type:
  - 1200 .. .. Single Solex B.30 PSEI
  - 13/60 .. .. Single sidedraught Stromberg 150 CD

Air filter .. .. AC pancake-type with replaceable element

Idling speed:
- 1200 .. .. 500 rev/min
- 13/60 .. .. 650 rev/min

IGNITION SYSTEM

Firing order	1–3–4–2
Sparking plugs:	
Type:	
Herald 1200	Champion L87Y
Herald 13/60	Champion N-9Y (or Lodge HNY)
Gap	.025 (.64)
Ignition timing:	
1200	15 deg BTDC
1200 (low compression)	9 deg BTDC
13/60	9 deg BTDC
Ignition coil:	
Type	Lucas HA.125195 (fluid filled)
Primary resistance	3.1 to 3.5 ohms at 20°C
Distributor:	
Type	Lucas 25D4
Lucas part No.:	
1200	41230
13/60	41127
Stanpart No.:	
1200	215046
13/60	212292
Rotation	Clockwise—viewed on rotor
Contact gap	.014 to .016 (.36 to .41)
Contact spring tension:	
1200	22 to 26 oz
13/60	17 to 21 oz
Capacitor	.18 to .23 mfd

COOLING SYSTEM

Pressure	7 lb/sq in (.49 kg/sq cm) or 13 lb/sq in after GA.240782E
Antifreeze	Must meet BSI.3151 or 3152 spec.

CLUTCH

Type	Borg and Beck 6½ in (16.51 cm) diaphragm spring operated
Adjustment	Self-adjusting
Repair	By replacement, must not be dismantled
Fluid	Castrol Girling Crimson Clutch and Brake Fluid to specification SAE.70.R3

GEARBOX

Type .. Four forward speeds, one reverse, synchromesh engagement on top three speeds only

Gear ratios:

Gear	Gearbox	Overall
Top	1.00	4.11
Third	1.40	5.74
Second	2.16	8.88
First and reverse	3.75	15.42

REAR AXLE AND REAR SUSPENSION

Rear axle:
  Type .. .. IRS using hypoid bevel gears
  Ratio 4.11:1
Camber angle .. .. 2 deg negative*
Toe-in .. .. 0 to $\frac{1}{16}$ (0 to 1.6)*
Road springs:
  Estate cars:
    Part No. 304860
    Number of blades 7
    Blade thickness .. .. .31 (7.87)
    Load .. .. 1735 lb (817.7 kg)
    Rate .. .. 510 lb/in (9106 kg/m)
    Laden camber .. .. 1.63 $\pm$.13 negative (41.4 $\pm$3.3)
  Saloons, etc.:
    Part No. 305945
    Number of blades 11
    Blade thickness .. .. .2188 (5.65)
    Load .. .. 1420 lb (66.47 kg)
    Rate .. .. 270 lb/in (4821 kg/m)
    Laden camber .. .. 1.94 $\pm$.13 negative (49.28 $\pm$3.3)
  Heavy duty:
    Part No. 305288
    Number of blades 12
    Blade thickness .. .. .2188 (5.56)
    Load .. .. 1420 lb (644.68 kg)
    Rate .. .. 295 lb/in (5267 kg/m)
    Laden camber .. .. 1.54 $\pm$.13 negative (39.12 $\pm$3.3)
  Saloon and Estate, competition:
    Part No. 305544
    Number of blades 7
    Blade thickness .. .. .31 (7.87)
    Load .. .. 1735 lb (817.7 kg)
    Rate .. .. 510 lb/in (9106 kg/m)
    Laden camber .. .. 2.25 $\pm$.13 (57.2 $\pm$3.3) negative
  Saloon and convertible, competition:
    Part No. 305543
    Number of blades 12
    Blade thickness .. .. .2188 (5.56)
    Load .. .. 1420 lb (644.68 kg)
    Rate .. .. 295 lb/in (5267 kg/m)
    Laden camber .. .. 2.5 $\pm$.13 (63.5 $\pm$3.3) negative
Dampers:
  Type .. .. Sealed, telescopic
  Part number:
    Saloon and convertible 123100
    Estate and heavy duty 132111
    Competition 209022

*Static laden with 150 lb (68 kg) weights in each seat

FRONT SUSPENSION AND STEERING

Camber angle .. .. 2 deg positive*
Castor angle .. .. 4 deg positive*
Toe-in .. .. 0 to $\frac{1}{16}$ (0 to 1.6)*
Steering axis inclination .. .. .. $6\frac{3}{4}$ deg

Steering:
   Type .. .. Rack and pinion, with telescopic column
   Lock .. .. Controlled by dimensions of steering unit. Wheels are at equal lock at 20 deg
      Shims for pinion .. .. .004 (.102) and .010 (.254) thick
      Shims for inner ball joints .. .. .002 (.05) and .010 (.254) thick

Springs and damper part numbers:

	Damper	Damper and spring
Saloon and convertible	206262	208176
Estate	208022	208178
Heavy duty	208022	209317
All models	134635	209679
Competition	209021	209030

Road springs:
   Estate and heavy duty:
      Part No. 209033
      Free length 10.97 (278.6)
      Fitted length .. .. 8.18 $\pm$ .09 (207 8 $\pm$ 2.29)
      Fitted load .. .. 790 lb (358.7 kg)
      Rate .. .. 284 lb/in (5071 kg/m)
      Identification .. .. Yellow
   Standard: Interchangeable
      Part No. 208056
      Free length 12.08 (306.8)   12.11 (307.6)
      Fitted length .. .. 8.18 $\pm$ .09 (207.8 $\pm$ 2.29)
      Fitted load .. .. 790 lb (358.7 kg)
      Rate .. .. 203 lb/in (3624 kg/m)
                                                                             201 lb/in (3590 kg/m)
      Identification .. .. White
   Competition:
      Part No. 209013
      Free length 10.47 (282)
      Fitted length .. .. 7.68 $\pm$ .09
      Fitted load .. .. 790 lb (358.7 kg)
      Rate .. .. 284 lb/in (5071 kg/m)
      Identification .. .. Black

Note. Packings, Part No. 125441, are fitted between upper spring plate and suspension bracket on both sides when 'heavy duty' springs are fitted. One packing only is fitted to the lefthand side only on lefthand drive models with standard springs.

*Static laden

BRAKES

Type .. .. Girling hydraulic system, front disc brakes and drum rear brakes
Fluid .. .. Castrol Girling Crimson Clutch and Brake Fluid to specification SAE.70.R3

Front disc brakes:
   Type .. .. 9 inch disc, 14LF caliper
   Adjustment .. .. Self-adjusting
   Swept area .. .. 205 sq inch
   Friction pad material .. .. .. Don 212
   Maximum disc run-out .. .. .. .002 (.0508)

Rear drum brakes:
   Type .. .. 7 x 1$\frac{1}{4}$ inch drum brakes
   Adjustment .. .. One adjustment point per brake
   Swept area .. .. 118 sq inch
   Friction lining material .. .. .. Don 242

ELECTRICAL

The electrical system is negatively earthed

Battery:
  Type:
    Home BT.7A
    Export .. .. BTZ.7A (supplied dry charged)
  Capacity:
    10 hour rate .. .. 38 ampere hours
    20 hour rate .. .. 43 ampere hours
  Plates per cell 7
  Electrolyte per cell .. .. 1 Imp pint (1.2 US pints) 570 cc
  Recharging current .. .. 5 amps, until battery gasses freely

Generator:
  Type .. .. Lucas C40.1, two brush, two pole
  Rotation .. .. Clockwise—viewed from front
  Field resistance .. .. 6 ohms approximately
  Brush tension .. .. 22 to 25 oz (.62 to .71 kg)
  Minimum brush length .. .. .. $\frac{9}{32}$ (7.0)
  Maximum output at 13.5 volts .. .. 22 amps on a load of .61 ohms at 2050 to 2250 rev/min

Generator control box:
  Type .. .. Lucas RB.106/2
  Cut-in voltage .. .. 12.7 to 13.3
  Drop-off voltage .. .. 9.3 to 11.2
  Open circuit settings .. .. ..

Ambient temperature	Voltage
10°C (50°F)	16.1 to 16.7
20°C (68°F)	16.0 to 16.6
30°C (86°F)	15.9 to 16.5
40°C (104°F)	15.8 to 16.4

  Current regulator setting .. .. 22 $\pm 1\frac{1}{2}$ amps

Starter motor:
  Type .. .. Lucas M.35G, four pole, four brush series wound
  Brush tension .. .. 32 to 40 ozs (.9 to 1.1 kg)
  Minimum brush length .. .. .. $\frac{5}{16}$ (8.0)

Performance data:

Armature speed rev/min	Torque lb ft	kg m	Current amps	Supply volts
Locked	10	1.38	420 to 440	7.9 to 7.3
1000	5.4	.75	250 to 270	9.3 to 8.9
7400 to 8500	No load		45	12

Windscreen wiper:
  Type .. .. Lucas DR.3A, shunt wound, single speed
  Light running speed .. .. .. 44 to 48 cycles per minute
  Light running current .. .. .. 2.7 to 3.4 amps
  Stall current .. .. 13 to 15 amps
  Field winding resistance .. .. 8.0 to 9.5 ohms at 20°C
  Brush tension .. .. 125 to 140 grammes
  Armature end float .. .. .. .008 to .012
  Maximum force to move rack cable .. 6 lb (2.7 kg)

Starter solenoid:
  Type .. .. Lucas 4.ST
  Winding resistance .. .. .. 2.3 to 2.8 ohms

Flasher unit FL5

Horns 9H

WEIGHTS AND DIMENSIONS

		1200	13/60
Weight:			
Dry:			
Saloon	.. ..	$15\frac{3}{4}$ cwt (800 kg)	16 cwt (815 kg)
Convertible	.. ..	$14\frac{7}{8}$ cwt (725 kg)	$15\frac{1}{2}$ cwt (785 kg)
Estate	.. ..	$16\frac{1}{8}$ cwt (820 kg)	17 cwt (865 kg)
Complete:			
Saloon	.. ..	16 cwt (810 kg)	$16\frac{3}{4}$ cwt (850 kg)
Convertible	.. ..	$16\frac{1}{4}$ cwt (790 kg)	$16\frac{5}{8}$ cwt (826 kg)
Estate	.. ..	$16\frac{7}{8}$ cwt (860 kg)	$17\frac{3}{4}$ cwt (900 kg)
Gross:			
Saloon	.. ..	23 cwt (1169 kg)	23 cwt (1169 kg)
Convertible	.. ..	23 cwt (1169 kg)	23 cwt (1169 kg)
Estate	.. ..	24 cwt (1229 kg)	24 cwt (1229 kg)

Overall length:
  All models .. .. 12 ft 9 inch (3.886 metres) except 1200 convertible which is 12 ft $8\frac{1}{2}$ inch (3.270 metres)

Overall width .. .. 5 ft (152.4 cm) all models
Overall height .. .. 4 ft 4 inch (132.0 cm) all models
  Height with hood down (convertibles only) .. 4 ft $\frac{1}{2}$ inch (123.19 cm)

CAPACITIES

	Imperial	*US*	*Metric*
Engine:			
From dry	8 pints	9.6 pints	4.6 litres
Drain and refill	7 pints	8.4 pints	4.0 litres
Gearbox	1.5 pints	1.8 pints	.85 litres
Rear axle	1 pint	1.2 pints	.57 litres
Cooling system (complete) ..	8.5 pints	10.2 pints	4.8 litres
Fuel tank:			
Standard	6.5 gall.	7.3 gall.	32 litres
Estate	9 gall.	10.8 gall.	41 litres

WHEELS AND TYRES

Do not intermix radial and crossply tyres as the mixture will affect the handling of the car to a dangerous degree

Rim section:
  All models except estate .. .. $3\frac{1}{2}$D
  Estate models .. .. $4\frac{1}{2}$J

Tyre size:
  All models except estate .. .. 5.20 x 13
  Estate models .. .. 5.60 x 13

Tyre pressures:
Figures are lb/sq in; figures in brackets are kg/sq cm.

	Saloon and convertible		Estate	
	Front	*Rear*	*Front*	*Rear*
2 up	21 (1.48)	24 (1.7)	21 (1.48)	25 (1.75)
4 up	21 (1.48)	28 (1.97)	21 (1.48)	30 (2.1)

The tyre pressures given are only recommendations. For competition high-speed work or different makes of tyres, the actual tyre makers' figures should always be used in preference to those given here.

TORQUE WRENCH SETTINGS

	lb ft	kg m
Engine:		
Chain wheel attachment	24 to 26	3.318 to 3.595
Clutch attachment	18 to 20	2.489 to 2.765
Connecting rod bolts	38 to 42	5.254 to 5.807
Cylinder head	42 to 46	5.807 to 6.36
Engine mounting to frame brackets	18 to 20	2.489 to 2.765
Flywheel mounting	42 to 46	5.807 to 6.36
Front engine bracket to engine plate	18 to 20	2.489 to 2.765
Gearbox and rear engine plate:		
$\frac{5}{16}$ UNF stud	12 to 14	1.659 to 1.936
$\frac{5}{16}$ UNF setscrew	14 to 16	1.936 to 2.212
Main bearing caps	50 to 55	6.913 to 7.604
Rear oil seal attachment	18 to 20	2.489 to 2.765
Rocker cover nuts	$1\frac{1}{2}$	.105
Rocker pedestals	24 to 26	3.318 to 3.595
Sump attachments	16 to 18	2.212 to 2.489
Sump to front and rear oil seals	10 to 12	1.383 to 1.659
Timing cover:		
$\frac{5}{16}$ UNF setscrew	14 to 16	1.936 to 2.212
$\frac{5}{16}$ UNF slotted screw	8 to 10	1.106 to 1.383
Gearbox:		
Clutch housing to gearbox	24 to 26	3.318 to 3.595
Coupling, operating shaft	6 to 8	.830 to 1.106
Extension to gearbox	14 to 16	1.936 to 2.212
Extension to top cover	12 to 14	1.659 to 1.936
Flange to mainshaft	70 to 80	9.678 to 11.06
Fulcrum, reverse lever	14 to 16	1.936 to 2.212
Mounting bracket to frame	18 to 20	2.489 to 2.765
Operating shaft to gearlever	6 to 8	.830 to 1.106
Rear axle and suspension:		
Bearing cap to housing	32 to 34	4.424 to 4.701
Mounting plate to housing	26 to 28	3.595 to 3.871
Pinion flange	70 to 85	9.678 to 11.752
Radius arm, and brackets	24 to 26	3.318 to 3.595
Rear axle mounting plate to frame	26 to 28	3.595 to 3.871
Rear damper: Lower attachment	30 to 32	4.148 to 4.424
Upper attachment	42 to 46	5.807 to 6.36
Rear hub to axle shaft	100 to 110	13.826 to 15.21
Road spring to axle	28 to 30	3.871 to 4.178
Road spring to vertical link	42 to 46	5.807 to 6.36
Vertical link to rear hub	42 to 46	5.807 to 6.36
Front suspension:		
Anti-roll bar link	38 to 42	5.254 to 5.807
Anti-roll bar stud	12 to 14	1.659 to 1.936
Anti-roll bar U-bolts	3 to 4	.415 to .553
Caliper mounting plate:		
To vertical link	18 to 20	2.489 to 2.765
and steering arm	32 to 35	4.424 to 4.839
Caliper to mounting plate	50 to 55	6.913 to 7.604
Lower front damper attachment	42 to 46	5.807 to 6.360
Stub axle to vertical link	55 to 60	7.604 to 8.295
Steering unit:		
Coupling pinch bolts	18 to 20	2.489 to 2.765
Impact clamp halves	6 to 8	.830 to 1.106
Impact clamp socket screw	18 to 20	2.489 to 2.765
Steering unit U-bolts	14 to 16	1.936 to 2.212
Miscellaneous: Wheel nuts	38 to 42	5.254 to 5.807

SPECIAL TOOLS

Special tools have been identified in the relevant sections as they are required. A list of tools which will make various operations much easier is given in the following.

General:
S.4221A   Handpress
               Adaptors for handpress as required

Engine:
60A   Valve guide removing and replacing
S.60A-2   Adaptor for 60A
S.60A-6   Adaptor for 60A
S.334A   Interference fit gudgeon pin remover and replacer
S.335   Crankshaft rear oil seal centralizer

Gearbox:
20.SM.90   Flange holding spanner
4235A   Impact remover
S.4235A   Input shaft remover adaptor
S.144   Gearbox mainshaft circlip remover
S.145   Gearbox mainshaft circlip replacer

Suspension and steering:
S.160   Ball joint separator
S.3600   Steering wheel remover
S.109C   Rear hub remover
S.300A   Rear hub needle bearing remover and replacer
S.304   Rear hub bearing replacer

     All the special tools for the models covered by this manual are obtainable from:
     Messrs V. L. Churchill & Co. Ltd., P.O. Box No. 3, London Road, Daventry, Northants, England.
     In addition to the normal hand tools and special tools a Dial Test Indicator, torque wrench and a selection of micrometer gauges will be required for accurate work and measuring wear on parts.

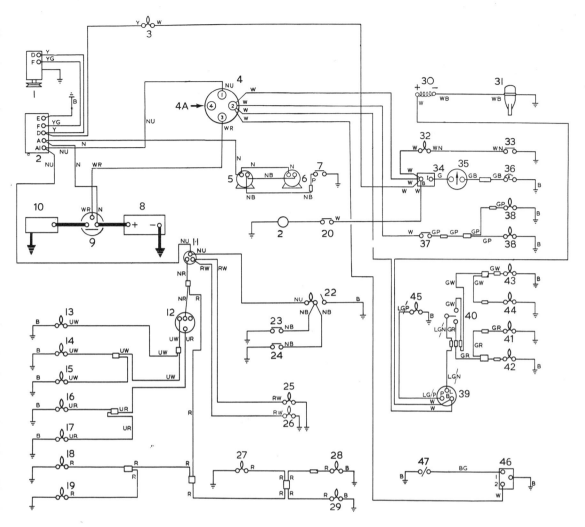

FIG 13:1 Herald 1200 wiring diagram

Key to Fig 13:1
1 Generator 2 Control box 3 Ignition warning light 4 Ignition/starter switch
4A Ignition/starter switch radio supply connector 5 Horn 6 Horn 7 Horn push 8 Battery
9 Starter solenoid 10 Starter motor 11 Master light switch 12 Column light switch 13 Main beam warning light
14 Main beam 15 Main beam 16 Dip beam 17 Dip beam 18 Front parking lamp 19 Front parking lamp
20 Heater switch 21 Heater motor 22 Facia lamp 23 Door switch 24 Door switch
25 Instrument illumination 26 Instrument illumination 27 Plate illumination lamp 28 Tail lamp 29 Tail lamp
30 Ignition coil 31 Ignition distributor 32 Oil pressure warning light 33 Oil pressure switch 34 Voltage stabilizer
35 Fuel indicator 36 Fuel tank unit 37 Stop lamp switch 38 Stop lamp 39 Flasher unit 40 Flasher switch
41 Lefthand flasher lamp 42 Lefthand flasher lamp 43 Righthand flasher lamp 44 Righthand flasher lamp
45 Flasher warning light 46 Windscreen wiper motor 47 Windscreen wiper switch

Cable colour code   N Brown   U Blue   R Red   P Purple   G Green   LG Light green   W White
Y Yellow   S Slate   B Black

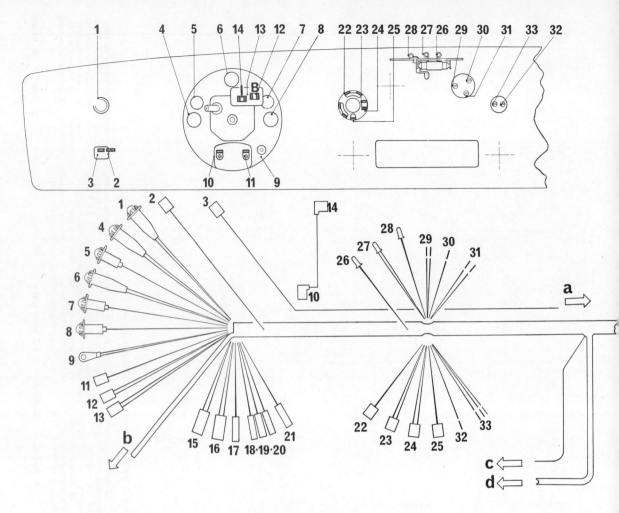

FIG 13:2 Herald 1200 facia connections

Key to Fig 13:2   1 LG/P and B—Bulb holder (flasher warning light)   2 W—Lucar (heater switch)   3 NW—Lucar (heater switch)   4 W and Y—Bulb holder (instrument–ignition warning light)   5 RW—Bulb holder (instrument illumination)   6 W and WN—Bulb holder (instrument–oil pressure warning light)   7 RW—Bulb holder (instrument illumination)   8 UW Bulb holder (instrument–main beam warning light)   9 B—Eyelet–2 wire (instrument)   10 G—Lucar (fuel indicator)   11 GB—Lucar (fuel indicator)   12 W—Lucar–2 wire (voltage stabilizer)   13 W—Lucar–2 wire (voltage stabilizer)   14 G—Lucar (voltage stabilizer)   15 NR and R—Double snap connector–2 wire (column light switch)   16 UW—Double snap connector–2 wire (column light switch)   17 UR—Snap connector (column light switch)   18 LG/N—3 way snap connector–3 wire (Flasher switch)   19 GR—3 way snap connector–3 wire (flasher switch)   20 GW—3 way snap connector–3 wire (flasher switch)   21 NB—Snap connector (horn push)   22 NU—Lucar (ignition/starter switch)   23 W—Lucar–2 wire (ignition/starter switch)   24 W—Lucar–2 wire (ignition/starter switch)   25 WR—Lucar (ignition/starter switch)   26 NU—Terminal end (facia lamp)   27 NB—Terminal end–2 wire (facia lamp)   28 B—Terminal end (facia lamp)   29 NU—Screw terminal–2 wire (master light switch)   30 NR—Screw terminal (master light switch)   31 RW—Screw terminal–2 wire (master light switch)   32 BG—Screw terminal (windscreen wiper switch)   33 B—Screw terminal–3 wire (windscreen wiper switch)
(a) NW–to heater motor   (b) W and GP–to stoplamp switch   (c) NB–to righthand door switch
(d) W, BG, B and B–to windscreen wiper motor

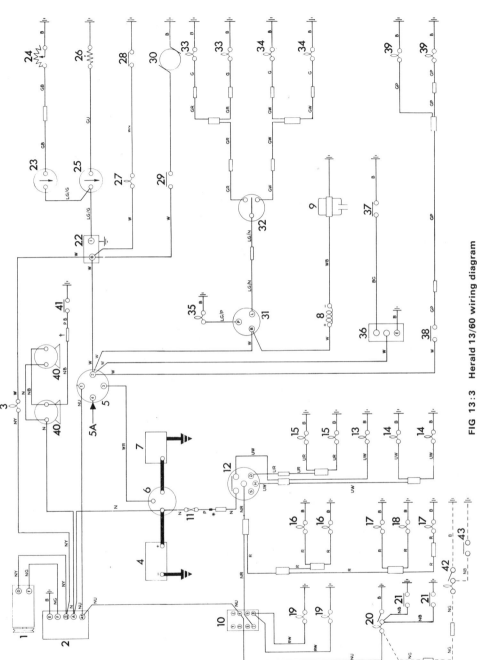

FIG 13:3 Herald 13/60 wiring diagram

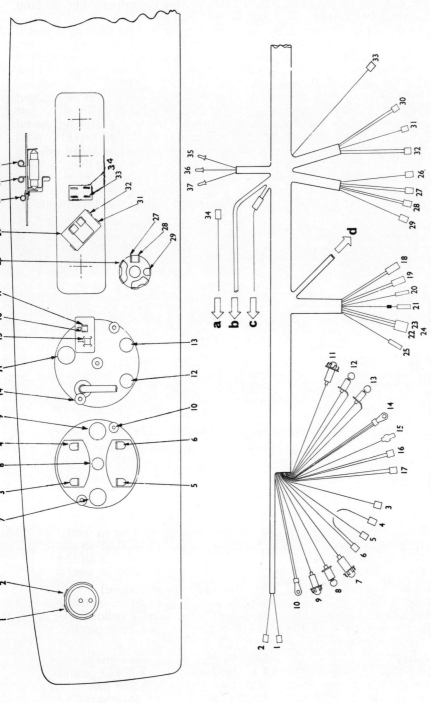

FIG 13:4 Herald 13/60 facia connections

Key to Fig 13:4 1 B—Lucar (windscreen wiper switch) 2 BG—Lucar (windscreen wiper switch) 3 GU—Lucar (temperature indicator) 4 LG/G—Lucar (temperature indicator) 5 GB—Lucar (fuel indicator) 6 LG/G—Lucar-2 wire (fuel indicator) 7 LG/P—Bulb holder (fuel/temperature instrument—flasher warning light) 8 RW—Bulb holder (fuel/temperature instrument) 9 UW—Bulb holder (fuel/temperature instrument—main beam warning light) 10 B—Eyelet—2 wire (fuel/temperature instrument—instrument illumination) 11 RW—Bulb holder (speedometer—instrument illumination) 12 W and WN—Bulb holder (speedometer—oil pressure warning light) 13 W and NY—Bulb holder (speedometer—ignition warning light) 14 B—Eyelet—3 wire (Speedometer) 15 LG/G—Lucar blade (voltage stabilizer) 16 W—Lucar—2 wire (voltage stabilizer) 17 W—Lucar—2 wire (voltage stabilizer) 18 NR and R—Double snap connector—2 wire (column light switch) 19 UW—Double snap connector—2 wire (column light switch) 20 UR—Snap connector (column light switch) 21 P with brown ident.—Snap connector (column light switch) 22 LG/N—3 way snap connector—3 wire (flasher switch) 23 GR—3 way snap connector—3 wire (flasher switch) 24 GW—3 way snap connector—3 wire (flasher switch) 25 NB—Snap connector (horn push) 26 NU—Lucar (ignition/starter switch) 27 W—Lucar—2 wire (ignition/starter switch) 28 W—Lucar—2 wire (ignition/starter switch) 29 WR—Lucar (ignition/starter switch) 30 NU—Lucar—2 wire (master light switch) 31 NR—Lucar (master light switch) 32 RW—Lucar—2 wire (master light switch) 33 W—Lucar (heater switch) 34 GY—Lucar (heater lamp) 35 NU—Terminal end (facia lamp) 36 PW—Terminal end (facia lamp) 37 B—Terminal end (facia lamp)

(a) GY—to heater motor (b) W, BG, B and B—to windscreen wiper motor (c) PW—to righthand door switch (d) W and GP—to stop lamp switch

RUNNING-IN

Whenever new parts are fitted to the engine they require careful bedding in. If these parts are submitted to the full load as soon as they are fitted they will not have the opportunity of being properly mated to the other working surface.

Power and performance will suffer, the working life of the engine will be shortened and it will always have a touch of 'roughness' about it if the running-in period is not complied with. New pistons and cylinder liners require full running-in. If only new piston rings or crankshaft bearings (including big-ends) have been fitted the running-in period is not so rigorous but the engine should still be treated with care for the first 1000 miles.

No specified speeds are recommended for running-in, but the engine should not be allowed to labour. Warm it up at a fast idle before driving away (this should be done at all times not just when running-in) and use the minimum choke sufficient to prevent the engine stalling. Avoid using full throttle at slow speeds. The running-in process is progressive but for the first 500 miles full power should not be used. The engine may be allowed to 'rev' fairly fast provided it is not under a heavy load. It is better to change down a gear and let the engine 'rev' fast than to make it 'slog' in a higher gear at lower rev/min. Full power may be used for short periods after the first 500 miles gradually extending the amount of time in full power as the engine becomes more responsive and the mileage reaches 1000 miles. After 1000 miles the engine may be considered to be fully run-in.

STANDARD MEASURE AND METRIC EQUIVALENTS

English to Metric (linear)
1 inch = 2.54 centimetres
1 foot = 30.4799 centimetres
1 yard = .914399 metre
1 mile = 1.6093 kilometre

English to Metric (square)
1 sq inch = 6.4516 sq centimetres
1 sq foot = 9.203 sq decimetres
1 sq yard = .836126 sq metres

English to Metric (cubic)
1 cu inch = 16.387 cc
1 cu ft = 28.317 litres
1 gallon = 4.546 litres
(.1605 cu feet)

English to Metric (weight)
1 pound = .45359 kilo
1 cwt = 50.8 kilo
1 ton = 1016 kilo

Torque loading
1 lb ft = .1382 kg metre

Metric to English (linear)
1 centimetre = .3937 inch
1 metre = 39.3702 inches
         = 1.0936 yard
1 kilometre = .62137 mile

Metric to English (square)
1 sq centimetre = .1550 sq inch
1 sq metre = 1550.01 sq inch
           = 10.7639 sq feet
           = 1.196 sq yard

Metric to English (cubic)
1 cc = .61 cu inch
1 litre = .22 gallons
(1000 cc) = 1.7598 pints

Metric to English (weight)
1 kilogramme = 2.20462 pounds
100 kilo = 1.968 cwt
1000 kilo = .9842 tons

1 kg metre = 7.2350 lb ft

Inches	Decimals	Milli-metres	Inches to Millimetres		Millimetres to Inches	
			Inches	mm	mm	Inches
1/64	.015625	.3969	.001	.0254	.01	.00039
1/32	.03125	.7937	.002	.0508	.02	.00079
3/64	.046875	1.1906	.003	.0762	.03	.00118
1/16	.0625	1.5875	.004	.1016	.04	.00157
5/64	.078125	1.9844	.005	.1270	.05	.00197
3/32	.09375	2.3812	.006	.1524	.06	.00236
7/64	.109375	2.7781	.007	.1778	.07	.00276
1/8	.125	3.1750	.008	.2032	.08	.00315
9/64	.140625	3.5719	.009	.2286	.09	.00354
5/32	.15625	3.9687	.01	.254	.1	.00394
11/64	.171875	4.3656	.02	.508	.2	.00787
3/16	.1875	4.7625	.03	.762	.3	.01181
13/64	.203125	5.1594	.04	1.016	.4	.01575
7/32	.21875	5.5562	.05	1.270	.5	.01969
15/64	.234375	5.9531	.06	1.524	.6	.02362
1/4	.25	6.3500	.07	1.778	.7	.02756
17/64	.265625	6.7469	.08	2.032	.8	.03150
9/32	.28125	7.1437	.09	2.286	.9	.03543
19/64	.296875	7.5406	.1	2.54	1	.03937
5/16	.3125	7.9375	.2	5.08	2	.07874
21/64	.328125	8.3344	.3	7.62	3	.11811
11/32	.34375	8.7312	.4	10.16	4	.15748
23/64	.359375	9.1281	.5	12.70	5	.19685
3/8	.375	9.5250	.6	15.24	6	.23622
25/64	.390625	9.9219	.7	17.78	7	.27559
13/32	.40625	10.3187	.8	20.32	8	.31496
27/64	.421875	10.7156	.9	22.86	9	.35433
7/16	.4375	11.1125	1	25.4	10	.39370
29/64	.453125	11.5094	2	50.8	11	.43307
15/32	.46875	11.9062	3	76.2	12	.47244
31/64	.484375	12.3031	4	101.6	13	.51181
1/2	.5	12.7000	5	127.0	14	.55118
33/64	.515625	13.0969	6	152.4	15	.59055
17/32	.53125	13.4937	7	177.8	16	.62992
35/64	.546875	13.8906	8	203.2	17	.66929
9/16	.5625	14.2875	9	228.6	18	.70866
37/64	.578125	14.6844	10	254.0	19	.74803
19/32	.59375	15.0812	11	279.4	20	.78740
39/64	.609375	15.4781	12	304.8	21	.82677
5/8	.625	15.8750	13	330.2	22	.86614
41/64	.640625	16.2719	14	355.6	23	.90551
21/32	.65625	16.6687	15	381.0	24	.94488
43/64	.671875	17.0656	16	406.4	25	.98425
11/16	.6875	17.4625	17	431.8	26	1.02362
45/64	.703125	17.8594	18	457.2	27	1.06299
23/32	.71875	18.2562	19	482.6	28	1.10236
47/64	.734375	18.6531	20	508.0	29	1.14173
3/4	.75	19.0500	21	533.4	30	1.18110
49/64	.765625	19.4469	22	558.8	31	1.22047
25/32	.78125	19.8437	23	584.2	32	1.25984
51/64	.796875	20.2406	24	609.6	33	1.29921
13/16	.8125	20.6375	25	635.0	34	1.33858
53/64	.828125	21.0344	26	660.4	35	1.37795
27/32	.84375	21.4312	27	685.8	36	1.41732
55/64	.859375	21.8281	28	711.2	37	1.4567
7/8	.875	22.2250	29	736.6	38	1.4961
57/64	.890625	22.6219	30	762.0	39	1.5354
29/32	.90625	23.0187	31	787.4	40	1.5748
59/64	.921875	23.4156	32	812.8	41	1.6142
15/16	.9375	23.8125	33	838.2	42	1.6535
61/64	.953125	24.2094	34	863.6	43	1.6929
31/32	.96875	24.6062	35	889.0	44	1.7323
63/64	.984375	25.0031	36	914.4	45	1.7717

UNITS	Pints to Litres	Gallons to Litres	Litres to Pints	Litres to Gallons	Miles to Kilometres	Kilometres to Miles	Lbs. per sq. In. to Kg. per sq. Cm.	Kg. per sq. Cm. to Lbs. per sq. In.
1	.57	4.55	1.76	.22	1.61	.62	.07	14.22
2	1.14	9.09	3.52	.44	3.22	1.24	.14	28.50
3	1.70	13.64	5.28	.66	4.83	1.86	.21	42.67
4	2.27	18.18	7.04	.88	6.44	2.49	.28	56.89
5	2.84	22.73	8.80	1.10	8.05	3.11	.35	71.12
6	3.41	27.28	10.56	1.32	9.66	3.73	.42	85.34
7	3.98	31.82	12.32	1.54	11.27	4.35	.49	99.56
8	4.55	36.37	14.08	1.76	12.88	4.97	.56	113.79
9		40.91	15.84	1.98	14.48	5.59	.63	128.00
10		45.46	17.60	2.20	16.09	6.21	.70	142.23
20				4.40	32.19	12.43	1.41	284.47
30				6.60	48.28	18.64	2.11	426.70
40				8.80	64.37	24.85		
50					80.47	31.07		
60					96.56	37.28		
70					112.65	43.50		
80					128.75	49.71		
90					144.84	55.92		
100					160.93	62.14		

UNITS	Lb ft to kgm	Kgm to lb ft	UNITS	Lb ft to kgm	Kgm to lb ft
1	.138	7.233	7	.967	50.631
2	.276	14.466	8	1.106	57.864
3	.414	21.699	9	1.244	65.097
4	.553	28.932	10	1.382	72.330
5	.691	36.165	20	2.765	144.660
6	.829	43.398	30	4.147	216.990

HINTS ON MAINTENANCE AND OVERHAUL

There are few things more rewarding than the restoration of a vehicle's original peak of efficiency and smooth performance.

The following notes are intended to help the owner to reach that state of perfection. Providing that he possesses the basic manual skills he should have no difficulty in performing most of the operations detailed in this manual. It must be stressed, however, that where recommended in the manual, highly-skilled operations ought to be entrusted to experts, who have the necessary equipment, to carry out the work satisfactorily.

Quality of workmanship:

The hazardous driving conditions on the roads to-day demand that vehicles should be as nearly perfect, mechanically, as possible. It is therefore most important that amateur work be carried out with care, bearing in mind the often inadequate working conditions, and also the inferior tools which may have to be used. It is easy to counsel perfection in all things, and we recognize that it may be setting an impossibly high standard. We do, however, suggest that every care should be taken to ensure that a vehicle is as safe to take on the road as it is humanly possible to make it.

Safe working conditions:

Even though a vehicle may be stationary, it is still potentially dangerous if certain sensible precautions are not taken when working on it while it is supported on jacks or blocks. It is indeed preferable not to use jacks alone, but to supplement them with carefully placed blocks, so that there will be plenty of support if the car rolls off the jacks during a strenuous manoeuvre. Axle stands are an excellent way of providing a rigid base which is not readily disturbed. Piles of bricks are a dangerous substitute. Be careful not to get under heavy loads on lifting tackle, the load could fall. It is preferable not to work alone when lifting an engine, or when working underneath a vehicle which is supported well off the ground. To be trapped, particularly under the vehicle, may have unpleasant results if help is not quickly forthcoming. Make some provision, however humble, to deal with fires. Always disconnect a battery if there is a likelihood of electrical shorts. These may start a fire if there is leaking fuel about. This applies particularly to leads which can carry a heavy current, like those in the starter circuit. While on the subject of electricity, we must also stress the danger of using equipment which is run off the mains and which has no earth or has faulty wiring or connections. So many workshops have damp floors, and electrical shocks are of such a nature that it is sometimes impossible to let go of a live lead or piece of equipment due to the muscular spasms which take place.

Work demanding special care:

This involves the servicing of braking, steering and suspension systems. On the road, failure of the braking system may be disastrous. Make quite sure that there can be no possibility of failure through the bursting of rusty brake pipes or rotten hoses, nor to a sudden loss of pressure due to defective seals or valves.

Problems:

The chief problems which may face an operator are:
1 External dirt.
2 Difficulty in undoing tight fixings
3 Dismantling unfamiliar mechanisms.
4 Deciding in what respect parts are defective.
5 Confusion about the correct order for reassembly.
6 Adjusting running clearances.
7 Road testing.
8 Final tuning.

Practical suggestion to solve the problems:

1 Preliminary cleaning of large parts—engines, transmissions, steering, suspensions, etc.,—should be carried out before removal from the car. Where road dirt and mud alone are present, wash clean with a high-pressure water jet, brushing to remove stubborn adhesions, and allow to drain and dry. Where oil or grease is also present, wash down with a proprietary compound (Gunk, Teepol etc.,) applying with a stiff brush—an old paint brush is suitable—into all crevices. Cover the distributor and ignition coils with a polythene bag and then apply a strong water jet to clear the loosened deposits. Allow to drain and dry. The assemblies will then be sufficiently clean to remove and transfer to the bench for the next stage.

On the bench, further cleaning can be carried out, first wiping the parts as free as possible from grease with old newspaper. Avoid using rag or cotton waste which can leave clogging fibres behind. Any remaining grease can be removed with a brush dipped in paraffin. If necessary, traces of paraffin can be removed by carbon tetrachloride. Avoid using paraffin or petrol in large quantities for cleaning in enclosed areas, such as garages, on account of the high fire risk.

When all exteriors have been cleaned, and not before, dismantling can be commenced. This ensures that dirt will not enter into interiors and orifices revealed by dismantling. In the next phases, where components have to be cleaned, use carbon tetrachloride in preference to petrol and keep the containers covered except when in use. After the components have been cleaned, plug small holes with tapered hard wood plugs cut to size and blank off larger orifices with grease-proof paper and masking tape. Do not use soft wood plugs or matchsticks as they may break.

2 It is not advisable to hammer on the end of a screw thread, but if it must be done, first screw on a nut to protect the thread, and use a lead hammer. This applies particularly to the removal of tapered cotters. Nuts and bolts seem to 'grow' together, especially in exhaust systems. If penetrating oil does not work, try the judicious application of heat, but be careful of starting a fire. Asbestos sheet or cloth is useful to isolate heat.

Tight bushes or pieces of tail-pipe rusted into a silencer can be removed by splitting them with an open-ended hacksaw. Tight screws can sometimes be started by a tap from a hammer on the end of a suitable screwdriver. Many tight fittings will yield to the judicious use of a hammer, but it must be a soft-faced hammer if damage is to be avoided, use a heavy block on the opposite side to absorb shock. Any parts of the steering system which have been damaged should be renewed, as attempts to repair them may lead to cracking and subsequent failure, and steering ball joints should be disconnected using a recommended tool to prevent damage.

3 It often happens that an owner is baffled when trying to dismantle an unfamiliar piece of equipment. So many modern devices are pressed together or assembled by spinning-over flanges, that they must be sawn apart. The intention is that the whole assembly must be renewed. However, parts which appear to be in one piece to the naked eye, may reveal close-fitting joint lines when inspected with a magnifying glass, and, this may provide the necessary clue to dismantling. Left-handed screw threads are used where rotational forces would tend to unscrew a right-handed screw thread.

   Be very careful when dismantling mechanisms which may come apart suddenly. Work in an enclosed space where the parts will be contained, and drape a piece of cloth over the device if springs are likely to fly in all directions. Mark everything which might be reassembled in the wrong position, scratched symbols may be used on unstressed parts, or a sequence of tiny dots from a centre punch can be useful. Stressed parts should never be scratched or centre-popped as this may lead to cracking under working conditions. Store parts which look alike in the correct order for reassembly. Never rely upon memory to assist in the assembly of complicated mechanisms, especially when they will be dismantled for a long time, but make notes, and drawings to supplement the diagrams in the manual, and put labels on detached wires. Rust stains may indicate unlubricated wear. This can sometimes be seen round the outside edge of a bearing cup in a universal joint. Look for bright rubbing marks on parts which normally should not make heavy contact. These might prove that something is bent or running out of truth. For example, there might be bright marks on one side of a piston, at the top near the ring grooves, and others at the bottom of the skirt on the other side. This could well be the clue to a bent connecting rod. Suspected cracks can be proved by heating the component in a light oil to approximately 100°C, removing, drying off, and dusting with french chalk, if a crack is present the oil retained in the crack will stain the french chalk.

4 In determining wear, and the degree, against the permissible limits set in the manual, accurate measurement can only be achieved by the use of a micrometer. In many cases, the wear is given to the fourth place of decimals; that is in ten-thousandths of an inch. This can be read by the vernier scale on the barrel of a good micrometer. Bore diameters are more difficult to determine. If, however, the matching shaft is accurately measured, the degree of play in the bore can be felt as a guide to its suitability. In other cases, the shank of a twist drill of known diameter is a handy check.

   Many methods have been devised for determining the clearance between bearing surfaces. To-day the best and simplest is by the use of Plastigage, obtainable from most garages. A thin plastic thread is laid between the two surfaces and the bearing is tightened, flattening the thread. On removal, the width of the thread is compared with a scale supplied with the thread and the clearance is read off directly. Sometimes joint faces leak persistently, even after gasket renewal. The fault will then be traceable to distortion, dirt or burrs. Studs which are screwed into soft metal frequently raise burrs at the point of entry. A quick cure for this is to chamfer the edge of the hole in the part which fits over the stud.

5 **Always check a replacement part with the original one before it is fitted.**

   If parts are not marked, and the order for reassembly is not known, a little detective work will help. Look for marks which are due to wear to see if they can be mated. Joint faces may not be identical due to manufacturing errors, and parts which overlap may be stained, giving a clue to the correct position. Most fixings leave identifying marks especially if they were painted over on assembly. It is then easier to decide whether a nut, for instance, has a plain, a spring, or a shakeproof washer under it. All running surfaces become 'bedded' together after long spells of work and tiny imperfections on one part will be found to have left corresponding marks on the other. This is particularly true of shafts and bearings and even a score on a cylinder wall will show on the piston.

6 Checking end float or rocker clearances by feeler gauge may not always give accurate results because of wear. For instance, the rocker tip which bears on a valve stem may be deeply pitted, in which case the feeler will simply be bridging a depression. Thrust washers may also wear depressions in opposing faces to make accurate measurement difficult. End float is then easier to check by using a dial gauge. It is common practice to adjust end play in bearing assemblies, like front hubs with taper rollers, by doing up the axle nut until the hub becomes stiff to turn and then backing it off a little. Do not use this method with ballbearing hubs as the assembly is often preloaded by tightening the axle nut to its fullest extent. If the splitpin hole will not line up, file the base of the nut a little.

   Steering assemblies often wear in the straight-ahead position. If any part is adjusted, make sure that it remains free when moved from lock to lock. Do not be surprised if an assembly like a steering gearbox, which is known to be carefully adjusted outside the car, becomes stiff when it is bolted in place. This will be due to distortion of the case by the pull of the mounting bolts, particularly if the mounting points are not all touching together. This problem may be met in other equipment and is cured by careful attention to the alignment of mounting points.

   When a spanner is stamped with a size and A/F it means that the dimension is the width between the jaws and has no connection with ANF, which is the designation for the American National Fine thread. Coarse threads like Whitworth are rarely used on cars to-day except for studs which screw into soft aluminium or cast iron. For this reason it might be found that the top end of a cylinder head stud has a fine thread and the lower end a coarse thread to screw into the cylinder block. If the car has mainly UNF threads then it is likely that any coarse threads will be UNC, which are not the same as Whitworth. Small sizes have the same number of threads in Whitworth and UNC, but in the $\frac{1}{2}$ inch size for example, there are twelve threads to the inch in the former and thirteen in the latter.

7 After a major overhaul, particularly if a great deal of work has been done on the braking, steering and suspension systems, it is advisable to approach the problem of testing with care. If the braking system has been overhauled, apply heavy pressure to the brake pedal and get a second operator to check every possible source of leakage. The brakes may work extremely well, but a leak could cause complete failure after a few miles.

Do not fit the hub caps until every wheel nut has been checked for tightness, and make sure the tyre pressures are correct. Check the levels of coolant, lubricants and hydraulic fluids. Being satisfied that all is well, take the car on the road and test the brakes at once. Check the steering and the action of the handbrake. Do all this at moderate speeds on quiet roads, and make sure there is no other vehicle behind you when you try a rapid stop.

Finally, remember that many parts settle down after a time, so check for tightness of all fixings after the car has been on the road for a hundred miles or so.

8 It is useless to tune an engine which has not reached its normal running temperature. In the same way, the tune of an engine which is stiff after a rebore will be different when the engine is again running free. Remember too, that rocker clearances on pushrod operated valve gear will change when the cylinder head nuts are tightened after an initial period of running with a new head gasket.

Trouble may not always be due to what seems the obvious cause. Ignition, carburation and mechanical condition are interdependent and spitting back through the carburetter, which might be attributed to a weak mixture, can be caused by a sticking inlet valve.

For one final hint on tuning, never adjust more than one thing at a time or it will be impossible to tell which adjustment produced the desired result.

GLOSSARY OF TERMS

AF	Across Flats. Width across the flats of nut or bolt heads, or between jaws of associated spanners.	Capacitor	Modern term for an electrical condenser. Part of distributor assembly, connected across contact breaker points, acts as an interference suppressor.
Allen key	Cranked wrench of hexagonal section for use with socket-head screws.	Castellated	Top face of a nut, slotted across the flats, to take a locking splitpin.
Alternator	Electrical generator producing alternating current. Rectified to direct current for battery charging.	Castor	Angle at which the kingpin or swivel pin is tilted when viewed from the side.
Ambient temperature	Surrounding atmospheric temperature.	cc	Cubic centimetres. Engine capacity is arrived at by multiplying the area of the bore in sq cm by the stroke in cm by the number of cylinders.
ANF	American National Fine screw thread.		
Annulus	Used in engineering to indicate the outer ring gear of an epicyclic gear train.	Clevis	U-shaped forked connector used with a clevis pin, usually at handbrake connections.
Armature	The shaft carrying the windings, which rotates in the magnetic field of a generator or starter motor. That part of a solenoid which is activated by the magnetic field.	Clockwise	In the direction of rotation of the hands of a clock, movement in the opposite direction is normally referred to as anti-clockwise.
Asymmetrical	Not symmetrical.	Collet	A type of collar, usually split and located in a groove in a shaft, and held in place by a retainer. The arrangement used to retain the spring(s) on a valve stem in most cases.
Axial	In line with, or pertaining to, an axis.		
BA	British Association screw thread.		
Backlash	Play in meshing gears.		
Balance lever	A bar where force applied at the centre is equally divided between connections at the ends.	Commutator	Rotating segmented current distributor between armature windings and brushes in generator or motor.
Banjo axle	Axle casing with large diameter housing for the crownwheel and differential.	Compression ratio	The ratio, or quantitative relation, of the total volume (piston at bottom of stroke) to the unswept volume (piston at top of stroke) in an engine cylinder.
Bendix pinion	A self-engaging and self-disengaging drive on a starter motor shaft.		
Bevel pinion	A conical shaped gearwheel, designed to mesh with a similar gear with an axis usually at 90 deg. to its own.	Condenser	See capacitor.
		Core plug	Plug for blanking off a manufacturing hole in a casting.
bhp	Brake horse power, measured on a dynamometer.	Crownwheel	Large bevel gear in rear axle, driven by a bevel pinion attached to the propeller shaft. Sometimes called a 'ring wheel'.
bmep	Brake mean effective pressure. Average pressure on a piston during the working stroke.		
Brake cylinder	Cylinder with hydraulically operated piston(s) acting on brake shoes or pad(s).	'C' Spanner	Like a 'C' with a handle. For use on screwed collars without flats, but with slots or holes.
Brake regulator	Control valve fitted in hydraulic braking system which limits brake pressure to rear brakes during heavy braking to prevent rear wheel locking.	Damper	Modern term for shock-absorber used in vehicle suspension systems to damp out spring oscillations.
		Depression	The lowering of atmospheric pressure as in the inlet manifold and carburetter.
BSF	British Standard Fine screw thread.	Dowel	Close tolerance pin, peg, tube, or bolt, which accurately locates mating parts.
BSW	British Standard Whitworth screw thread.		
		Drag link	Rod connecting steering box drop arm (pitman arm) to nearest front wheel steering arm in certain types of steering systems.
Bypass filter	Oil filter—one which cleans a small volume of oil from the pump and returns it to the sump.		
Camber	Angle at which a wheel is tilted from the vertical.	Dry liner	Thinwall tube pressed into cylinder bore.

Dry sump	Lubrication system where all oil is scavenged from the sump, and returned to a separate tank.
Dynamo	See Generator.
Electrode	Terminal part of an electrical component, such as the points or 'electrodes' of a sparking plug.
Electrolyte	In lead-acid car batteries a solution of sulphuric acid and distilled water.
End float	Or end play. The endwise movement between associated parts.
EP	Extreme pressure. In lubricants, special grades for heavily loaded bearing surfaces, such as gear teeth in a gearbox, or crownwheel and pinion in a rear axle.
Fade	Of brakes. Reduced efficiency due to overheating.
Field coils	Windings on the polepieces of motors and generators.
Fillets	Narrow finishing strips usually applied to interior bodywork.
First motion shaft	Input shaft from clutch to gearbox.
Fullflow	Oil filters. Filters all the oil pumped to the engine. If the element becomes clogged, a bypass valve operates to pass unfiltered oil to the engine.
FWD	Front wheel drive.
Gear pump	Two meshing gears in a close fitting casing. Oil is carried from the inlet round the outside of both gears in the spaces between the gear teeth and the casing to the outlet, the meshing gear teeth prevent oil passing back to the inlet, and the oil is forced through the outlet port.
Generator	Modern term for 'dynamo'. When rotated produces electrical current.
Grommet	A ring of protective or sealing material. Can be used to protect pipes or leads passing through bulkheads.
Gudgeon pin	Shaft which connects a piston to its connecting rod. Sometimes called 'wrist pin', or 'piston pin'.
Halfshaft	One of a pair transmitting drive from the differential gearing to the wheel hubs.
HC	High-compression. See Compression ratio.
Helical	In spiral form. The teeth of helical gears are cut at a spiral angle to the side faces of the gear wheel.
Hot spot	Hot area that assists vapourisation of fuel on its way to cylinders. Often provided by close contact between inlet and exhaust manifolds.
HT	High Tension. Applied to electrical current produced by the ignition coil for the sparking plugs.
Hydrometer	A device for checking specific gravity of liquids. Used to check specific gravity of electrolyte.
Hypoid bevel gears	A form of bevel gear used in the rear axle drive gears. The bevel pinion meshes below the centre line of the crownwheel, giving a lower propeller shaft line.
Idler	A device for passing on movement. A free running gear between driving and driven gears. A lever transmitting track rod movement to a side rod in steering gear
IFS	Independent Front Suspension.
Impeller	A centrifugal pumping element. Used in water pumps to stimulate flow.
Journals	Those parts of a shaft that are in contact with the bearings.
Kerosene	Paraffin.
Kingpin	The main vertical pin which carries the front wheel spindle, and permits steering movement. May be called 'steering pin' or 'swivel pin'.
Layshaft	The shaft which carries the laygear in the gearbox. The laygear is driven by the first motion shaft and drives the third motion shaft according to the gear selected. Sometimes called the 'Countershaft' or 'Second motion shaft'.
lb ft	A measure of twist or torque. A pull of 10 lb at a radius of 1 ft is a torque of 10 lb ft.
lb/sq in	Pounds per square inch.
LC	Low Compression. See 'Compression ratio'.
Little end	The small, or piston end of a connecting rod. Sometimes called the 'Small end'.
ls	Leading shoe in brake drum. Tends to wedge into drum, when applied, so increasing the braking effect.
LT	Low Tension. The current output from battery.
Mandrel	Accurately manufactured bar or rod used for test or centring purposes.
Manifold	A pipe, duct, or chamber, with several branches.
Needle rollers	Bearing rollers with a length many times their diameter.
Oil bath	Reservoir which lubricates parts by immersion. In air filters, a separate oil supply for wetting a wiremesh element and holding the dust.
Oil wetted	In air filters, a wiremesh element lightly oiled to trap and hold airborne dust.

Overlap	Period during which inlet and exhaust valves are open together.
Panhard rod	Bar connected between fixed point on chassis and another on axle to control sideways movement.
Pawl	Pivoted catch which engages in the teeth of a ratchet to permit movement in one direction only.
Peg spanner	Tool with pegs, or pins, to engage in holes in the part to be turned.
Pendant pedals	Pedals with levers that are pivoted at the top end.
Phillips screwdriver	A cross-point screwdriver for use with the cross-slotted heads of Phillips screws.
Pinion	A small gear, usually in relation to another gear.
Piston-type damper	Shock absorber in which damping is controlled by a piston working in a closed oil filled cylinder.
Preloading	Preset static pressure on ball or roller bearings not due to working loads.
Radial	Radiating from a centre, like the spokes of a wheel.
Radius rod	Pivoted arm confining movement of a part to an arc of fixed radius.
Ratchet	Toothed wheel or rack which can move in one direction only, movement in the other being prevented by a pawl.
Ring gear	A gear toothed ring attached to outer periphery of flywheel. Starter pinion engages with it during starting.
Runout	Amount by which a rotating part is out of truth.
SAE	Society of Automotive Engineers.
Semi-floating axle	Outer end of rear axle halfshaft is carried on bearing inside axle casing. Wheel hub is secured to end of shaft.
Servo	A hydraulic or pneumatic system for assisting, or augmenting a physical effort. See 'Vacuum Servo'.
Setscrew	One which is threaded for the full length of the shank.
Shackle	A coupling link, used in the form of two parallel pins connected by side plates to secure the end of the master suspension spring, and absorb the effects of deflection.
Shell bearing	Thin walled, steel shell lined with anti-friction metal. Usually semi-circular and used in pairs for main and big-end bearings.
Shock absorber	See 'damper'.
Silentbloc	Rubber bush bonded to inner and outer metal sleeves.
Socket-head screw	Screw with hexagonal socket for an Allen key.
Solenoid	A coil of wire creating a magnetic field when electric current passes through it. Used with a soft iron core to operate contacts or a mechanical device.
Spur gear	A gear with teeth cut axially across the periphery.
Stator tube	A stationary tube inside the steering column, carrying wiring to steering wheel controls.
Stub axle	Short axle fitted at one end only.
Tachometer	An instrument for accurate measurement of rotating speed. Usually indicates in revolutions per minute.
TDC	Top Dead Centre. The highest point reached by a piston in a cylinder, with the crank and connecting rod in line.
Thermostat	Automatic device for regulating temperature. Used in vehicle coolant systems to open a valve which restricts circulation at low temperatures.
Third motion shaft	Output shaft of gearbox.
Three-quarter floating axle	Outer end of rear axle halfshaft flanged and bolted to wheel hub, which runs on bearing mounted on outside of axle casing. Vehicle weight is not carried by the axle shaft.
Thrust bearing or washer	Used to reduce friction in rotating parts subject to axial loads.
Torque	Turning or twisting effort. See lb ft.
Track rod	The bar(s) across the vehicle which connect the steering arms and maintain the front wheels in their correct alignment.
ts	Trailing shoe, in a drum brake assembly. Tends to be pushed away from drum.
UJ	Universal joint. A coupling between shafts which permits angular movement.
UNF	Unified National Fine screw thread.
Vacuum Servo	Device used in brake system, using difference between atmospheric pressure and inlet manifold depression to operate a piston which acts to augment pressure as required. See 'Servo'.
Venturi	A restriction or 'choke' in a tube, as in a carburetter, used to increase velocity to obtain a reduction in pressure.
Vernier	A sliding scale for obtaining fractional readings of the graduations of an adjacent scale.
Welch plug	A domed thin metal disc which is partially flattened to lock in a recess. Used to plug core holes in castings.
Wet liner	Removable cylinder barrel, sealed against coolant leakage, where the coolant is in direct contact with the outer surface.
Wet sump	A reservoir attached to the crankcase to hold the lubricating oil.

INDEX

A
Acceleration pump, Solex 28
Acceleration pump, Stromberg 31
Air cleaners 33
Antifreeze 45
Anti-roll bar 75
Armature, generator 102
Armature, starter 106

B
Balljoints 78
Battery testing 100
Beam-setting, headlamps 108
Belt tension 43
Big-end bearings 19
Bleeding the brakes 97
Bleeding the clutch 51
Bonnet adjustments 116
Brake adjustment 92
Brake disc 93
Brake drum 95
Brake master cylinder 48
Brushes, generator 101
Brushes, starter 106
Brushes, wiper motor 107

C
Cable rack, windscreen wiper 107
Caliper maintenance 93
Camshaft 16
Camshaft driving chain 14
Capacities 132
Capacitor, distributor.. 37
Carburetter adjustment, Solex 28
Carburetter adjustment, Stromberg .. 33
Carburetter operation, Solex 28
Carburetter operation, Stromberg .. 31
Carburetter servicing, Solex 29
Carburetter servicing, Stromberg .. 31
Clutch master cylinder 48
Clutch linings 52
Clutch removal 17
Clutch release mechanism 52
Clutch slave cylinder 50
Commutator, generator 101
Commutator, starter 106
Compression ratio 125
Contacts, control box 103
Contacts, distributor 36
Control box, generator 102
Crankshaft bearings, big-end.. 19
Crankshaft bearings, main 21
Crankshaft end float 21
Crankshaft oil seals 22
Cylinder bore.. 19
Cylinder head nut sequence 12

D
Damper, Stromberg carburetter maintenance.. 25
Damper (shock absorber) front 80
Damper (shock absorber) rear 72
Damper, steering rack 86
Decarbonizing 13
Diaphragm, fuel pump 28
Diaphragm, Stromberg carburetter .. 32
Diaphragm spring, clutch 47
Dimensions 132
Disc brake friction pads 93
Disc removal 76, 93
Distributor adjustment 35
Door glass 114
Door locks 115
Door removal.. 112
Door trim 112
Drum brake adjustment 92

E
Electrolyte, battery 100
Engine description 9
Engine removal 12
Engine reassembly 22

F
Facia 117
Fan belt 43
Fan blades 43
Field coils, generator 102
Field coils, starter 106
Field coils, wiper motor 107
Firing order 128
Flywheel ring-gear 17
Friction linings, clutch 52
Friction linings, drum brake 94
Friction pads, disc brake 93
Front hubs, adjustment 78
Front hubs, lubrication 76
Front suspension geometry 82, 129
Front road springs 80
Front road spring data 130
Front wheel alignment 87
Fuel filtration 25
Fuel gauge 109
Fuel pump 25
Fuel pump testing 28
Fuses 108

G
Gasket, cylinder head 13
Gearbox description 53
Gearbox lubrication 53
Gearbox selector mechanism 62
Generator bearings 102
Generator brushgear 101
Generator maintenance 100
Generator testing 101
Glossary of terms 143
Grading of pistons 20, 125
Grinding-in valves 13
Gudgeon pins 20, 21
Guides, valve.. 14

H

Handbrake adjustment	95
Handbrake cables	97
Headlamps	108
Head nut tightening sequence	12
Head removal and replacement	12
Heater controls	119
Heater removal	118
Hints on maintenance and overhaul	141
Horn adjustment	108
Hub bearings, front	76
Hub bearings, rear	68
Hydraulic system, brakes	91
Hydraulic system, clutch	47
Hydrometer	100

I

Idling adjustment, Solex	28
Idling adjustment, Stromberg	33
Idling speeds	127
Ignition faults	36
Ignition leads	39
Ignition timing	38
Impact clamp, steering column	88
Instruments	118

J

Jets, Solex carburetter	29
Jet, Stromberg carburetter	32

L

Lighting circuit faults	109
Lock door	115
Lock, steering	83, 84
Low-tension circuit, ignition	37

M

Main bearings	21
Master cylinder clutch and brakes	48
Mixture control, Solex	28
Mixture control, Stromberg	33

N

Needle, Stromberg carburetter	31
Needle valve, Solex carburetter	29
Needle valve, Stromberg carburetter	32

O

Oil filter	18
Oil pressure	127
Oil pressure relief valve	18
Oil pump	18
Oil seals, crankshaft	22
Oil seals, differential	69

P

Parking windscreen wipers	106
Pistons	20
Piston grades	20, 125
Piston rings	20, 126
Propeller shaft	67
Pump, fuel	25
Pump, oil	18
Pump, water	43

R

Rack adjustment	84
Rack lubrication	84
Radiator	43
Rear axle oil leaks	69
Rear dampers	72
Rear brake drums	95
Rear brake adjustment	92
Rear brake linings	94
Rear road spring	73
Rear road spring data	129
Rear suspension	65
Regulator, control box	103
Regulator, door window	114
Removing engine and gearbox	12
Remote control door lock	115
Rocker gear, engine	12

S

Seat belts	112
Selector mechanism, gearbox	62
Shock absorbers (see Dampers)	
Slave cylinder, clutch	50
Slow-running, Solex	28
Slow-running, Stromberg	33
Sparking plugs	39
Sparking plug makes	128
Specific gravity, battery	100
Sprockets, timing	14
Springs, road	73, 80
Springs, valve	13
Starter motor	104
Starter solenoid	106
Steering column removal	88
Steering column servicing	89
Steering rack removal	84
Steering rack servicing	84

T

Tappets	12
Temperature gauge	109
Thermostat	45
Timing chain	14
Timing, ignition	38
Timing valves	14
Torque wrench settings	133
Track, front wheels	87
Trim removal, door	112
Tyres and tyre pressures	132

U

Universal joints, transmission	66
Universal joint, steering	88

V

Vacuum control ignition	35
Valve clearances	22
Valve data, engine	126
Valve guides	14
Valve seat renovation	13
Valve springs	126
Voltage stabilizer (instruments)	109

W

Water circulation	41
Water drain taps	42
Water filler cap	41
Water pump	43
Wheels and tyres	132
Window glass, door	114
Window glass, backlight and quarter light	115
Windscreen	115
Windscreen wiper motor	107
Windscreen wiper wheel boxes	107
Wiring diagrams	135

NOTES

THE AUTOBOOK SERIES OF WORKSHOP MANUALS

Alfa Romeo Giulia 1600, 1750 1962 on
Aston Martin 1921-58
Auto Union Audi 70, 80, Super 90, 1966 on
Audi 100 1969 on
Austin, Morris etc. 1100 Mk. 1 1962-67
Austin, Morris etc. 1100 Mk. 2, 3, 1300 Mk. 1, 2, 3 America 1968 on
Austin A30, A35, A40 Farina
Austin A55 Mk. 2, A60 1958-69
Austin A99, A110 1959-68
Austin J4 1960 on
Austin Maxi 1969 on
Austin, Morris 1800 1964 on
Austin, Morris 2200 1972 on
Austin Kimberley, Tasman 1970 on
Austin, Morris 1300, 1500 Nomad 1969 on
BMC 3 (Austin A50, A55 Mk. 1, Morris Oxford 2, 3 1954-59)
Austin Healey 100/6, 3000 1956-68
Austin Healey, MG Sprite, Midget 1958 on
Bedford CA Mk2 1964-69
Bedford Beagle HA Vans 1964 on
BMW 1600 1966 on
BMW 1800 1964 on
BMW 2000, 2002 1966 on
Chevrolet Corvair 1960-69
Chevrolet Corvette V8 1957-65
Chevrolet Corvette V8 1965 on
Chevrolette Vega 2300 1970 on
Chrysler Valiant V8 1965 on
Chrysler Valiant Straight Six 1966-70
Citroen DS 19, ID 19 1955-66
Citroen ID 19, DS 19, 20, 21 1966 on
Colt 1970 on
Daf 31, 32, 33, 44, 55 1961 on
Datsun 1200 1970 on
Datsun 1300, 1400, 1600 1968 on
Datsun 240C 1971 on
Datsun 240Z Sport 1970 on
De Dion Bouton 1899-1907
Fiat 124 1966 on
Fiat 124 Sport 1966 on
Fiat 125 1967 on
Fiat 128 1969 on
Fiat 500 1957 on
Fiat 600, 600D 1955-69
Fiat 850 1964 on
Fiat 1100 1957-69
Fiat 1300, 1500 1961-67

Ford Anglia Prefect 100E 1953-62
Ford Anglia 105E, Prefect 107E 1959-67
Ford Capri 1300, 1600 OHV 1968 on
Ford Capri 1300, 1600, 2000 OHC 1972 on
Ford Capri 2000, 3000 1969 on
Ford Classic, Capri 1961-64
Ford Consul, Zephyr, Zodiac, 1, 2 1950-62
Ford Corsair Straight Four 1963-65
Ford Corsair V4 1965-68
Ford Corsair V4 2000 1969-70
Ford Cortina 1962-66
Ford Cortina 1967-68
Ford Cortina 1969-70
Ford Cortina Mk. 3 1970 on
Ford Escort 1967 on
Ford Falcon 6 1964-70
Ford Falcon XK, XL 1960-63
Ford Falcon 6 XR/XA 1966 on
Ford Falcon V8 (U.S.A.) 1965-71
Ford Falcon V8 (Aust.) 1966 on
Ford Pinto 1970 on
Ford Maverick 1969 on
Ford Maverick V8 1970 on
Ford Mustang 6 1965 on
Ford Mustang V8 1965-71
Ford Thames 10, 12, 15 cwt 1957-65
Ford Transit 1965 on
Ford Zephyr Zodiac Mk. 3 1962-66
Ford Zephyr Zodiac V4, V6, Mk. 4 1966-72
Ford Consul, Granada 1972 on
Hillman Avenger 1970 on
Hillman Hunter 1966 on
Hillman Imp 1963-68
Hillman Imp 1969 on
Hillman Minx 1 to 5 1956-65
Hillman Minx 1965-67
Hillman Minx 1966-70
Hillman Super Minx 1961-65
Holden V8 1968 on
Holden Straight Six 1948-66
Holden Straight Six 1966 on
Holden Torana 4 Series HB 1967-69
Jaguar XK120, 140, 150, Mk. 7, 8, 9 1948-61
Jaguar 2.4, 3.4, 3.8 Mk. 1, 2 1955-69
Jaguar 'E' Type 1961 on
Jaguar 'S' Type 420 1963-68

Jaguar XJ6 1968 on
Jowett Javelin Jupiter 1947-53
Landrover 1, 2 1948-61
Landrover 2, 2a, 3 1959 on
Mazda 616 1970 on
Mazda 808, 818 1972 on
Mazda 1200, 1300 1969 on
Mazda 1500, 1800 1967 on
Mercedes-Benz 190b, 190c, 200 1959-68
Mercedes-Benz 220 1959-65
Mercedes-Benz 220/8 1968 on
Mercedes-Benz 230 1963-68
Mercedes-Benz 250 1965-67
Mercedes-Benz 250 1968 on
Mercedes-Benz 280 1968 on
MG TA to TF 1936-55
MGA MGB 1955-68
MGB 1969 on
Mini 1959 on
Mini Cooper 1961 on
Morgan 1936-69
Morris Marina 1971 on
Morris (Aust) Marina 1972 on
Morris Minor 2, 1000 1952-71
Morris Oxford 5, 6 1959-71
NSU 1000 1963 on
NSU Prinz 1 to 4 1957 on
Opel Ascona, Manta 1970 on
Opel GT 1900 1968 on
Opel Kadett, Olympia 993cc 1078cc 1962 on
Opel Kadett, Olympia 1492, 1698, 1897cc 1967 on
Opel Rekord C 1966 on
Peugeot 204 1965 on
Peugeot 304 1970 on
Peugeot 404 1960 on
Peugeot 504 1968 on
Porsche 356A, B, C 1957-65
Porsche 911 1964-69
Porsche 912 1965-69
Porsche 914 S 1969 on
Reliant Regal 1952 on
Renault R4, R4L, 4 1961 on
Renault 6 1968 on
Renault 8, 10, 1100 1962 on
Renault 12, 1969 on
Renault R16 1965 on
Renault Dauphine Floride 1957-67
Renault Caravelle 1962-68
Rover 60 to 110 1953-64
Rover 2000 1963 on
Rover 3 Litre 1958-67
Rover 3500, 3500S 1968 on
Saab 95, 96, Sport 1960-68
Saab 99 1969 on
Saab V4 1966 on
Simca 1000 1961 on
Simca 1100 1967 on

Simca 1300, 1301, 1500, 1501 1963 on
Skoda One (440, 445, 450) 1955-70
Sunbeam Rapier Alpine 1955-65
Toyota Corolla 1100 1967 on
Toyota Corona 1500 Mk. 1 1965-70
Toyota Corona 1900 Mk. 2 1969 on
Triumph TR2, TR3, TR3A 1952-62
Triumph TR4, TR4A 1961-67
Triumph TR5, TR250, TR6 1967 on
Triumph 1300, 1500 1965 on
Triumph 2000 Mk. 1, 2.5 PI Mk. 1 1963-69
Triumph 2000 Mk. 2, 2.5 PI Mk. 2 1969 on
Triumph Dolomite 1972 on
Triumph Herald 1959-68
Triumph Herald 1969-71
Triumph Spitfire, Vitesse 1962-68
Triumph Spitfire Mk. 3, 4 1969 on
Triumph GT6, Vitesse 2 Litre 1969 on
Triumph Toledo 1970 on
Vauxhall Velox, Cresta 1957-72
Vauxhall Victor 1, 2, FB 1957-64
Vauxhall Victor 101 1964-67
Vauxhall Victor FD 1600, 2000 1967 on
Vauxhall Victor 3300, Ventora 1968 on
Vauxhall Victor FE Ventora 1972 on
Vauxhall Viva HA 1963-66
Vauxhall Viva HB 1966-70
Vauxhall Viva, HC Firenza 1971 on
Volkswagen Beetle 1954-67
Volkswagen Beetle 1968 on
Volkswagen 1500 1961-66
Volkswagen 1600 Fastback 1965 on
Volkswagen Transporter 1954-67
Volkswagen Transporter 1968 on
Volkswagen 411 1968 on
Volvo 120 1961-70
Volvo 140 1966 on
Volvo 160 series 1968 on
Volvo 1800 1960 on

NOTES